DREAD POETRY AND FREEDOM

'David Austin offers nothing less than a radical geography of black art in his (re)sounding of Linton Kwesi Johnson. You don't play with Johnson's revolutionary poetry, Austin teaches, and *Dread Poetry and Freedom* is as serious, and beautiful, as our life.'
—Fred Moten, poet, critic and theorist

'A moving and dialogic musing on freedom. Austin's richly textured study reads LKJ's poetry in relation to an expansive tradition of black radical politics and poetics. It captures both the urgency of Johnson's historical moment and his resonance for ours.'
—Shalini Puri, Professor of English, University of Pittsburgh

'With the intensity of a devotee and the precision of a scholar, David Austin skilfully traverses the dread terrain of Linton Kwesi Johnson's politics and poetry, engaging readers in an illuminating dialogue with diverse interlocutors who haunt the writer's imagination.'
—Carolyn Cooper, cultural critic, author of *Noises in the Blood: Orality, Gender and the 'Vulgar' Body of Jamaican Popular Culture*

'*Dread Poetry and Freedom* offers an expansive exploration of Caribbean political and cultural history, from Rastafari in Jamaica and Walter Rodney and Guyana to the Cuban Revolution with impressive articulations of the significance of Fanonism. Caribbean political theory is animating literary and cultural studies diasporically; this work demonstrates this elegantly.'
—Carole Boyce Davies, author of *Caribbean Spaces*, Professor of Africana Studies and Literature at Cornell University

DREAD POETRY AND FREEDOM

Linton Kwesi Johnson and the Unfinished Revolution

David Austin

PLUTO PRESS

and

Between the Lines

First published 2018 by Pluto Press
345 Archway Road, London N6 5AA

www.plutobooks.com

Copyright © David Austin 2018

The right of David Austin to be identified as the author of this work has
been asserted by him in accordance with the Copyright, Designs and
Patents Act 1988.

British Library Cataloguing in Publication Data
A catalogue record for this book is available from the British Library

ISBN   978 0 7453 3814 9   Hardback
ISBN   978 0 7453 3813 2   Paperback
ISBN   978 1 7868 0348 1   PDF eBook
ISBN   978 1 7868 0350 4   Kindle eBook
ISBN   978 1 7868 0349 8   EPUB eBook

Published in Canada 2018 by Between the Lines
401 Richmond Street West, Studio 281, Toronto, Ontario, M5V 3A8

www.btlbooks.com

Cataloguing in Publication information available from Library and
Archives Canada

ISBN   978 1 77113 401 9   Paperback
ISBN   978 1 77113 403 3   PDF eBook
ISBN   978 1 77113 402 6   EPUB eBook

This book is printed on paper suitable for recycling and made from
fully managed and sustained forest sources. Logging, pulping and
manufacturing processes are expected to conform to the environmental
standards of the country of origin.

Typeset by Stanford DTP Services, Northampton, England

Simultaneously printed in the United Kingdom and United States of
America

For Méshama and Alama

In memory of my grandmother, Ms. James and Aunt Pearl

and

Richard Iton, Franklyn Harvey, Abby Lippman
and Myrtle Anderson

CONTENTS

ACKNOWLEDGEMENTS

To quote the words of Sam Cooke, *Dread Poetry and Freedom: Linton Kwesi Johnson and the Unfinished Revolution* has 'been a long time coming'. I would like to thank the team at Pluto Press, and especially editor David Shulman, for his support and trust in the outcome.

Yael Margalit graciously read the entire manuscript and I am very fortunate to have benefited from her precision and keen insights on poetry and the English language. Malik Noël-Ferdinand provided critical feedback on Chapter 3 in relation to Aimé Césaire, as did Alissa Trotz on Chapter 4 related to Walter Rodney and Guyana. Many students have sat through my 'Poetry and Social Change' courses at John Abbott College over the years as some of the book's ideas were reconsidered in the classroom. I would especially like to signal Maranatha Bassey and Stefan Florinca who helped to keep the class alive as I stumbled my way through that very first course in the winter of 2013, and Katya Stella Assoe, Anne Bojko, and Diego Ivan Nieto Montenegro who affirmed, without them realizing, why I was writing this book.

Friends, family and colleagues have been a presence, suffered through my musings, or offered, often unaware, words of encouragement, disagreement, and insight on poetry, politics, music, and theory. I would like to mention the following: Amarkai Laryea and d'bi young anitafrika, both of whom were present when I first embarked on writing this book in Havana; Ceta Gabriel, Vincent Sparks, Amanda Maxwell, Cleo Whyne and Garth Mills, and the rest of the old Youth in Motion crew who are always in my thoughts. Robert Hill, a friend and scholar's scholar. Mariame Kaba, for among other things, putting up with my incessant play of LKJ many years ago; Nigel Thomas and the Logos Readings (formerly Kola); Binyam Tewolde Kahsu and

Anastasia Culurides, Nantali Indongo, Kai Thomas, Amarylis Gorostiza, Xismara Sánchez Lavastida, Teeanna Munro, Karen Kaderavek, Sujata Ghosh, Tamar Austin, Hyacinth Harewood, Shalini Puri, Roy Fu, Sarwat Viqar, Neil Guilding (aka Zibbs), Jason Selman, Kaie Kellough and Jerome Diman; Scott Rutherford, Patricia Harewood (thanks) and Pat Dillon; Koni Benson, Melanie Newton, Alberto Sanchez, Astrid Jacques, Kagiso Molope, Beverley Mullings, Samuel Furé, Peter Hudson, Sunera Thobani, Sayidda Jaffer, Aziz Choudry, Ameth Lo, Stefan Christoff, Isaac Saney, Désirée Rochat, David Featherstone, Karen Dubinsky, Paul Di Stefano, Eric Shragge, Hillina Seife, Frank Francis, Kelly McKinney, Aaron Kamugisha, Irini Tsakiri, Minkah Makalani, Karen Dubinsky, Candis Steenbergen, Frank Runcie, Mario Bellemare, Debbie Lunny, Alissa Trotz, Sara Villa; Rodney Saint-Éloi (le poète), Yara El-Ghadban for those many conversations on Mahmoud Darwish; Adrian Harewood and Ahmer Qadeer for checking in, and Shane Book, the poet among us.

I would also like to acknowledge my grandmother, Rose Denahy, my parents, Sonia Jackson and Lloyd Austin; Michael Archer and Norman Austin, Tony Denahy and Jeff Denahy – childhood memories of music on Selbourne Road in Walthamstow, East London

Laneydi Martinez Alfonso has been a sounding-board and co-conspirer. She gave critical feedback on the manuscript and patiently listened to my late night ramblings on it. *¿Qué haría yo sin ti?*

The impending birth of my daughter Méshama was the initial inspiration for this book, and many years later she also assisted in transcribing interviews, including an interview with Linton Kwesi Johnson. My son Alama was perhaps once LKJ's youngest fan who also alerted me to the profile resemblance between Johnson's image on the Penguin Modern Classics selection of his poetry and the image of Thelonious Monk on the album *Monk's Dream*. He was also quick to remind me not to neglect the brilliant Jamaican poet Michael Smith as I wrote. This book is for both of you.

Finally, were it not for Richard Iton, this book, in all likelihood, would not have been written. His intellectual acumen was matched only by his sincerity as a friend. Richard, may your restless spirit continue to haunt us.

PREFACE

Several specific experiences directly influenced my motivation to write *Dread Poetry and Freedom: Linton Kwesi Johnson and the Unfinished Revolution.* Part of the book's origins lie in South Africa, where in August 2001 I was part of a team that accompanied ten Montreal youth to participate in the World Conference Against Racism (WCAR). I had just finished an intense and exhausting three years of work with a youth organization in Montreal that plunged me into an existential crisis.

In this moment of deep introspection, I was forced to pose some difficult personal, political and organizational questions. Some of these questions touched on the relationship between theory and practice, the meaning of social change and the practical process involved in realizing change in an environment in which real lives are at stake. I was pondering these issues in South Africa as I visited sites where some of the most important rebellions and uprisings against apartheid had occurred, often with youth as young as those with whom I had worked with over the years in Montreal at the forefront. Organized by a local youth organization that specialized in the arts, the trip to South Africa was structured as an exchange in which youth from Montreal were paired with youth from Johannesburg-Soweto. The experience was an eye-opener for the youth who participated in it, and for the adults, and it provided an international forum to discuss the issues of race, class, colonialism and imperialism. Perhaps, were it not for the events of 9/11, the impact of the conference would have had more traction and far-reaching significance in its aftermath.

After a week participating in the WCAR in Durban we then travelled to Port Elizabeth, Cape Town, and finally back to Johannesburg where we had initially landed. As someone whose consciousness had been shaped by the anti-apartheid struggle and anti-apartheid reggae songs such as Peter Tosh's 'Apartheid', and who had participated in the tail end of the global anti-apartheid movement as a university student, the trip put a face to the country that had once been infamous for its policies of white supremacy. I also gained a better understanding of the impact that apartheid had, and continues to have, on the entire society.

During a visit to Seanna-Marena High School in Soweto we encountered young students in a crammed and underequipped classroom, but who nonetheless seemed to teem with the very energy and spirit that helped to topple official apartheid. Following brief introductions, the WCAR conference partic- ipants were asked, 'Do you think racism will ever end?' The question was met with an almost deafening silence. We had already experienced the perplexing shock of how little so many young South Africans seemed to recall about the horrors of the apartheid system that had ended only a few short years before. Given the silence that greeted the question, I felt compelled to say that, while I did not think that there was a definitive answer to the very difficult question, if there was ever an example of how change can come about, the struggle to end official apartheid was it. The rest of the experience was a strange one. I actually found myself talking to these young South Africans about how young women and men like them who had struggled to eliminate apartheid had inspired people across the globe to struggle against injustice.

What happened when I finished talking still moves me to this day. The responses to the previous questions had been punctuated by applause from the over one hundred students that sat in the overflowing room. But my seemingly innocuous intervention was followed by a deafening silence. You could hear a pin drop. Something that I had said had somehow struck a chord with the students in a manner that was similar to another experience that I would have in Cape Town sixteen years later,[1] and they simply stared at me in an apparent self-reflexive gaze.

When the classroom session ended the students and guests gathered outside the school to talk and take pictures together.

A young student, Portia Mohale, who had sat quietly in her seat during the classroom exchange, approached me to thank me for my comments. My remarks, she said, reminded her that there were people in other parts of the world who were concerned about the well-being of South Africa. She then insisted that the struggle for a more just and equal society would continue: that they, meaning she and her peers, would be successful in creating the kind of society they desired – the obvious inference being that the society that they desired had yet to come into being.

It was not what Portia said that struck me so much as the conviction with which she said it. She was fifteen years of age and spoke with the determination and force of a young Winnie Mandela who, despite being ridiculed and reviled in the press, clearly remained very popular among many young black South Africans, especially in Johannesburg and Soweto.

We returned from South Africa via New York on 10 September 2001, and made our way back to Montreal from JFK Airport by van. As we passed what were then the twin towers of the World Trade Center, some of the Montreal youth expressed an interest in stopping in New York to do some sightseeing, a proposal that the adults of the group politely vetoed. In fact, the only reason why I remember the proposition at all is because of what happened the following morning. Tired as I was after an eighteen-hour direct flight from South Africa and an almost eight-hour drive from New York, I turned on the television almost just in time to witness the second plane crash into the second tower. At least this is how I remember it.

Reposing at home that week after stepping away from the mentally and physically exhausting job at the youth centre, I watched and listened to countless radio and television programmes in which people of all walks of life attempted to come to terms with what had happened in New York. America was shell-shocked, and voices of reason were few and far between in the mainstream media (as I remember it, poet Maya Angelou, who cautioned people to think and attempt to understand the 'why' of what had happened, was one such voice of reason). In addition to the visit to South Africa and the work at the youth centre, the first draft of this book was sparked, not so much by the 'why' of the events of September 11, but by 'what' and 'how' questions, such as what kind of society do we envision for ourselves as a departure from the politics and economics of madness that currently prevail, and how do we consciously act to bring this society into being?

Cuba also played an important part in the production of this book. It was in Cuba where I wrote the first drafts on Johnson's poems on socialism in light of its collapse in Eastern Europe. Given the history of the Cuban Revolution, and particularly its post-Soviet history, it is not hard to imagine why Cuba would be a fitting place to reflect and write about socialism. As I wrote in the January 2002 version of the manuscript:

> Drafting these lines … in the sanctuary of a kind and generous family in Havana, I cannot help thinking about the current socio-economic situation in Cuba, its historic relationship with the former Soviet Union and the parallels between this Caribbean island and its former Cold War ally. Cuba benefitted tremendously from technical and economic assistance from the former Soviet Union and the two states developed what appeared to be an indelible link between them. This relationship is exemplified in the former Soviet embassy in Havana, an imposing, multi-storied space-like edifice, towering over the district of Miramar, the once up-scale neighborhood of the Cuban bourgeoisie that was expropriated by the revolutionary government after 1959. The embassy sits alongside a church amidst palms trees, peering down on the inhabitants of the area and dwarfing even larger hotels in the vicinity. Built in the 1980s as a symbol of the lasting ties between the two countries, the structure is a glaring reminder of the potential price of economic dependence, irrespective of its source or rationale. Echoes of the past resonate throughout the hallways of the building, a souvenir of the historic relationship between the Soviet Union and Cuba and a reminder of a time when the world was immersed in a Cold War.[2]

I went on to discuss Cuba's dogged efforts to hold on to the gains of the revolution in a highly unfavourable political and economic climate, with few allies to turn to for support, and concluded with the voice of Esteban Montejo, a staunch supporter of the Cuban Revolution and a loyal follower of Fidel, echoing in my ear. In 1968, Esteban Montejo, the 108-year-old former runaway slave who lived for years alone, wandering in the forests in order to elude recapture, gave an interview with Jamaican writer Andrew Salkey. Montejo had seen a great deal in his lifetime – he was a slave, experienced the Cuban independence war and the US invasion of the country which subverted a Cuban victory against the Spanish, and witnessed the Cuban Revolution unfold. His fascinating life and thoughts were recounted to and subsequently captured in a book by Cuban poet and writer, Miguel Barnet. In the Salkey interview, Montejo, who was very close to the Cuban Revolution and friends with many of its leading figures, makes a startling statement, suggesting that there would be another revolution in Cuba. In fact, he suggested that 'The day we lose the Revolution, we will not have another Fidel. We will have another Revolution, because our history says so, but we will not have the same Fidel on the scene. There is only one Fidel, and that's the one we've got right now. That one man alone,' he continues, 'like Fidel, can help to carry a nation, like Cuba, is a very incredible thing. I am not saying that that is a very good thing.'[3] As if anticipating the question that people in Cuba, and all over the world, began to ask as Castro grew older, Montejo stated, 'I think he needs help. When he goes who will take over?'[4]

In conclusion I wrote:

Yet today Cuba faces a crisis of the highest order. It is a crisis that threatens to dissolve the tremendous social gains that have been made in that country over the past 40 years and one that is already bringing to the surface all the old antagonisms enmeshed in the race/class nexus that have plagued the Americas since European contact with the indigenous peoples of the Americas and the enslavement of Africans in the New World.

And that:

> For the Cuban Revolution to survive and grow it will have to turn directly to its people. Cuba will have to further develop creative and popular approaches to social development and management, tapping into the creative efforts ... that make the utmost use of the population's abilities and its tested resilience.

A great deal has changed in Cuba since 2002, but the challenges remain the same, and mirror those of so many other parts of the world: what is freedom, and how do we exercise it? How is it possible to expand a revolution and the entitlements it engenders and acknowledge and embrace the spirit and meaning of freedom that socialism is supposed to represent, in the current capitalist conjuncture and its imperial designs and, in Cuba's case, in the absence of close powerful allies?

The most immediate contributing factor to writing *Dread Poetry and Freedom* was the news, shortly after returning from South Africa, that I was going to be a parent. Faced with the prospect of a child in a new century that demonstrated no signs of being markedly different from the old; amid a climate of environmental, social, political and economic degradation; and in an era of unbridled bloodletting, sanitized by the term 'ethnic cleansing' and numbed by the unrestrained bravado of what appeared to be, at the turn of the millennium, the world's sole superpower – I was forced to ask myself what kind of world do I envision for my daughter? What kind of world will she and her generation contribute to changing, I hope, for the better? *Dread Poetry and Freedom* is also an attempt to respond to those questions.

PROLOGUE

SOMETIME IN 1993 a friend, Richard Iton, who would later author the fabulous book *In Search of the Black Fantastic: Politics and Popular Culture in the Post-Civil Rights Era*, asked me whether or not I was familiar with Linton Kwesi Johnson's work. I wasn't, and Richard's sense of disbelief was obvious, as if to suggest 'you can't be serious'. His incredulous expression was not completely unfounded. He knew that I was born in London, England and that I had lived there for the first ten years of my life. Also, given my 'socialist proclivities' and political involvement at the time – I was an undergraduate university student who was active in both campus and community politics, and Richard and I, along with two other friends, were co-hosts of a radio programme (*Soul Perspectives*) on CKUT Radio that combined music with cultural and political commentary – it seemed only natural that I would have heard of Johnson, one of the deans of 'dub poetry'. Add to this the fact that I had been familiar with the work of Jamaican poets Mutabaruka and Oku Onuora and was aware of well-established Toronto-based poets Lillian Allen, Afua Cooper and Clifton Joseph, I too began to wonder why I was not familiar with Johnson's poetry. One day, just before one of our weekly radio shows, Richard handed me a cassette tape of Johnson's classic *Dread Beat an' Blood*, the album that first brought the poet international attention. Given Richard's persistence, I was now keen to listen, and when I did finally listen to the tape, I was stunned. I had not heard anything like it before.

There are not many artists like Johnson, and few have been as effective in blending creative talent with politics. Since his emergence on the poetry scene in the 1970s, Johnson has produced some of the best received and bestselling reggae recordings of his generation. He has developed a following throughout the world – South Africa, Japan, Brazil, among other places – and he is particularly well known and respected in France, where he has performed before thousands, as well as in Germany, Italy and other parts of Europe. His poetry has also been translated into German and Italian, and in 2002, a collection of his poetry was published under the Penguin Modern Classics series, making him only the second living poet at the time to be published in this series (the Polish poet Czesław Miłosz is the other). Johnson has influenced a whole generation of poets, hip-hop artists and political activists. In Britain, he has been described as 'the most conscientious godfather' of black British arts, and in 1987 he was nominated for a Grammy for the album *LKJ Live in Concert with the Dub Band.*

Listening to Johnson for the very first time in 1993 was a thoroughly new experience for me. First, the reggae music that accompanied his ominous verse was mystical and foreboding, but also decidedly urban compared to the Jamaican-based reggae that I grew up listening to as a child in the South London district of Peckham and in the streets and record shops in Brixton. The music gripped me as if I had been transposed into the place and time in which his poetry and music was set.

Second, the cadence of Johnson's monotone baritone voice was also surprisingly sonorous and his haunting chants had an almost wailing effect, reflecting the pain, suffering and woe of the people 'down below', that is to say his generation of black youth in Britain and the sufferers in Jamaica. His poetry not only resonated in Babylonian Britain where black youth confronted brutal police officers and their batons, but across the Atlantic in Canada where police killings of black youth have been carried out with impunity. In fact, unbeknownst to me at the time, the then Montreal-based Bahamian poet Michael Pintard had adopted a line from Johnson's 'Reggae fi Peach' to highlight the killing of black youth in the city. And such was the allure of the militant tone and the pulsating baseline of the musical accompaniment to his poetry that he had developed an underground following among young punks and skinheads in the UK.

Third, Johnson's verse was graphic, vivid and very compelling, and alongside his adept deployment of metaphors he left little doubt as to his thoughts on the internecine violence that had cast a shadow over London's black youth, and the all-too-common brutal police attacks on young blacks.

Fourth, unlike many of his dub poetry counterparts – Johnson himself has never fully embraced this term as a description of his poetry – I discovered in his verse a very familiar underlying phenomenological spirit. The theme of *Dread Beat an' Blood* was about the violence of the 'babylonian tyrants', fratricide, and, ultimately, the violence that he warned would be unleashed against the police and the state by their victims if the British bobbies and the government did not cease terrorizing them. But beneath his testimony on the fraternal bloodletting and the violence that Johnson had himself experienced at the hands of the police, and underneath his apparent call to arms, lay an underlying sense of human possibilities. In other words, he did not simply describe what *is* but also what can *be* within that delicate continuity and tension between being and becoming. Johnson projected the feeling that, despite the prevailing circumstances of dread, no situation was static and that genuine social change was not only desirable but necessary and also possible.

There were obvious parallels between Johnson's analysis of violent phenomena in Britain and Frantz Fanon's *The Wretched of the Earth*, and particularly the first chapter of that book, 'On Violence'. The similarities were too conspicuous to ignore, and later I discovered Johnson's 1976 essay, 'Jamaican Rebel Music', published in the UK journal *Race & Class*, in which he outlined the parallels between Fanon's phenomenological probe of violent phenomena under colonialism and his own assessment on the contemporary conditions in Jamaica. This now classic essay on the sociology of reggae not only confirmed my suspicion that his poetry has been profoundly influenced by Fanon's prose, but it also alerted me to his ability to step outside his art and analyse some of the very themes that his poetry addressed, but this time in poetic prose.

Linton Kwesi Johnson is not only a poet. He is, or at least has been, a political *engagé*, a French word that in this context is preferable to activist, as the latter has a ring of professionalism as if to suggest that 'activism' or activist work is a special vocation that only a select minority can undertake, as opposed to being engaged out of political necessity. Johnson has been actively engaged in grassroots political work since the early 1970s. His political life has infused his poetry, permitting an organic legitimacy that has nourished and sustained his art over the years and that is evident in his description of the plight of black British youth in England and the emergence of a black British bourgeoisie, as well as in his accounts of working-class struggles, the rise of Solidarity in Poland, the demise of the Soviet Union and the Eastern bloc, and the future of socialism. It is hard to imagine another poet who has contributed more to our political understanding of such a wide range of political events and phenomena, qualifying him, in my estimation, as a 'political poet par excellence', an accolade that he once accorded the esteemed Guyanese poet Martin Carter.

Johnson's early poetry forewarns of a new day, at times anticipating violent reactions to colonial oppression in Britain, at other times blending a Jamesian socialist critique with biblical metaphors deployed as an artistic and political motif, as he does in the poem 'Di Good Life'. His poetry reflects, but is in no way reducible to, the sum total of the personalities, literary and political figures, and experiences that have touched his life: from his grandmother and the Bible during his childhood in Jamaica, the poetic chanting of the Jamaican reggae chanter Big Youth; the writings of W.E.B. Du Bois, Frantz Fanon, and C.L.R. James whom he discovered as a member of the British Black Panther Movement in London, and his involvement in the political organization Race Today; to the contributions of his mentors in Britain – the poet-publisher John La Rose and poet-novelist Andrew Salkey – and the poetry of Aimé Césaire, Amiri Baraka, The Last Poets and Kamau Brathwaite.

When all is said and done, *Dread Poetry and Freedom* is about social change – the need for dramatic change in our time, and

Johnson is the vehicle through which I explore this issue in so far as his poetry typifies Brathwaite's description of artists as seers or harbingers of change who often perceive and anticipate developments long before they actually unfold; and Aristotle's description of the universal character of poetry and its ability to 'to describe what can happen, that is, what is possible because it is either likely or necessary'. Of all art forms, I suggest that poetry is particularly well placed to articulate society's needs and to at least hint at social developments to come. In some cases, this ability not only reflects artists' rare gifts but also their freedom to articulate in verse, and particularly in dread or destitute times, what others dare not say, or cannot see. Society often turns to its poets to shed light on the contemporary social situation, to pose difficult questions and, at times, to provide answers, or at least present political possibilities. Great artists are often well placed, even best placed, to assist us as we probe human possibilities, and poets are particularly well suited for this role.

'A poem is grounded in its time, whether it articulates its consciousness of this or not, and it does not have to manifest a direct awareness of its historical situation in order to be significant and to fulfill a rich definition of poetry.' But in addition to its context, the poetic image 'eludes causality' and is self-created in ways that cannot be reduced to being the product of external influences outside of the poetic images themselves.[1] Poets' great gifts include the ability to perceive what is often imperceptible to most and to project those observations in artistic form, but they can never be *fully* conscious of *all* the various strains, vibrations, events and influences that shape, motivate and compel them to do what they do because much of this creative process often happens behind their backs, leading to 'something larger than its author's conscious purpose, and something remote from its origins', according to T.S. Eliot, one of Linton Kwesi Johnson's favourite poets.[2] In this sense, the creative imagery of poetry enters into our consciousness as a phenomenon, a phenomenology of the heart and soul, produced by 'a flicker of the soul' that grips our being according to Gaston Bachelard,[3] imagery that we internalize as it touches our imaginations.[4] The end result is varied interpretations that may differ from the poet's presumed meaning.[5] Eliot goes as far as to suggest that not only may the reader's interpretation of a given poem differ considerably from the poet's, but that this interpretation may be both 'equally valid' or 'may even be better' than the author's, and in some instances might provide poets with insight into their own work.[6] All of this provides fertile ground for critical interpretation, including of the particular social-political context that has presumably shaped the poet's work. While it would be more than presumptuous for me to suggest that my interpretation of Johnson's poems are even better than his own, and given that this book is grounded in the lofty desire to make a modest contribution towards creating a just and equitable world, *Dread Poetry and Freedom* is not about Linton Kwesi Johnson's poetry; or put another way, it is about his poetry in so far as his poetry *qua* poetry is an expression of politics, or provides poetic insight into politics, again, premised on the presumption that poets are well placed to inform our understanding of political possibilities. In this spirit, this is not solely a book of criticism, but is written with what Bachelard refers to as 'pride', that is to say a phenomenological 'soulful' appreciation of the poet that is partial to the poetic aesthetics of his politics.[7]

I certainly take some poetic licence with Johnson's poetry, and although I would like to think that he would appreciate at least some of this book's insights, and at the risk of becoming what Sylvia Wynter once described as 'maggots' who feed 'on the decaying corpse of that which gives it a brief predatory life',[8] my main preoccupation here is to open a space for political reflection through poetry. However, as a meditation on the dynamics of social transformation I in no way want to suggest that social change is inevitable. The insanity that presently governs the world is real, coupled by a technological capacity that almost three decades after the end of the Cold War, still threatens to destroy the planet as we know it. Yet sinking into a calamitous sea of despair is neither desirable nor helpful. Change does not fall from the sky or miraculously appear in a single sweeping, cataclysmic flourish. As Johnson constantly reminds us, it is the 'each an evry wan a wi' that makes change and possibilities for change often emerge 'like a thief in the night', as a wise man once said, when it appears least likely to. Dread and destitute times can anticipate better days ahead.

* * *

I began writing the first draft of this book in October/November 2001 and completed the first draft (is a draft ever completed?) on 17 May 2002. That unwieldy draft was written in a moment of brooding self-reflection. After paring it down to a reasonable size I attempted to find a publisher. Several expressed interest but then ultimately declined – including the current publisher – on the basis that the manuscript did not fit within the conventional academic boundaries of literary criticism, politics or the social sciences in general. After several failed attempts I let the manuscript sit for over eleven years before returning to it in fits and starts. However, as my late Jamaican grandmother Ethilda James was fond of saying, 'nothing comes before time', and I have benefited from both recent work on Johnson and the kind of intellectual maturity that, one hopes, comes with the passage of time.

Having said that, this book would perhaps have been published earlier were it not for two other books: Fred Moten's *In the Break: The Aesthetics of the Black Radical Tradition* and Richard Iton's *In Search of the Black Fantastic: Politics and Popular Culture in the Post-Civil Rights Era*. In different ways, both books were important in terms of rethinking the relationship between art and politics in general, and in relation to Afro diasporic peoples in particular.

Drawing on the work of various poets, philosophers, poet-philosophers and political and cultural theorists, Chapter 1 probes the ways in which poetry permits us to think beyond the here and now and to envision new possibilities, at times precisely because the possible and impossible appear to be least possible. The chapter then turns to Johnson's poetic and political evolution in the 1970s in London, including the impact of the British Black Panther Movement and Race Today and the life and work of W.E.B. Du Bois, John La Rose, Frantz Fanon and C.L.R. James on the poet's work.

Chapter 2 draws on Johnson's early essays on Jamaican popular music and Rastafari to explore the apocalyptic concept of dread and the impact of dread dialectics, via Rastafari and the Bible, on the poet, despite the fact that he is an atheist. As we shall see, the concept of dread – in both its Jamaican/Rastafarian and English-language sense of the word – is crucial to appreciating the poet's early work. The chapter also examines the phenomenology of the reggae aesthetic and gender dynamics through the prism of several Caribbean and Afro diasporic 'dread' poets, including Jean Binta Breeze and d'bi young anitafrika.

Chapter 3 probes Frantz Fanon's phenomenology – Fanonmenology – of violence and Aimé Césaire surrealism – Césairealism – in Johnson's 'blood poems' of dread. In invoking Fanon, not only does Johnson posit a notion of violence that describes the police brutality and state oppression that proscribed black youth life chances in the 1970s, but in so doing, he proffers a vision of social change as a dynamic, unfolding dialectical process that casts light on Fanon's conception of humanism and freedom.

Chapter 4 explores Johnson's *Making History* poems and his deployment of the elegy as a form of poetic-political expression in the poem 'Reggae fi Radni', a poem about the late Guyanese pan-Africanist, Marxist, historian and political figure, Walter Rodney. Rodney was killed in Guyana in June 1980. In the poem, his life becomes the embodiment of eclipsed dreams, but also the possibility of new possibilities if – as both Johnson and C.L.R. James suggest – we can learn from Rodney's political practice and the circumstances under which his unseemly death occurred.

Originally written in the municipality of Vedado in Havana in December–January 2002 as Cuba grappled with its socialist past and attempted to chart a course for a renewed socialist future, Chapters 5 and 6 scan Johnson's *Tings an' Times* in which he meditates on past struggles, the impending collapse of apartheid, the collapse of the former Soviet Union and the relevance of socialism. Drawing on C.L.R. James's conception of socialism as self-organization – as well as biblical lore as metaphor, including the symbolism of Moses and the promised land and the birth, death and resurrection of Christ, and nursery rhymes that harken back to his childhood – the poet interprets the rise and fall of the communist wall as part of the cycle of death and rebirth and as a precursor to genuine socialism or freedom in our time.

Chapter 7 probes the concepts of time, technology, mortality and the relationship between leisure and the human capacity to creatively create. Johnson's elegy 'Reggae fi May Ayim' and the poem 'More Time' are examined alongside the work of several theorists (John La Rose, David Harvey and Jonathon Martineau, among others) in order to probe the relationship between alienation, time and politics.

Continuing from the previous chapter, Chapter 8 concludes by positing a vision of social change that is influenced by the creative capacity that is inherent in poetry. I argue that if fundamental social change is indeed possible, we will have to break with outmoded notions that hamper or stifle our creativity and the ability to build healthy communities and societies, and that poetry, and art in general, often points the way towards new horizons of possibility.

Chapter 1

THE POET'S ROUTES

Poetry is not only dream and vision; it is the skeleton architecture of our lives. It lays the foundations for a future of change, a bridge across our fears of what has never been before.

Audre Lorde

… No, poetry,
Do not hide yourself away in the grottoes of my being
espouse life
Break the invisible bars of my prison
open the gates of my being through and through
and leave…

Amilcar Cabral

I must be given words to refashion futures
like a healer's hand

Edward Kamau Brathwaite

'In the beginning was the word, and until you can conceive of change, then that change will not come about.' This declaration by the renowned Barbadian poet Kamau Brathwaite captures the spirit of words – poetry – as the quintessential embodiment of the power of the word as a harbinger of rebellion, change and freedom.[1] Brathwaite was inspired by the Kongo concept of *nommo*, or what he describes as calling upon or naming change in words – in poetry – in order that change can be, and we can think about the significance of poetry and social change through the particular experience of specific groups because poetry is local, particular and time sensitive. Its timelessness is tied to the era in which it is produced, and to the 'language of the tribe' that produces it, according to C.L.R. James. For James: 'Poetry comes from deep down in the social consciousness and attitudes of the population', even if poets are not fully conscious of the extent to which their words give voice to the time and place where the poet is situated.[2]

Poetry is 'distilled life', according to the great American poet Gwendolyn Brooks. It has the capacity to move our spirits and inspire hope that the change we desire and desperately require is indeed possible even when, and sometimes precisely because, we believe it is least likely. Poets are both imaginers and diviners who draw on cosmic sources and everyday experience,[3] the ultimate form of expression for the renowned Barbadian poet Kamau Brathwaite, or the 'primal impulse' that gives birth to all other art forms. It 'begins with the heartbeat. If the heart beats, poetry begins. If you open eyes and see the light, the trees, the shadows, poetry begins.' Poetry also sustains 'distance' or what he describes as 'a longer sense of time and space' that permits changes in terms of rhythms, venues and moods; and the poet is a philosopher whose words 'reorganize the world' and even resurrect the world by foreshadowing the possibilities that are available within a community because the poet is of the community and understands it, but also recognizes that the 'tidalectic' of time and space suggests that poets cannot always be certain of their certitude.[4]

Like, Brathwaite, Édouard Glissant suggests that 'The poet is one who has a vision and a conception of the world' and he too privileges poetry over theory, fiction or theatre 'because poetry cannot be conceived as anything but the exercise, the attempt, of uncovering hidden truths or hidden dimensions of existence – at any rate, those which are not apparent to people in any common way'.[5] Poetry permits us to avoid the prison of 'socio-historical situations' and to 'to enter the poem of the world', to 'enter into *all* of reality'.[6] Poetry is life itself for Glissant, or at least it is 'the breath of the living, of that which lives' but 'cannot speak … cannot write … cannot sing',[7] or, as the American poet Adrienne Rich suggests, poets are endowed 'to speak for those who do not have the gift of language, or to see for those who – for whatever reasons – are less conscious of what they are living'.[8] It is 'the breath of the volcanoes, of the mountains, of the rivers, of the seas, of the cultures' and, according to Glissant, the poet 'feels that in the world'.[9] Poetry is also life for the French philosopher Jacques Derrida, or at least it breathes life into language: 'Each poem is a resurrection, but one that engages us to a vulnerable body, one that may be forgotten again', or resurrects language when it is near dead or dormant, a sentiment that Derrida shared with the American and British poet and playwright T.S. Eliot.[10]

Poetry, at its best, is not predictable. We can never be sure how a poem might touch our minds and souls because poetry has a life of its own, reaching 'into the realm of chance' according to the American poet and critic C.K. Williams, and it is the poet's ability 'to fuse the unlikely with the undeniable' that gives poetry meaning through 'the intensity of metaphor', among other things.[11] Poets perform the daunting task of forging an 'uncreated consciousness', to borrow a phrase from James Joyce,[12] and in this same spirit, cultural critic and feminist theorist bell hooks simply describes poetry as 'the place of transcendence',[13] or what the Jamaican poet Jean Binta Breeze succinctly describes as 'truth'.[14] Again, it is through its particularity that we hear the poet's universality, a language, an art form that is premised on the peculiarity of the poet's literary voice that speaks from and through the poet's experience. In this spirit, as the Jamaican cultural theorist Carolyn Cooper reminds us, poetry 'is not a language of generalities' but 'a celebration, in the making, of particulars',[15] that is to say poetry is experiential, rooted in the context (time and space) in which it is written and in the experiences and consciousness of the poet, but the poem 'does not have to manifest a direct awareness of its historical situation in order to be significant and to fulfill a rich definition of poetry'.[16]

Poetry is experiential and Gaston Bachelard speaks of the 'exuberance and depth' of the poem and the poem as a 'resonance-reverberation doublet'.[17] The experience of exuberance awakens new depths within us, reverberating through language in ways that resonate with our being as we feel the poetic creativity in the depths of our souls.[18] In this sense poetry is sensuous and experiential, not simply intellectual. Poetry is also experimental in so far as it explores new forms, or old forms in new contexts and guises, refashioning old language in novel ways that often transcend established norms. According to great Palestinian poet Mahmoud Darwish, poetry rebels against the critic and reason,[19] although for Fred Moten the line that separates poetry from critical theory is blurred.[20] Either way, if we think of the musicality of poetry in terms of rhythm and message, the audience is an important part of the 'musicking' process – that is, the act and process of making and participating (both musician/singers and audience) in music-making through interpretation and understanding[21] – because it adds meaning and interpretation that often extends outside and beyond the artist's intentions and imagination,[22] and even as poets write in isolation they both consciously and unconsciously consider their audience's expectations and desires.

Poetic knowledge and experience also represents 'the astonishing mobilization of human and cosmic powers' that appeals to our unconsciousness and, according to the Martiniquan poet Aimé Césaire, 'contains within it the original relationships that unite us with nature'. It is the poet who possesses the capacity to restore humanity to universal harmony[23] and 'who marries a human florescence to universal florescence'; in this sense, 'poetry is a blossoming' that also 'returns language to its pure state' as words create revolutionary images that break through barriers on the path to truth.[24] Put another way, poets paint with words that touch our imaginations, they possess the capacity to expand our sense of what is humanly possible, or permit us to imagine that the impossible is possible, that rare gift of the seer or soothsayer, or the poet as prophet, a prominent phenomenon in poetry from Isaiah to Milton to Tupac, and, again, particularly in times of dread.[25] The rhythm and music of poetry is internally driven and contains sound but cannot be reduced to its aurality, according to Césaire.[26] It is a music that sits 'latent in the common speech of its time' and latent in the common speech of the poet's *place*', according to T.S. Eliot, for whom this music conveys meaning

that is tied to the common, changing language of the people
to whom the poet belongs or who surround the poet, creating
melody and harmony from the sound of the language.[27]

The German philosopher Martin Heidegger also argues that
poetry represents the quintessential art and that all art is essen-
tially a poetry that reveals that which is concealed but present
as 'language alone brings what is, as something that is, into
the Open for the first time'.[28] Poetic language unconceals or
unlocks new possibilities and desires and reveals what can be
while anticipating what is to come, and in doing so it synthesizes
the interconnectedness between the past, present and future. It
is a unique ability 'to describe what can happen, that is, what is
possible because it is either likely or necessary' that defines the
poet according to Aristotle.[29] But this apparent gift of foresight
is actually the gift of sight, an acute ability to tap into the spirit
of the existing moment and to hone in on and sense our joy,
pain or anger and disaffection or the capacity to inspire us to
project beyond the present and imagine what can be despite
or often because of what is. It is through the poet, in the eyes
of the Chilean poet Pablo Neruda, that 'freedom and the sea |
will make their answer to the shattered heart'.[30] For the French
philosopher Alain Badiou, the poem is 'active thinking' and it
effectuates the infinite power of language 'by delving into the
latent song of language, in the infinity of its resources, in the
novelty of its assemblage', but it also 'stops language in its tracks
and prohibits its squandering in the vast commerce that is the
world today. Against the obscenity of "everything to be seen" and
"everything to be said," the showing, polling, and commenting
of everything, the poem is the guardian of the decency of the
saying', or what he describes as 'a delicacy of language against
language' or 'a delicate touching of the resources of language'.[31]

If the poets' appreciation of the present and the past facilitates
their capacity to project into the future, this ability is especially
important in times of dread, one of those curious words to which
we will return. As the Grenadian and American feminist and poet
Audre Lorde wrote, 'poetry is not a luxury. It is a vital necessity
of our existence. It forms the quality of the light within which

we predicate our hopes and dreams towards survival and change, first made into language, then into idea, then into more tangible action. Poetry is the way we help give name to the nameless so it can be thought. The farthest horizons of our hopes and fears are cobbled by our poems, carved from the rock experiences of our daily lives'.[32] While Lorde was referring specifically to poetry's significance for women, her remarks speak to the role of the poet and what poetry can do in general in times of dread and crisis when the poetic imagination becomes a human necessity. This is what the American poet Amiri Baraka meant when he argued that poets possess the ability to 'raise the sun every morning' and raise the level of human 'comprehension of the world' in moments of 'absolute darkness', that is to say, 'raising the level of human consciousness' about the need for revolution. For Baraka, poets carry the message that humans can make leaps beyond the moment (Baraka was speaking at a time when George W. Bush was in power in the US, but his remarks clearly speak to Trump times and the overall global political climate).[33] And as Baraka's fellow poet and kindred Maoist dialectician, the Englishman J.H. Prynne, has suggested, to be a poet 'is to be in direct potential communication with every part of the world's action, including, without doubt, all its misery'.[34] Indeed, poetry can guide us through the misery, through times of dread or what the German poet Friedrich Hölderlin via Heidegger describes as 'destitute times'. Poets jump into the abyss in such times, tracing the steps along the trail that leads into the light while bringing us closer to understanding the labour necessary to enter it.[35] But whereas Heidegger dismisses those descriptions that reduce poetry to 'whimsicalities' or 'a flight of mere notions and fancies into the realm of the unreal',[36] it is precisely the fanciful and unreal that draw us to some poets because they permit us to escape an undesirable present and to anticipate another reality. In this spirit we must abandon the false dichotomies between the real/unreal or surreal, or between spiritual and material existence. Poetry and poetic lyricism often work in mysterious ways, bringing together the real, unreal, surreal, spiritual and material worlds, thereby acknowledging that these phenomena have never truly parted ways. Poetry is cosmic and mystical, or at least can be, and it ventures into the world of the marvellous which resides in the poet, taking the mythical seriously in appreciation of the reality that there is so much that science and reason cannot explain while incorporating the heart and reason, fragmentation and the whole, and the false and the true. This is poetry's gift according to Césaire.[37]

When the destitute and the damned find their form and act in times of dread it is often the poet who gives creative expression to and validates their actions because, as Darwish once argued, poetry is also rooted in a sense of social justice for the victimized.[38] The Mexican poet Octavio Paz tells us that *'When History wakes, | image becomes act, the poem happens: poetry moves into action'*,[39] sometimes in order to critically assess, chide and even chastise history's actors and not simply romanticize and celebrate those who make history. As Badiou suggests, 'Poets are those who try to make a language say what it seems incapable of saying' while naming that which has been nameless and sharing the gift of language with the people for the common good: 'A tense, paradoxical, violent love of life in common; the desire that what ought to be common and accessible to all should not be appropriated by the servants of Capital. The poetic desire that the things of life would be like the sky and the earth, like the water of the oceans and the brush fires on a summer night – that is to say, would belong by right to the whole world.' For Badiou, poetry should be offered 'to the mute, to the stutterer, to the stranger ... and not to the chatterbox, to the grammarian, or to the nationalist. It is to the proletarian ... that we must give the entire earth, as well as all the books, and all the music, and all the paintings, and all the sciences' along with 'the poem of communism'. Of course, embedded in Badiou's remarks is the idea that poetry must be bestowed upon or shared with the dispossessed, but in the case of Caribbean poetry and the dread poetry of Jamaica, it is precisely this caste of outcasts and the evicted, who, because of their outsider status, have been a major source of creative expression, including poetic and musical expression.[40]

If poetry is the product of the interplay between the artist's creativity and the social, cultural and political environment in which the artist lives, it is also true that the physical environment is important to poetry and art in general. The Cuban writer Alejo Carpentier certainly thought so when he wrote the following about the Cuban painter Wifredo Lam: 'it had to be a painter from the Americas, Wifredo Lam, to show us the magic of tropical vegetation, the unbridled Creation of Forms of our natural world, with all its metamorphoses and symbioses, in monumental canvases of expressiveness unique in contemporary painting'.[41] For Lam and his friend Aimé Césaire, the natural world served as metaphor for the magnificent and malevolent embodied in what the Martiniquan surrealist theorist Suzanne Césaire (née Lacascade) referred to as the plant-man that is 'dead but being reborn'.[42] In this spirit, Lam's poetic painting *The Jungle* represents a metaphorical jungle in Cuba in which two symbols of exploitation – sugarcane and the sex trade – merge.

Art, then, including poetry, is an expression of the material-ideological and ecological world, which is given further expression in the creative process of its production. This also raises the question of form, in this case the form of poetic expression in relation to ideology and politics. While poetry assumes its own form and structure, tied to but not wholly dependent on the ideologies that have assisted in its creation, the ideology also changes in the process of producing art.[43] This is perhaps what Derrida means when he suggests that a poet is one who surrenders to the truth of language with its own inner meaning that is separate from what we might describe in this case as the poem's ideological meaning;[44] and in the process, the poet resurrects language and breathes life into it so that it may speak to us, even if its speech exists in codes that are sometimes difficult to decipher.

If a poem is a product of its time and place, even when its context is not consciously acknowledged by the poet,[45] and if it speaks to the soul as 'a kind of song, a fugue of thoughts, emotions, perceptions, beliefs, ideals, hopes', according to C.K. Williams, and is 'too grand' for 'even the philosophical mind, to grasp'[46] – if this is so, then it is important to understand that context in which the early poetry of Linton Kwesi Johnson emerged and how the poetry of this 'political poet par excellence' came into being.

* * *

In 1981 riots erupted in cities across England: Brixton in London, Chapeltown in Leeds, Toxteth in Liverpool, Moss Side in Manchester and Handsworth in Birmingham. Police officers were attacked and properties in neighbourhoods were burned to the ground during the days of rage, and while the triggers of these urban rebellions varied, they were all tied to ongoing racial tension and animosity with the police, a primary point of contact between working-class black British youth and the state. The rebellion captured the attention of people across the world, and caught the British public by surprise, but at least one poet had anticipated these explosive rebellions and warned whomever chose to listen that the state of racial oppression in England could not be endured by young blacks and that their pent-up anger and frustration, often expressed in internecine violence, would at some point erupt against the state.

As I have suggested, destitute times, times of dread and times of revolt, revolution and the euphoria associated with upheaval have been particularly important for the production of poetry. Poetry, and particularly poetry that is explicitly political, flourished during the anti-colonial liberation struggle in Namibia,[47] in Grenada during its short-lived revolution between 1979 and 1983,[48] in Cuba in the early days of its revolution,[49] in South Africa during the anti-apartheid struggle[50] and among African Americans during the Civil Rights-Black Power continuum, to name just a few examples. In Jamaica poets such as Dennis Scott, Bongo Jerry and Lorna Goodison emerged as Jamaica grappled with the legacy of slavery and colonialism in the post-independence period, but most of Jamaica's poetic expression in the 1970s took the form of lyricism associated with reggae music. It was reggae, along with African American poetry, Césaire and the poetics of Fanon, that were important for Linton Kwesi Johnson as the young poet emerged in those dread days in London in the 1970s. Not only would his poetry reflect the feelings of young blacks, and particularly young male members of the UK black population, but it was his poetry that presaged the days of rage that rattled urban Britain in the early 1980s, even though, as the poet himself has acknowledged, 'you didn't have to be a prophet to know what happens if you keep pouring oil on a fire: the beatings, brutalisations, frame-ups'.[51]

Johnson's poetry exemplifies the role that poetic insight and foresight can play in articulating politics that capture a given historical moment while foreshadowing human possibilities that are largely unapparent, or at least less apparent, to most. This is a peculiar privilege of some artists, including visual artists, but it is perhaps particularly true of artists who paint images with words, and especially poets. In Johnson's case, his poetry has been rooted in his active participation in the very politics that he has given expression to in his writing, and in this sense he defies the stereotypical notion of aloof poets who are largely disconnected from the movements that inspire them. In this spirit, he might be described as the 'political poet par excellence', a title he once bestowed on the Guyanese poet Martin Carter,[52] and the antithesis of what the British Guyanese poet Fred D'Aguiar describes as artists who 'retreat to an aestheticized corner of the planet' and 'merely create the illusion in the body politic of having escaped the earth's gravitational pull'.[53] Johnson's poetry has been grounded in the desires, defeats and victories of the black British population in England, the aspirations of the working class and in a socialist ethos that poses the question: what is the good life and how do we arrive at it?

From the outset of his poetic life, Johnson dismissed the notion of 'art for art's sake', as writing for him was 'a political act and poetry a cultural weapon in the black liberation struggle'.[54] He has argued that his insights regarding the relationship between culture and politics were rooted in the ideas of the

Guinea-Bissauan revolutionary leader and theorist Amilcar Cabral, who also wrote poetry.[55] Although Johnson does not elaborate on exactly how Cabral informed him,[56] he is perhaps alluding to the importance that Cabral attached to culture as a tool of emancipation. For Cabral, 'Culture is simultaneously the fruit of a people's history and a determinant of history, by the positive or negative influence it exerts on the evolution relations between man and his environment and among men or human groups within a society, as well as between different societies.' While Cabral was speaking about culture as a product of material circumstances, determined by a given mode of production,[57] it is not difficult to see how, for Johnson, this might be applied to poetry as a product of a given society (England or Jamaica, the latter in terms of its 'rebel music'), but which can also influence that society.

As D'Aguiar argues, politics is Johnson's 'muse, an organizing principal, an ethical foundation and vibe for his sound'.[58] But in more recent years, Johnson has come to appreciate poetry's range,[59] and even in the 1970s he was unwilling to absolutely subsume poetry to politics, cautioning against propagandistic or didactic poetry in which craft is sacrificed for politics: 'If politics creeps into art unconsciously, without the writer trying, that's often the most powerful' expression of politics, 'But when the artists try to *be* political in their art it usually ends up badly, whether in poetry or in a novel or other art forms. People don't like to be preached at.'[60]

Throughout the 1970s and well into the dusk of the twentieth century, Johnson articulated many of the major social and political concerns of the times, and in the process he has helped to raise the level of public political consciousness of British people, at times anticipating what is to come while suggesting the possibility of better days ahead.[61] This combination of acute artistic sensitivity and his active involvement in politics has fostered what Amor Kohli refers to as his 'poetics of participation' – the use of language and rhythm designed to raise the political consciousness of the poet's audience.[62] Writing on the poetics of Kamau Brathwaite, critic June D. Dobbs has argued that he 'submerges the individual self, and his voice is always the voice of the community. Through his voice the contemporary pains and possibilities of his community are distilled and added to the archives of ancestral memory. Brathwaite adopts the mask of the African griot. He is a seer who is the repository of a people's wisdom, culture, and vision.'[63] However, a mask implies a hidden presence, whereas Johnson's poetry has served to expose the mask that shields society's inequalities while emphasizing black and working-class self-activity in the struggle for social change, and for socialism, in Europe and the Caribbean.

Johnson's poetry is part of the cultural and political praxis that Caribbean and Afro diasporic people continue to engage with in Britain as part of what the Jamaican poet Louise Bennett once described as 'colonizin in reverse'.[64] In the arena of music, this process was inaugurated in the post-Second World War period with the invasion of ska, and in particular Jamaican singer Millie Small's hit, 'My Boy Lollipop'.[65] Small's youthful voice, backed by an uptempo ska rhythm, topped the British charts and broke into the international market in 1964, opening the gates for other Jamaican artists and laying the groundwork for the reggae surge that dramatically influenced the British music industry – there is no punk music without ska – and the cultural politics of British society in general. Colonizing in reverse was part of an ongoing process of diasporization. Having been dragged to the Caribbean from Africa during slavery, Afro Caribbean women and men lived a double displacement in which, out of economic necessity, they found themselves in Britain in search of opportunities that were not available to them at home because of the political-economic legacy of slavery and colonialism. After the Second World War, West Indians were encouraged to immigrate to England in order to rebuild a devastated country, and yet despite their 'Britishness' and the long history of blacks in England dating at least as far back as the sixteenth century,[66] they faced economic hardship and fierce, even brutal racial reprisals.

UK Black

England of the 1960s and 1970s was teeming with racial tension, and the growing presence of blacks increasingly became a social problem that many white Britons believed needed to be contained. The British MP Enoch Powell called for the deportation of blacks and a halt to black emigration. But emigration was a product of the process in which blacks shifted from producers of surplus labour on the slavery plantation to surplus labourers. Caribbean women and men sought opportunities in the UK in the post-emancipation and post-Second World War era that were not available to them in the Caribbean because of the legacy of slavery, colonialism and underdevelopment under capitalism, only to find themselves exiled, alienated, often unemployed and the target of hostile whites in the UK, presumably for taking jobs that whites assumed were rightly theirs, even if these were jobs that whites either did not want or were in some instances underqualified to assume. As the incomparable Caron Wheeler, the former lead singer of the British group Soul II Soul, sang in her 1990 black British anthem 'UK Black', the streets were not paved with gold as many believed when they crossed the Atlantic to the UK, but despite the disappointment and hostility they faced, blacks were forced to forge a life for themselves.[67] The character Hortense Roberts came to terms with this same reality in Andrea Levy's lovely novel *Small Island*.[68]

Consistent with Powell's words were the actions of the National Front and the rise of neo-fascism – a phenomenon captured in Johnson's anti-fascist poem 'Fite dem Back' – that went beyond rhetoric and led to physical attacks against people of African and Asian descent.[69] The character of Britain was changing as Caribbean, African and Asian migrants planted roots in the country, and racial antagonisms and tensions would later magnify and eventually explode. Police brutality was a major issue as the police abused young blacks with impunity, aided and abetted by Britain's so-called 'sus laws', a throwback to the nineteenth-century Vagrancy Act that permitted the police to stop, search and detain 'suspicious' looking characters.[70] In the watershed 1978 study *Policing the Crisis: Mugging, the State, and Law and Order* written by Stuart Hall, Chas Critcher, Tony Jefferson, John Clarke and Brian Roberts, the authors argued that a combination of intense policing and surveillance and incendiary headlines about mugging and crime led to high arrest rates and harsh sentencing in reaction to the presumed pervasiveness of criminality (despite statistics that suggested the contrary), all of which contributed to a tense and volatile atmosphere in the UK.[71] The police used questionable tactics that led to the disproportionate arrests and detention of black youth for muggings or loitering with the intent to steal, all of which led to a deterioration in police–black relations and the swamping of black neighbourhoods by the Special Patrol Group (SPG) while reinforcing the alarmist perception of blacks as a threat to 'law and order'. Locked in Giorgio Agamben's permanent state of exception,[72] this was part of the disciplining, punishing and dehumanizing of blacks – whose image, Paul Gilroy suggests, was associated with 'squalor', 'sordid sexuality' and the fear of 'miscegenation' in ways that precipitated the perception of Afro Britons as criminals[73] – by the state and its instruments such as the SPG, the Special Branch, and the Illegal Immigration Intelligence Unit in Britain, and by racists and neo-fascists who physically attacked blacks with impunity.[74] These attacks were also consistent with what I have referred to elsewhere as biosexuality or the biosexual sense of dread that the physical presence of black bodies – in this sense perceived to be devoid of intellect, the life of the mind, and morality – have historically engendered in Europe and the Americas which, dating back to the history of slavery, persists in slavery's afterlife in the form of the dread of black–white solidarity and black–white interracial mixing and overall racial animosity.[75] This, alongside high rates of unemployment among black and immigrant groups, the intense scrutiny of black communities by the media, violent attacks, including the firebombing of black communities, xenophobic rants by politicians like Powell[76] and the threat of physical violence from the neofascist National Front led to a untenable situation that would inevitably explode as young blacks became increasingly radicalized and politicized.

Johnson has characterized this moment in two poems, 'Fite dem Back' and 'Sonny's Lettah'. 'Fite dem Back' is an anti-fascist poem in response to attacks against people of African and Asian descent in Britain in which the speaker parodies or 'vintrilo-quizes',[77] to use Peter Hitchcock's word, the English (cockney) of a violent racist neofascist chant – 'we gonna smash their brains in I cause they ain't got nofink in 'em'.[78] Ashley Dawson's describes 'Fite dem Back' as a reaction 'to neofascist attacks with a militant assertion of the black community's ability to meet racist violence with effective resistance in a striking affir-mation of collective power' while testifying 'to the acuity of Frantz Fanon's discussion of the humanizing effect of counter-violence within a context of racial domination and terror'.[79] 'Sonny's Lettah' is a harrowing poem that captures the sense of dread and frustration that black British youth felt in the late 1970s and into the 1980s. When Johnson joined his mother, Sylvena, a machinist and dressmaker, in Brixton in 1963 it was the centre of London's Caribbean population. The Jamaican language, Patwa, and other Caribbean creoles were widely spoken among the growing Caribbean population and the cultural life in Brixton helped ease the transition for Johnson as it did for many Caribbean families.[80] But the poet became intimately familiar with the reality of police violence as he had been beaten by officers in the back of a police van and then charged with two counts of assault when he attempted to com-municate with black youth who had been arrested by the police, as he had been trained to do in the Panthers.[81] 'Sonny's Lettah' begins with the greeting 'Dear Mama I Good day I I hope dat wen I deze few lines reach yu I they may find yu in de bes af helt'.[82] Like any normal letter, the sender's address is indicated in the right-hand column of the page. But the letter's feigned innocence is reminiscent of Prince Buster's 'Ghost Dance' which begins in a similar fashion (Dear Keithus, my friend, good day I Hoping you're keeping the best of health) followed by a series of sombre greetings, commentaries and queries offered by an apparent ghost who, for reasons unknown, has passed on but seemingly has unfinished business among the living.[83] But the revolutionary theorist George Jackson's prison letters to his mother are perhaps closest to the tenor and tone of Johnson's poem. The English edition of *Soledad Brother* was published in 1971[84] and was part of the British Black Panther Movement's (BBPM) required reading list.[85] In this 'poem of experience', as the British author and educator Chris Searle has described the book, Jackson frequently begins with the same greeting as 'Sonny's Lettah' – 'Dear Mama' – after which he too inquires about his mother's health. But in both cases the routine greeting is interrupted by the reality of incarceration. Sonny is writing from a Brixton prison cell, having been charged with murder. As he informs his mother, despite his best efforts to take care of his brother, he and Jim have been arrested and he proceeds to describe the circumstances surrounding his detention, contrasting the hustle and bustle of the rush hour period with the seemingly innocuous activity of two brothers waiting at a bus stop. A black maria (police van) pulls up to the stop and the officers proceed to arrest Jim without cause, and Jim attempts to wriggle himself free. Sonny then details the officers' brutal beating of his brother and how he jumped to his defence, resulting in the death of one of the officers. The poet's sombre voice combines with a melancholy melody that is punctuated by abrupt breaks in the music, producing a dramatic, almost theatrical effect. While it might seem more natural to draw parallels between the poem and reggae don Peter Tosh's 'Watcha Gonna Do?' or perhaps Tupac's 'Dear Mama' or Kendrick Lamar's 'Collect Calls', an obvious but not so obvious parallel would be The Clash's 1979 song 'The Guns of Brixton',[86] written and sung by the punk rock group's bass player Paul Simonon, a white Englishman who grew up among blacks in Brixton where he gained an appreciation for reggae music. In what Paul Gilroy has described as a particular moment of black–white solidarity expressed culturally in the punk 'appropriation of black style and their hostility to both racist nationalism and nationalist racism in several records which recast reggae music in their own idiom'[87] – a solidarity perhaps expressed in Bob Marley's song 'Punky Reggae Party'[88] – The Clash also covered Lee 'Scratch' Perry's song 'Police and Thieves', made famous by the legendary Jamaican falsetto Junior Murvin. Aside from the obvious fact that 'The Guns of Brixton' is set in Brixton, Simonon raises the question of what is the appropriate response to police violence and brutality – whether to die guns blazing when the police knock down the door, ultimately ending up dead or on death row for murder, or to passively submit to the police, running the risk of being killed. In response to the question, Simonon invokes the spirit of the singer turned gangster Ivan, the lead character (played by the legendary Jamaican singer and reggae pioneer Jimmy Cliff) in the 1972 film *The Harder They Come*, who was killed in a fury of gunfire exchange with Jamaican police. The ultimate answer: police brutality will have to contend with the guns of Brixton, which can literally mean those with guns in Brixton, but figuratively suggests the 'young guns' of Brixton, which is to say assertive and confident youth who are unwilling to passively endure police brutality and simply turn the other cheek.

Parallels with Queen's 'Bohemian Rhapsody' and Ella Fitzgerald's version of 'Miss Otis Regrets' also come to mind here, not in terms of lead singer Freddie Mercury's mercurial voice and remarkable range, or Fitzgerald's melodic phrasing, but in the caesurae, the pauses and the sense of timing, momentarily occupying the spaces between the words and lines as the speaker ponders in the moment, and in so doing compels us to dwell in it too as we meditate on the gravity of the events or anticipate the tragedy that is about to unfold.[89] The point here is that the printed verse and the music-accompanied recording of 'Sonny's Lettah' represent different versions of the same poem. 'Sonny's Lettah' is a poem to be heard more so than read, both in terms of the cadence of the poet's voice and for how the music both serves the poem and speaks on its own terms as, for example, when the thumping sound of the bass drum simulates the repetitive and monotonous everydayness of Jim's experience with the police, including the blows that Jim receives from the officers, and the licks in kind that Sonny administers to one of the officers. The overdubbed baseline and the ominous-sounding harmonica provide a haunting sense of foreboding. This, along with the poet's characteristic caesura, the 'breaks', that compel us to dwell and linger in the moment long enough to ponder with the poet – all of this can only be inadequately represented but not reproduced on the printed page.[90]

The most direct correspondence to 'Sonny's Lettah' is 'Dear Mama' by the Jamaican and Canadian poet, actor and playwright d'bi young anitafrika. Not only was the poem inspired by 'Sonny's Lettah' but it was also dedicated to Johnson, and like 'Sonny's Lettah', it too begins with a greeting ('dear mama | good afternoon | I hope you are happy and well | I have something to tell | you'), though not from a prison cell in Brixton, but from an undisclosed Canadian location. But the polite greeting, witty rhyme scheme and the speaker's curiosity about her family members and the neighbours back home contrasts with the tone of the entire poem in which the speaker struggles to share her tragic news with Mama. As in 'Sonny's Lettah', the poet's repeated use of the words 'Mama' and 'you' followed by an ellipsis that emphasizes the importance of the personal relationship between mother and child and anticipates the failed desire of the child to live up to Mama's expectations. The fact that she was sent to Canada to establish a better life is overshadowed by an HIV test that she took nine months ago that indicated that she is HIV positive. The nine months associated with the birthing cycle that brings life into being is juxtaposed with tragic news that is compounded by the speaker's observation that, as a black woman, the irony is that AIDS doesn't discriminate, and that the absence of discrimination works against her in this instance.

The rest of the poem recounts a litany of reactions and misconceptions concerning AIDS, including ridicule by her friends, the assumption that AIDS is a gay white male disease, ostracism as well as rumour-mongering at her expense.[91] But the poem is also about a woman's relationship with her mother and a yearning for home, coupled by a sense of dread and the mortal fear that family members and friends will discover the news.[92] 'Dear Mama' is not simply a gendered or feminist rendering of Johnson's poem: it is about sexuality, homosexuality and the dread of HIV-AIDS, and like young's poem 'Blood', it is also about shame, in this case the shame associated with contracting the virus.

Blooded

The Black Panther Party was at the forefront of black struggles in the United States in the late 1960s and early 1970s. Internationally, the Panthers became a strident symbol of radical social change, and inspired by the Panther's militancy, similar groups emerged in the Caribbean and Europe, and in India among the Dalits or 'untouchable' caste. Britain was no exception, and Linton Kwesi Johnson became an active member of the youth league of the British Black Panther Movement, one of several Black Power organizations in England and part of a long history of black political organizations in the UK,[93] while he was still in secondary school. Despite being a bright student in Jamaica, like so many other black students, he was quickly channelled into a vocational stream in England, which he eventually worked his way out of. He joined the BBPM's Youth League after being impressed with one of its leaders, Althea Jones-Lecointe, when she participated in a debate at his high school, Tulse Hill, and the BBPM played a central role in his political awakening ('I don't think I would be the kind of person that I am today if it wasn't for having been through the Black Panther Movement').[94] He participated in the organization's various meetings, sold its newspaper and canvassed door-to-door for the movement, raising awareness about police brutality, stop and searches, housing and employment, and African liberation struggles in Mozambique, Guinea (likely Guinea-Bissau) and other places.[95] He also participated in study sessions in which the group read various texts – the writings of C.L.R. James's *The Black Jacobins*, Frantz Fanon's *The Wretched of the Earth* and writings by Mao Tse-Tung were among the required readings – within the context of contemporary social and political developments in England and internationally. All of this was part of the poet's political experience: 'It was a tremendous education for me', he recalls, as 'that is where I got blooded, if you like, in political practice and what it is to be in an organization and to organize campaigns and to take part in demonstrations and this kind of thing'.[96]

When interviewed by the Jamaican poet and critic Mervyn Morris in 1982, Johnson stressed that the BBPM addressed 'the politics of race ... which was obviously a limitation. We were never anti-white ... but we always put a great stress on blackness. ... We preached black consciousness and black pride and being proud of ... your blackness and your African ancestry'.[97] Here we encounter a curious bifurcation in which the poet posits the BBPM's 'race work' as a 'limitation' despite the fact that race and class have been inextricably linked with the history of slavery in the Americas. This is precisely the point that C.L.R. James and Eric Williams made in their classic studies of slavery, *The Black Jacobins* and *Capitalism and Slavery* respectively, and the separation of race and class is perhaps at the root of the poet's assertion that the presence of Britain's black middle class and black Members of Parliament is an indication that blacks are now 'fully integrated into British society'.[98] This assertion not only appears to conflate integration with liberation, but also fails to acknowledge those blacks that continue to sit on the margins as outsiders peering into a society that they have not been permitted to fully enter, although in fairness to Johnson, he has made other statements that contradict these remarks.

In a recent interview the poet reframed his analysis of the BBPM, arguing that, in addition to its fight against racial justice and anti-black oppression, the organization also developed a working-class analysis.[99] As part of the process of developing this race-class and working-class approach within the Panthers he also read E.P. Thompson's *The Making of the English Working Class* and Du Bois's *Black Reconstruction*.[100] In this version of the BBPM's history – and this is important in terms of thinking about the politics of memory and remembering – the poet situates the organization within the global anti-imperialist movement that highlighted the convergence of race *and* class[101] in the fight against police brutality and racism and discrimination in the workplace and in education. Here 'race politics' becomes an opening as opposed to a limitation in the local and global struggle for social change, and this particular rewinded version selects and includes the experiences of people of Asian origin, and particularly the UK's Indian and Pakistani population, as part of the black experience. While this conception of blackness and Afro and Indo solidarity – which was anticipated musically when the Jamaican and Alpha Boys School-trained saxophonist Joe Harriott and the Indian violinist and composer John Mayer collaborated to produce an Indo-jazz fusion in England in the 1960s – was more ideological than actual in terms of how most people of African and Asian descent related to each other and experienced race, for critic Michael Eldridge, Johnson has been a leading exponent of this notion of blackness as racial solidarity, even if in practice, the experiences of people of Asian descent were generally underrepresented within the group.[102] In this context, racial divisions were not felt simply along 'ethnic' lines – ethnic in the spirit of Stuart Hall's plurality of ethnicities and the idea that we all wear ethnic identities, including the dominant group (in this case the English of European descent)[103] – but also in terms of class. But today, as the gap between people of Asian and African descent has grown and Asians find themselves, at least relatively speaking, in a more advantageous economic position according to Eldridge,[104] the political definition of blackness has given way to its more conventional meaning that is tied to the Afro diasporic population.

For Eldridge, black identity and the struggle to assert it in opposition to hegemonic whiteness has now transitioned into a battle for Englishness.[105] As he poetically writes, the 'metaphorical nation, founded as the antithesis of "white Britain," couldn't dance around its own constituent tensions. Its hip-hop/trip-hop, jungle/bungle, jazzstep/hardstep successors have moved from countering to "versioning" – the long established "dub" practice, rooted in reggae DJs and dance halls, of stripping down and building back up again, reassembling and remixing, creating new takes on old times.'[106]

In a 2013 interview Johnson remixed BBPM history once again, arguing that the BBPM influenced a generation of black people who went on to do significant political work outside of the organization, and that the organization dissolved as it developed a class analysis, or more accurately, as it transitioned into the Black Workers' Movement (BWM) and towards a working-class consciousness that attempted to build a working-class movement across racial lines.[107] Here again class is emphasized, but not at the expense of anti-racist politics, but in concert with them. But in the Morris interview, conducted in 1982 but only published in 1987, Johnson also made the point that there were problems within the BBPM leadership (he doesn't elaborate), and that some of its members were deported by the state or imprisoned while others were incorporated into the state through the ruse of government grants.[108] His more favourable assessment of the BBPM in 2013 again hints at the complexities associated with memory and history in general that I have discussed elsewhere,[109] and perhaps has something to do with the fact that the interview was conducted by youth as part of a research project on the BBPM and that Johnson may have been cautious about tarnishing the organization's legacy in the mind's of a younger generation looking to draw inspiration from that history.[110]

Black Souls

When Linton Kwesi Johnson discovered W.E.B. Du Bois's *The Souls of Black Folk* in the BBPM library the book had a visceral, almost traumatic impact on him, shaking him to the core. It was 'one of the most beautiful things I had ever read. ... It just ... blew my mind', and he was struck by the book's poetic language.[111] Up until that point he was unaware that there was such a thing as black literature and, equally remarkable, but not necessarily surprising, he assumed that books were only written by Europeans.[112]

    The Souls of Blacks Folk is a classic in American literature and thought that has influenced generations of thinkers and writers, including the black British composer Samuel Coleridge-Taylor who, like Johnson many years later, also drew inspiration from the African American poet Paul Dunbar.[113] The book was first published in 1903 by one of the century's most eminent scholars, a point that I insist on here as far too often 'black' is used as a stigmatized qualifier that limits the significance and scope of Afro diasporic and African thinkers. In the spirit of C.L.R. James's 1970 interview with the American author and broadcaster Studs Terkel, it is important to emphasize that Du Bois was not only a great black leader, but 'one of most distinguished citizens of the twentieth century – Black, white, yellow, or anything'.[114] For Alexander G. Weheliye, Du Bois was the original deejay dub mixer in that *The Souls of Black Folks* anticipated hip-hop by mixing, cutting and collating African American and Euro American literary genres and poetics alongside the aurality of musical notation.[115] The combination of musical and printed epigrams that inaugurate each chapter of the book serves as a leitmotif, binding the series of cultural and political essays to one another as an expression of Du Bois's commitment to a unified arts, or what Anne E. Carroll, drawing on theorist Richard Wagner, describes as the 'total work of art' – the combination of spirituals and poetry as equivalents, that is to say artistically equal forms: 'these spirituals were as expressive as poetry and, in fact, had a greater power to move their audiences than written words'.[116] This 'total' approach is perhaps expressed in the way Johnson combines prose with poetry in his 1975 essay 'The Politics of the Lyrics of Reggae Music' and the 1976 essay 'Jamaican Rebel Music', and in the way that he combines poetry and music to create a unique aural-literary, emotional-intellectual sensibility. These essays are classics, not only in terms of their sociological analysis of Jamaican popular music, but also in terms of their conjoining of poetry and prose in a form that, it could be argued, represents a unique genre of writing of its own. His printed poetry possesses its own voice, but the music-accompanied poetry presents another side, a unique version of his poetry that cannot be adequately reproduced in the printed form.

It was in *The Souls of Black Folks* that Du Bois made his famous declaration that 'The problem of the twentieth century is the problem of the color-line – the relations of the darker races of men in Asia and Africa, in the Americas and the islands of the sea.'[117] Du Bois then describes the peculiar circumstances in which African Americans found themselves situated, declaring that, 'After the Egyptian and Indian, the Greek and Roman, the Teuton and Mongolian, the Negro is a sort of seventh son, born with a veil, and gifted with second sight in this American world, – a world which yields him no true self-consciousness, but only lets him see himself through the revelation of the other world. It is a peculiar sensation,' he continues, 'this double-consciousness, this sense of always looking at one's self through the eyes of others, of measuring one's soul by the tape of a world that looks on in amused contempt and pity. One ever feels this two-ness, – an American, a Negro; two souls, two thoughts, two unreconciled strivings; two warring ideals in one dark body, whose dogged strength alone keeps it from being torn asunder.'[118] Du Bois was describing the recently emancipated ex-slave who, in the afterlife of slavery, represented what Sylvia Wynter refers to as the 'embodiment of symbolic death' and the Other to the 'symbolic life'.[119] To be a professional 'Negro' was to be anti-Negro, according to Wynter and, like Fanon, Du Bois took a leap in consciousness, waging war against the silence of double-consciousness: a war against the self and against segregation and the colour-line, colonialism and imperialism. In other words, Du Bois was at war with both his own consciousness and also the dominant way of being and seeing in the world as he attempted to reconstitute his humanity and that of the black dispossessed.[120] True, double-consciousness emphasizes the psycho-social impact of the legacy of slavery and segregation in the United States, but as political theorist Anthony Bogues points out, the dialectic of double-consciousness not only opens a window into the African American experience of existential angst, but also represents 'second sight', that is to say a heretical perspective on both dominant and radical discourses.[121]

Du Bois's double dialectic of simultaneity reflects both the inner and outer worlds that we occupy, and his discussion on the veil, his eloquent, poetic prose, his combining of music, folk culture and politics and his appreciation of the role that biblical lore has played in African American consciousness stirred something inside Johnson, compelling the future poet to express his thoughts and feelings about the experiences of young Afro Britons. *If*, as T.S. Eliot has argued – in a manner that no doubt reflects his spirited xenophobia – poetry differs from other art forms in that it is much more localized and closely tied to the poet's 'race' and language,[122] then Johnson embodies this idea as someone who has felt compelled to write for members of his community, and in their idiom: 'I've never been through such a deep emotional experience with any other piece of work or art by anybody. I just felt I wanted to write too, to express and say something about what was going on in England with young people, and how black people were being treated, and so on.'[123] The poet fitted Du Bois's notion of double-consciousness into another context, adeptly adapting it to the precarious existence of English blacks – a poem in which silence and being silenced is not only synonymous with invisibility and Du Bois double-consciousness, but also a prelude to the shattering of the silence, presaging the eruption of rebellion.

Beacon of Hope

In many ways, Johnson is a child of the Caribbean Artists Movement (CAM). He came under the tutelage of two of its co-founders, the Jamaican novelist and poet Andrew Salkey, and especially John La Rose, the Trinidadian poet, publisher and founder of New Beacon Books.[124] As a poet, *engagé* and thinker, La Rose played a central role in Johnson's poetic-political and personal life. Johnson discovered a number of poets at New Beacon: Christopher Okigbo from Nigeria and Tchicaya U Tam'si from the Congo, along with African American poets such as Amiri Baraka, Gwendolyn Brooks, Langston Hughes and Sonia Sanchez, and Martinique's Aimé Césaire whose surrealist-like poem *Notebook on a Return to My Native Land*, in Johnson's own words, 'absolutely freaked me out'.[125] As early as 1974, long before he became internationally known, two Johnson poems – 'Dread Beat an' Blood' and 'Time Come' – were published in CAM's journal, *Savacou*.[126] Both poems reflect the poet's early experimentation with Césaire's independent brand of surrealism – let's call it Césairealism – and Fanon's dramatic phenomenology, or Fanonmenology, of violence. In CAM Johnson was also exposed to poets Paul Laurence Dunbar of the US, Martin Carter of Guyana and Edward Kamau Brathwaite of Barbados, another major influence on him[127] and someone whom he imitated in his early verse.[128] And although he admits that he finds Derek Walcott's work 'a bit more difficult to get into', Johnson also acknowledges it, and particularly *In a Green Night* and *Star-Apple Kingdom*.[129] Johnson also met Sam Selvon through CAM, author of *The Lonely Londoners*, a path-breaking work of Caribbean fiction set in post-Second World War England. When Johnson expressed his insecurity about his lack of formal training in poetry, Selvon pointed out to him that this apparent lack was in fact a virtue as it meant he could write with his own unique aesthetic voice.[130] Further, while Johnson often mentions C.L.R. James's *The Black Jacobins* as an important political impact on him, he has also described James's novel *Minty Alley* as an important literary influence.[131]

Minty Alley demonstrates James's keen eye for the life of 'people down below' and his ability to not only capture that life, but recognize it as a source of resistance, strength and liberation. Moreover, his acute sense for the possibilities of so-called everyday people was a trait that would characterize his work in later years. The novel's chief protagonist, Mr Haynes, is a middle-class Afro Trinidadian (in this context, middle class often meant living one pay cheque away from poverty) who works in the book business. Having fallen on hard financial times, Haynes is forced to rent out his home and lodge in another. He lands at number two Minty Alley, some metres from his own house. There he is exposed to a life, a class and, in many respects, a culture that had hitherto had eluded him. Fascinated with the gossip and intrigues of the house, he finds himself drawn to some of its residents. In a manner reminiscent of James's boyhood days when he observed the world from his bedroom window, which faced a cricket pitch, Haynes takes steps to ensure that he keeps abreast of the comings and goings in the home. He removes 'his pillow from the top of his bed to the bottom, fixed his elbows on it and glued his eyes to his peephole which he enlarged and arranged (and camouflaged)' in order to 'command a wide and comprehensive view of the whole yard'.[132] Haynes is essentially an outsider looking in, and it is the women of Minty Alley who initiate him into a conscious understanding of the world via their experiences as members of the Caribbean underclass.

Johnson also notes an anthology of African American poets such as Gwendolyn Brooks, Countee Cullen, Langston Hughes, Claude McKay, Don L. Lee[133] and The Last Poets, to whom he was introduced as a member of the BBPM. To an extent, reggae has been for blacks in England what the blues has represented for African Americans. But the two aesthetics have been mutually beneficial to Afro diasporic groups on both sides of the Atlantic. The Last Poets were the 'prototype Rappers' according to Amiri Baraka, although the same could be said of Baraka, whose vocal inflection in the jazz-inflected 'Nation Time' sounds remarkably like Kendrick Lamar on 'Alright'. The early reggae deejays such as King Stitt, U-Roy, Big Youth and I-Roy, among others, are also forerunners to hip-hop with Jamaican Kool Herc (Grand-master Flash and Afrika Bambaataa also have deep Caribbean roots) serving as the direct links to the sound systems in Jamaica and the emergence of hip-hop culture in New York.[134] Inspired by The Last Poets, Johnson too began combining his voice in Jamaica's vernacular language, Patwa, with music, initially performing to the percussion of Rasta Love (several of his early poems such as 'Dread Beat an' Blood' and 'All Wi Doin is Defendin' were written over the drummers' music) before eventually setting his poetry to music in the studio under the title Poet and the Roots.[135] Not only does the name contain an echo of its American counterpart, but Johnson's poems 'Reggae Sounds' and 'Bass Culture' might be described as the reggae complement of The Last Poets' 'Jazzoetry' which describes the experiential nature of jazz music, and perhaps even 'Bird's Word', a tribute to the jazz greats.

Amiri Baraka stands out as an important American influence on Johnson, and as with The Last Poets, their trans-Atlantic links are part of the ongoing cross-fertilization that characterizes the Afro diasporic experience that forged reggae and rap music as well as Afro diasporic poetics-politics in general. Baraka was a connoisseur of jazz who made a profound contribution to literature. In the words of the poet-novelist-critic Ishmael Reed, Baraka 'did for English syntax what Monk', that is to say Thelonious Monk, did for musical chords,[136] and like Johnson in relation to reggae and Jamaica, Baraka made a significant contribution to our understanding of the blues-jazz aesthetic in America. Like Johnson, Baraka was an atheist, a point he makes explicitly in his irreverently sacrilegious poem, 'When We'll Worship Jesus' in which he writes:

jesus need to be busted
jesus need to be thrown down and whipped
till something better happen
jesus aint did nothing for us
but kept us turned toward the sky [...][137]

Baraka also viewed poetry as a 'revolutionary weapon' that, deployed otherwise, represented 'a distraction, an ornament the imperialists wear to make a gesture toward humanity'.[138] Revolutionary poetry 'directly describes the situation of the people and tells us how to change it. That shows us our lives and gives us the responsibility for mobilizing them around life and revolution rather than drifting impotently in support of death and bourgeois rule.'[139] Again like Johnson, but albeit coming from a different background, Baraka engaged in political organizing alongside producing verse. Poetics and politics are clearly intertwined in much the same way that religion and politics have been conjoined within the broad Afro diasporic experience, and as the political theorist Richard Iton has argued, it would be a mistake to separate 'the politics of poetry and the poetics of politics' and, in the case of Baraka (and like Johnson), he embodied, with all of his contradictions, the spirit of poetry as politics and politics as poetics, exemplifying the poet as a political organizer who combined the 'word' and the 'act'.[140] Baraka was a socialist who, once he transitioned from various forms of black nationalism to Marxist-Leninism in the mid-1970s, never looked back, although he never renounced the centrality of black struggles in his cultural and political work.[141] Perhaps his most important poetic Marxist declaration is 'Das Kapital':

> we mull them over as we go to sleep,
> the skeletons of dollar bills, traces of dead used up
> labor, lead away from the death scene until we remember a
> quiet fit that everywhere is the death scene. [...][142]

Baraka and Johnson would later become friends, and Baraka was moved and inspired by Johnson's verse when he was first exposed to it, once he was able to adjust his ear to 'Jamaican English', as he described it. He would later recall that Johnson's poetry was the 'baddest stuff I'd heard'[143] and, compared to his own and other jazz-blues inflected poetry, a 'more developed form' of music to poetry that was more integrated and in tune to the music, recalling for him the 'fundamental relationship between the poet and his people's speech'.[144] While recognizing the 'correspondences' between the poets on different sides of the Atlantic, for Baraka, Johnson and his fellow Jamaican poets Michael Smith and Oku Onuora 'added a great inspirational factor to what we were doing in the United States',[145] and in his elegy for Smith he wrote 'Mikey Smith's poetry spoke the truth in the rhythms and accents of the masses. This is why his poetry was so dangerous to imperialism. This is why the whole dub poetry movement is so important. This is why Reggae is so important. The artist can make truth irresistible!'[146] Baraka himself experimented with the reggae aesthetic in the poems 'Reggae or Not' and 'Wailers', in which he invokes the memory

of Bob Marley and playfully toys with the phonetics of wailer/
whalers.[147]

Johnson also recalls reading Bongo Jerry's poems 'Sooner
or Later' and 'Mabrak' in *Savacou*. Both poems captured his
imagination[148] and perhaps influenced the apocalyptic tenor
of some of his early poems as well as his resolve to counteract
the influence of the English canon in Caribbean poetry and
to speak in his own voice.[149] As Jerry writes in 'Mabrak' (black
lightening), 'mostofthestraighteningisinthetongue', that is to say
that it is language, which is also a reflection of thought, and not
necessarily cosmetic attempts to 'look white', that is a central
expression of the legacy of colonialism.

Jamaican singers such as Ken Boothe, Leroy Sibbles of
the Heptones and Pat Kelly, and American songs like James
Brown's 'Say it Loud, I'm Black and I'm Proud', Syl Johnson's
'Is it Because I'm Black?', Marvin Gaye's 'What's Going On'
and Curtis Mayfield and the Impressions' 'People Get Ready'
also influenced Johnson as he contemplated becoming a
reggae singer, but he abandoned these ambitions when his
voice broke.[150] Mayfield in particular stands out here as a poet/
songwriter who, like Johnson, was partial to poet Paul Dunbar,
and as someone asserting his artistic independence by establish-
ing his own record label (as Johnson would later do as an act of
self-activity and autonomy), and Johnson's Grammy-nominated
LKJ in Concert with the Dub Band is in some ways comparable to
Mayfield's classic album, *Curtis/Live!*[151]

This said, the most direct and immediate poetic influence on
Johnson was the work of reggae deejays who were part of the
sound system culture in Jamaica.[152] The rival sound systems
were a central part of Jamaican cultural life, and deejays would
play the latest hits in an effort to undo their rivals in competing
for the souls of the people. The disc jockey/selector was like a
shepherd and the people his flock and together they engaged
in this spiritually ritualist séance, as Clinton Hutton eloquently
describes the early days of the sound system phenomenon:
thousands of revellers would 'participate in a community of
movement to sound, engendering and languaging a common

national emotional, psychological, aesthetic ethos, transcending the epistemology and ontology of coloniality and its power to alienate subjected peoples from themselves, from their physicality and metaphysicality, from the sovereignty of their imagination, from their lineality'.[153] These toasters 'made ingenious use of the aesthetic traditions of Jamaican verbal arts and [were] influenced by the American radio disc jockey, as well as the jazz and blues and verbal expression of Black America.' Count Machuki (otherwise known as Winston Cooper) was the founding figure of the Jamaican sound system art form. According to Hutton, he selected, played and choreographed 'dancehall movements to the rhythm, the beat, the spaces of recorded sound intersected at transformed, improvisational spaces, with his toasting, his jiving, his ring shouting, his scatting, and 'created in the process, a modern popular verbal-music art form'.[154] Machuki laid the groundwork for deejays such as I-Roy, whom Johnson would later immortalize ('di mitey poet I-Roy woz on di wire') in his wicked, sardonic poem 'Street 66', U-Roy and Big Youth, all of whom were a crucial part of Johnson's poetic-political awaking. He has also identified Big Youth's lyricism in particular as a source of inspiration as he began to write about his generation's experiences in the Jamaican language while incorporating reggae music into his poetry, prodding the production of his unique form of poetic expression.[155] Johnson's goal was to create a form of poetry that drew on his Jamaican heritage, but also to use the country's vernacular language, almost as a musical instrument through which the music of dub, or reggae – its baseline and rhythms – could be heard even when the actual music was absent.[156] This autonomous creative spirit guided his work and his attitude towards publishing, and he refused to seek literary recognition from mainstream publishers in the early days, instead turning to the culture and community that inspired his work, and to this end his early work was published by Bogle-L'Ouverture and other small independent presses such as Race Today Publications.[157]

Race Today

Linton Kwesi Johnson has distinguished himself as a politically engaged poet, writer, radio broadcaster and music producer. This mixing of mediums shatters the stereotypical image of the aloof, disengaged, self-absorbed and distant artist, and as I have suggested, his poetic voice stems from his own active engagement in the very issues he addresses in his poetry. The organization that facilitated his political involvement in the aftermath of the BBPM was the Race Today Collective, which was aptly located on 74 Shakespeare Road in Brixton, and the poet immortalized the organization's founder and leader Darcus Howe in the poem 'Man Free'.[158] Johnson became associated with the organization in 1973, eventually becoming the arts and poetry editor of its popular journal, *Race Today*.[159] Throughout the 1970s and well into the 1980s, the Race Today Collective and a circle of people centred around John La Rose and the New Beacon publishing house and bookstore[160] was arguably the most active and vibrant voice on black British popular politics and, tied to this work and equally important, was at the centre of social justice struggles in the country: 'We not only published a magazine that documented the struggles of black people in this country and internationally, it was also an organ to mobilize people for action, and we were involved in building mass organisations up and down the country. It gave me a focus, and it gave me a sense of stability.'[161] As the poet remarked in a 2011 interview, 'It was not just the politics of race, it was also the politics of class. The analysis from which we were working was that we were part of a working-class struggle. So from an ideological point of view, the fact that it was a class oriented organization, as opposed to one simply dealing with race meant that I was more likely to join than not'.[162] The Race Today Collective drew on the spirit of C.L.R. James's socialist, pan-African and pan-Caribbean politics as well as his appreciation of art, literature and sport. The extent of James's impact on the organization is obvious in terms of the articles he contributed to *Race Today*, the numerous allusions to his work in the journal and in terms of the journal's overall approach (James wrote histories, produced political theory and books on sport and criticism, and also wrote a play on Toussaint L'Ouverture and the Haitian Revolution). Johnson's 1986 description of the Race Today Collective gives us an idea of the polymath's impact on the organization: 'only an independent movement of workers can present an alternative to what exists; and we agree with C.L.R. James's position that the only structures that exist, the only formations that exist, are the black movement itself, to a certain extent the shop stewards' movement, and the women's movement. These, we believe, point possibilities to the way forward', adding the caveat that 'blacks don't live in a vacuum, and we can't transform our situation independent of other groups in society. And the things that affect us are things that affect white working-class people, only our situation is more acute because it's compounded by the question of race.'[163] This was less a simplistic rerun or version of the old clarion call 'black and white unite and fight' and more of an appreciation of the interconnections of race and class and how they converge in political struggles. The poet's statement also shows an awareness of the central role that black labour has played in the development of and in resistance to capitalist exploitation dating back to the slave plantation, if not before in the bottom of slave ships; an analysis can also be traced back to James's seminal study of the Haitian Revolution, *The Black Jacobins*. Johnson has also noted that the collective was inspired by James's notion that 'every cook can and *should* govern', and despite the Race Today Collective's relatively small size it was evident to the poet that the organization could have a big social impact.[164]

The Race Today Collective worked with parents and groups of African and Asian descent in order to address problems that their children confronted in the school system, and on issues such as police brutality as well as racially motivated physical attacks. As a popular journal, *Race Today* published a range of articles that sensitized readers to issues that not only affected blacks in England, but also global developments in the realms of politics, the arts, and sports. The political and social themes addressed in Johnson's poetry often coincided with campaigns centred on specific issues in which the Race Today Collective had been directly involved. These 'campaign' or 'protest' poems chronicle events, sometimes tragic ones, in Britain, Europe and the Caribbean and, in many cases, describe black British and working-class responses to adversity and persecution. Many of these poems were initially published or reproduced in *Race Today*. 'It Dread inna Ingland', for example, dealt with the arrest of George Lindo, a black factory worker in Bradford who was framed for the robbery of a betting shop in 1978, a story that was covered extensively in *Race Today*. Other poems such as 'Man Free', 'Reggae fi Peach', 'Forces of Victory' and 'New Craas Massahkah' also reflect events, incidents and political campaigns of one kind or another in which the poet was directly involved. These experiential poems are the product of the creative labour of writing through the politics of the moment. An immanent undercurrent flows through many of his poems as they reveal injustice and archive struggles for social change in times of dread.

Chapter 2

DREAD DIALECTICS

The sufferer does not need any 'marxist' to tell him about class, expropriation, or the social relations of production. He may even be able to tell the 'marxist' a thing or two for herein lies the fundamental basis of his experience and existence.

Linton Kwesi Johnson

Every artist and every conscious person in developing society must have the full range of *all* resources, not only language resources but economic, political, ideational – the whole lot.

Edward Kamau Brathwaite

God is the answer to all the questions that science can't answer, so God, like science, is here to stay.

Linton Kwesi Johnson

Linton Kwesi Johnson is a dread poet whose dread dialectic was inspired by the dread dub poetry and lyricism of Jamaica that he described in his 1976 essay 'Jamaican Rebel Music'. For the poet the dread lyricism of Jamaican music is *poetic*, or what Édouard Glissant refers to as 'natural poetics', that is to say 'any collective yearning for expression that is not opposed to itself either at the level of what it wishes to express or at the level of the language that it puts into practice'.[1] It is a legitimate form of poetic expression whose apocalyptic lyricism reflects the suffering, crisis and woe of the people down below. It is about defiance, despair and deliverance in times of dread:

The lyricism of Jamaican music, which is a part of as well as being informed by the wider Jamaican oral tradition, gives poetic or lyrical expression to what the music expresses. It is a lyricism which laments the human suffering, the terrible torments, the toil, a lyricism whose imagery is that of blood and fire, apocalyptic and dread – images that are really pictures of a brutal existence in the 'land of Sodom and Gomorrah'. Songs of hope in suffering, songs of utter despair, songs of praise, songs of defiance, dread dub-poetry, songs that speak of the historical endurance of the black Jamaican, songs that are as prophetic as they are true – such is the nature of the poetry of Jamaican music.[2]

In his 1975 essay 'The Politics of the Lyrics of Reggae Music', the poet wrote: 'when the people hear the music they also live it; for they find within it their pain, their anguish, their bitterness their hope and despair … they feel the dread and the violence that it cries'.[3] As James Baldwin succinctly wrote, 'Dread stalks our streets | and our faces'.[4] We can call this experience the dread dialectic of the sufferer, and as the poet of dread suggests, the sufferers do not need Marxism to explain class oppression, and they may in fact have something to tell Marxists as the dread of the sufferer is a lived experience in which race and class converge.[5] The Rasta is 'a dialectical representation of the contradictions of a society and indeed of an entire epoch of history',[6] and the dialectic of dread involves a struggle between the denigrated denizens of Jamaica who have been discarded and denied even a whiff of genuine democracy, and the colonial/post-colonial bourgeoisie and large-scale landowner.

Dread is one of those curious, simple yet complex words that possess multiple meanings within the continuum between English and Jamaica's popular national language. In English, the noun dread means extreme fear while the verb dread means to anticipate with great fear. But the word assumes another significance in Jamaican: it can mean someone who adheres to the Rastafarian faith – a Rasta – or dreadlocks, or simply dreads, which refers to the uncropped locks that Rastafarians sport; a dread beat in music can mean an exceptionally good beat, but to suggest that a situation is dread is to imply a dreadful or bad situation – really bad. If poets often possess that uncanny capacity to guide us through dread and destitute times, then it is in this sense and in the tradition of the dread dub lyricists of Jamaica such as Big Youth, U-Roy and I-Roy that Johnson is a dread poet. This is particularly true of his earliest published and recorded poetry that largely captures the spirit of dread in England, as does the poem 'It Dread Inna Inglan',[7] and in Jamaica, though to a lesser degree. These dread poems were inspired by the music of dreads (Rastas) and the dread/dub culture that confounded middle- and upper-class Jamaica by confronting the condition of dread in the language of dread. If Johnson's dread poetry is tied to the aurality and orality of Jamaican popular music, his is a voice that speaks within the continuum between English and Jamaican, the latter including dread talk, or Rasta talk, what the Jamaican writer Velma Pollard describes as a 'lexical expansion within the Creole system', and what is sometimes referred to as the lyaric or a 'livalect' (as opposed to 'die-alect'). In Jamaica's more recent history, the unique linguistic infusions introduced into Jamaican by dread talk has not only expanded the language's vocabulary, but also added new philosophical meanings that have found a place in popular music and poetry, including Linton Kwesi Johnson's.[8] 'Yout Scene' is one of the best examples of the infusion of dread talk and dread imagery in the poet's work. A young man takes a walk through Brixton in order to link up with his 'bredrin' – dread talk for male members of the same group, or brothers in the colloquial sense of the word in English:

> as usual, a look pretty;
> dem a lawf big lawf
> dema a talk dread talk
> dem a shuv an shuffle dem feet,
> soakin in di sweet musical beat.

This is a ritual moment, ritual in the sense that it is a norm, a public form of custom involving socializing in front of a popular cultural institution, in this case Desmond's Hip City record shop on Atlantic Road. But it is precisely because the culture is lived and experienced in public, on the streets, that it offends the sensibilities and raises the alarm of Babylon – a term of derision, borrowed from the Bible, which refers to oppressors or the police – as, given the distrust of 'difference', this popular display of culture is perceived as menacing, a virus to be contained before it contaminates the wider society. (For the same reason, the private performance of culture at a blues dance is also attacked, in part because the music breaks through the walls of Babylon, making noise that 'pollutes' the public space.) Naturally, the ritual is interrupted when the 'wicked come', a dread reference to the equally dread Babylon (police) who bestow a beating on the bredrin, before sending them 'paas justice' and 'to prison walls of doom, another obvious Rasta resonance'.[9] Dread talk is also evident in the use of words such as 'site' (to see, acknowledge or understand) as well as the greetings 'hail' and 'love' and the word 'fahwod' (to leave or move) in the poem 'Double Scank';[10] and the words 'ganja' (weed/marijuana) and 'dread' in 'Dread Beat an' Blood'[11] are repeated along with 'kally' (weed/marijuana) and 'babylonian tyrants' in 'Five Nights of Bleeding';[12] and the words 'man-son', 'dread', 'dread I', 'irie' (to feel good) and 'raas claat' (literally ass cloth, but it is also a strong and vulgar curse).[13]

For Louis Chude-Sokei, Rasta mysticism is rooted in African cosmologies that have parallels with the Negritude movement initiated by Aimé Césaire, among others. Negritude and Rastafari stressed the repossession of African identity in response to its suppression under colonization, and both movements possess(ed) the metaphysical and/or surreal that is rooted in the creative manipulation of language. While in Rasta's case, this involved the creative use of Jamaican vernacular, including linguistic inversions such as 'downpressed' (as opposed to oppressed), Césaire's poetics were largely rooted in the creative manipulation of French, and not Martiniquan Creole.[14] We will hear much more about Johnson in relation to Césairealism in Chapter 3, but my point here is that as a dread poet in the 1970s Johnson was inspired by the dread lyricism of Jamaica, and captured the experience of dread in England by combining the elements of reggae, Rastafari and Césaire's surrealism in his apocalyptic synoptic of dread in England and Jamaica.

The dreads, that is to say the Rasta and people down below, are destitute because they have been denied sovereignty, that is to say the right to existence and to not simply exist. As the Guyanese critic Gordon Rohlehr wrote in the early 1970s, dread is 'a brooding melancholy which seems always on the verge of explosion, but which is under some sort of formal control'.[15] It is also 'the historic tension between slaver and slave, between the cruel ineptitude of power on the part of the rulers, and introspective menace and the dream of Apocalypse on the part of the downtrodden. This is why', for Rohlehr, 'Dread remains a constant quality in Jamaica's creative life'.[16] The state of dread confronts the dread's humanity and the Rasta is treated as what Sylvia Wynter refers to as the 'absolute zero of social and metaphysical value'.[17] In this sense, dread is about non-being, being and becoming a dread in the process of confronting the state of dread, by pushing against and ultimately overcoming the terror of dread associated with slavery-colonization-neo-colonization. In this sense, dread is what Father Joseph Owens described as 'an experience: the awesome, fearful confrontation of a people with a primordial but historically denied racial selfhood',[18] and a negation of the ethos of white supremacy and imperialism, which would explain why Fidel Castro has occupied a prominent place within Rasta. For the Caribbean sociologist turned philosopher Paget Henry, the Danish philosopher Søren Kierkegaard's concept of dread concerns 'anxiety that paralyzes the human self as it senses its aloneness in the face of the cosmic dance of life'. These are moments of non-being that shake the being to the core and that may also unmask or reveal the true self by threatening the existing self with collapse; relief from this suffering comes from a relationship with god.[19] But while the dread of Rastafari is also intimately tied to god, it is not an anxious relationship of dread per se, but the product of injustice and social oppression that stems 'from the dance of social life; from the unjust and impersonal conventions of Jamaican society that threaten the identity of many of its members with insignificance'.[20] In other words, the dread's anxieties are not cosmic. They stem from the dread of society and are rooted in concrete social experience of dread and the dialectic of class and cultural warfare against the dread of colonialism and post-colonial violence. But as Henry suggests, it is within this concrete context that dreads reconstitute their egos and their sense of being in the world through various rituals including, among other things, invoking the divinity of Emperor Haile Selassie I of Ethiopia in the place of the British monarchy.[21]

Despite the fact that Marcus Garvey shunned the Rastafari movement in the 1930s, the influence of Garvey's 'Ethiopianism' – that is to say his attack on Eurocentric conceptions of history and interpretations of the Bible, along with his emphasis on the diaspora's ties to Africa and black uplift – was profoundly important for Rastafari.[22] Garvey is a prophet for Rastas, and his prophesies are captured by the legendary Rasta reggae artist Burning Spear who canonized Garvey in his classic song 'Marcus Garvey'.[23] It is no coincidence, then, that the reggae deejay Big Youth chose the dub version of 'Marcus Garvey' to declare in 'Marcus Garvey Dread', in typical dread dialectic and Fanonian form, that the righteous will come into self-consciousness, into being, when their backs are against the wall; and to warn that blood will run in Babylon as Garvey prophesied and that, in quintessential dread talk, the blackhearts (the righteous) will stand while the weakhearts (the unrighteous) will fall.[24] In the Garveyite spirit, Rastas have reinterpreted the Bible, drawing on the historical connection between Ethiopia and Israel, including the fact that Moses was married to an Ethiopian woman. They trace their roots through the lineage of Ethiopian Jews and the Solomonic line back to King Solomon himself, the Queen of Sheba and the birth of Menelik I to whom Haile Selassie is claimed to be a descendant; and some Rastas follow the strict Leviticus Judaic practices and make direct links to events that are described or foretold in the Bible to their social, historical and economic experiences.[25]

Prior to his coronation in 1930, Selassie was known as Ras Tafari Makonnen, and in adopting the name Rastafari the dreadlocks Rasta sanctified their link with the monarch through the spiritual power of the word. If the emperor's coronation was a catalyst for the movement, his visit to Jamaica in 1966 represented something of a crowning moment for Rastas there, vindicating the dread mission while contributing to a cultural boon that closely allied reggae music with the dreadlocks Rasta. But dread is the product of a social crisis that has its roots in the history of slavery and the forced migration of captive labour throughout the Caribbean and the Americas. It is rooted in the crisis-ridden reality of capitalism that demands and discards labour according to its needs without regard for the dispossession that it reproduces. It was this perpetual crisis and the overall nature of capitalist underdevelopment in the Caribbean that has led to the ongoing migration of Jamaicans and other Caribbean peoples to European and North American cities in search of opportunities that were not afforded them at home. This lack in the Caribbean represented an opportunity for England during its reconstruction process following the devastation of the Second World War, and Linton Kwesi Johnson's presence in London is a product of this mass migration process (he joined his mother, Sylvena, in 1963, and he credits his mother for much of what he has achieved in life).[26]

In combining the words 'dread', 'dub' and 'poetry' in his 1975 and 1976 essays on Jamaican popular music, Johnson introduced the term 'dub poetry', a term that, despite his own resistance to it, is now indelibly tied to his own poetry. In 1977 he used the term to describe Oku Onuora's poetry[27] and reserved the term reggae poetry for his own poetic style because of the influence that reggae lyricists such as Big Youth, I-Roy, U-Roy, King Stitt and Prince Buster, among others, had on him as an aspiring poet.[28] But because these lyricists would, at least initially, toast or chant over instrumentals in a somewhat spontaneous fashion, Johnson termed this musical style dub poetry or dub lyricism, arguing as early as 1974 'that what they were doing was really poetry, and that it had a lot in common with traditional African poetry in so far as it was spontaneous, improvisatory and had a music base'.[29] The word dub is synonymous with reggae, but also represents the 'B' side or the instrumental 'version' side of a reggae 45 record. Dub means doubling, that is to say copying a reggae track in a studio and deconstructing, stripping down the track to its bare essentials and then reconstructing or reworking the track by adding echo, loops, reverb, overdubbing or exaggerated bass and other sounds effects in order to produce a new version of the original track. In other words, despite its 'rootsy' association and the perception of 'primitivism' and the 'pre-modern', dub/reggae recordings, like jazz – the production of John Coltrane's *A Love Supreme* is an example of this in so far as it mirrors Coltrane's poem 'A Love Supreme', combining composition and improvisation with the mixing and piecing together of the final version in the studio, including Coltrane's voice[30] – are rooted in technology, creativity and innovation.[31] Dub, and dread, is 'sound as syntax, as syncopation, "sonority contrasts" (Brathwaite), and instrumentation'.[32] It is a sound archive, a music that captures, embodies and reflects the experience of the Black Atlantic, according to critic-theorist Phanuel Antwi,[33] and is the musical precursor to hip-hop, drum 'n' bass, dancehall reggae, reggaeton and what is today known as dub poetry.[34]

For Johnson, his own 'reggae poetry' differed from the dub poetry of the reggae lyricist. As his poetry developed, he would write with reggae music in mind as opposed to poetically chanting over a 'dub' version of a song, and in this process the music became an integral part of his poetry,[35] so much so that the music is evident when we read the poem on the page. But while dub poetry has been almost inextricably linked with reggae music (generally speaking, the poet has both resisted and acquiesced to the term dub poetry, ultimately preferring to simply describe himself as a poet),[36] Johnson has expressed his concern that the one-drop 4/4 reggae rhythm limits the structure and creativity of poetry (so too has Jean Binta Breeze).[37] For the poet-critic Kwame Dawes, the overdependence on what he describes as the tyranny of the backbeat rhythm has resulted in predictable lines and the absence of variation in terms of rhythmic pacing and tone.[38] But at its best, dub poetry draws on the range of the reggae aesthetic which, like the jazz or blues aesthetic in the context of the US, and as a reflection of the Jamaican social, cultural and political environment that produced the music, is rhythmic, structural, ideological and thematic, according to Dawes,[39] and includes the dialogical dynamic between what Dawes refers to as the melodic bass line and the staccato of the drum[40] that is characteristic of much of Johnson's recorded poetry. With time the poet, backed by the remarkable Dennis Bovell Band, has combined a blend of music with his lyricism, including elements of jazz, the blues and calypso, and reviewers have identified musical influences including South Africa, Hungary, Algeria, New Orleans zydeco and Cuban funk.[41]

Referring to Johnson as a dread poet both situates him within the dread history of Jamaica and its rebel music while capturing a spirit of resistance and subaltern politics that his poetry embodies, including the relationship between dread/ Rastafari and the Bible. As J. Edward Chamberlain has noted, the literary and liturgical language of the Bible has been profoundly important for Caribbean poetry.[42] In Johnson's case, he was attracted to poetry as a child but the verse he was taught in primary school in Jamaica did not appeal to him because it was taught by rote and was largely unrelated to the experiences of the Caribbean.[43] But like most people in the Caribbean, the Bible was a central part of his social and aesthetic development. As Johnson recalls:

> When I began to write verse, a lot of it was full of 'thou' and 'thee' and 'thy' ... because, as I said, my primary literary influence was the Bible. I say literary but, of course, in the Caribbean the Bible is part of the oral tradition; there are people who are illiterate who can recite and quote entire sections of the Bible by heart, so as far as the Bible is concerned it has become a part of the oral tradition in the Caribbean.[44]

The poet acquired a fondness for the Bible's lyricism at an early age reading it to his grandmother, Miss Emma, with whom he lived on a farm at the foot of the Bull Head Mountain in Sandy Hill in the deep rural parish of Clarendon in Jamaica.[45] Miss Emma was particularly fond of Psalms, Proverbs and the Songs of Solomon, and she bequeathed Johnson an appreciation for the poetic language of the Old Testament, and especially the lyricism of the Song of Solomon.[46] She played a major role in his life and it was from her that he gained an appreciation for Jamaican folk and oral culture. But in the absence of a radio or television and books, with the exception of the Bible and school materials, it was the musicality and lyricism of the Bible along with his grandmother's duppy (a Jamaican word for ghost) stories and riddles that kept the family (Johnson, his sister and his grandmother) entertained.[47]

As Rastafari attests, the Bible is as much a literary text as it is a religious book for Jamaicans (Jamaica is said to have the largest number of churches per square mile in the world). As part of the country's oral-literary tradition the Bible is embedded in the everyday language of Jamaicans, who habitually relate its well of parables and stories to their own lives and circumstances, including people who cannot read but yet can recite entire passages from the Bible from memory, invoking it with wit or invective to exalt, condemn or redeem. Johnson's familiarity with the Bible found its way into his early poetry in which, drawing on its apocalyptic language and Early Modern English, he combined a sparse, economic use of language with vivid and evocative imagery rooted in his native rural Jamaican culture, his childhood familiarity with the Bible and his intimate knowledge of reggae music and Rastafari, which he encountered in the concrete jungle of London.

Rastas are not immune to the contradictions that riddle wider Jamaican society, and literal interpretations of the Bible, along with prevailing attitudes towards gender, have meant that the unequal status of women mirrors that of the wider society in terms of, among other things, women taking care of the children while at the same time, in many instances, being the breadwinner.[48] But Rasta women have been challenging those conservative Judaic principles that support Rastafari – for example the ascetic practice of isolating women during their menstruation cycles among the Bobo Shanti, or domestic violence and childrearing responsibilities[49] – while confronting the norms of Babylon. There has been a shift towards more equality within the movement according to Imani M. Tafari-Ama,[50] and it is also true, as Julia Sudbury's *Other Kinds of Dreams: Black Women's Organisations and the Politics of Transformation* suggests, that Rastafarian women were among the most actively militant black activists in England in the 1970s and 1980s – the period in which Johnson's dread poetry was forged – embracing the ital (loosely translated as a healthy, natural, usually vegetarian diet) and communal side of Rasta in a somewhat more secularized Rastafari movement. In the process, these women challenged conventional feminist assumptions about the expression of sexuality and freedom.[51]

Rasta women's resistance to patriarchy, both within Rasta communities and wider society, has also been part and parcel of the resistance to colonization and oppression in Jamaica. Stories of rebellion and resistance in the Bible have been a major source for Jamaica's insurrectionary spirit, and it could be argued that Johnson's early poetry owes as much of its phenomenological poetics and politics, its dramatic sense of dread and its revolutionary verve to the apocalyptic language of the Bible as invoked by Rastafarians and reggae artists as it does to Frantz Fanon's *The Wretched of the Earth*. As the poet himself wrote in 1976,

> That the language of the poetry of Jamaican music is rastafarian or biblical language cannot simply be put down to the colonizer and his satanic missionaries ... the historical experience of the Afro-Jamaican is a deeply spiritual experience, a religious experience in the wildest sense of the word. The quest for spiritual well-being, this impelling need to be free of the inner pain, the inner tension, the oscillation between the psychic states of despair and rebellion does not necessarily oppose the physical quest for liberation. The historical phenomenon called Rastafarianism which is saturating the consciousness of the oppressed Jamaican – which represents

a particular stage in the development of the consciousness of
the oppressed – is in fact laying the spiritual and the cultural
foundations from which to launch a struggle for liberation.[52]

The poet's faith in the ability of the linguistic-poetics of Rastafari
to express the material and spiritual aspirations of Jamaica's dis-
possessed Afro Jamaican population is obvious, but is somewhat
diminished here by a dialectical reasoning that both celebrates
the movement for raising and reflecting the political conscious-
ness of Jamaicans while positing it as a stage to be overcome – a
kind of false consciousness – en route towards the 'real' liberation
struggle. However, as the Jamaican historian Robert Hill's
work shows, Rasta *is* a politics of existence and part of a global
pan-African movement that is deeply rooted in a vision, which
is really a version, of Africa and in the history of rebellion in
the African diaspora.[53] It represents a cultural-spiritual-political
movement embedded within the historical experience of slavery,
colonialism, state oppression and neoliberal globalization in the
post-independence era, and in this sense theorist Colin Wright
is right to suggest that the combination of religion and reggae
challenges French philosopher Alain Badiou's assumption that
culture-aesthetics and politics are incompatible.[54] In capturing
the imaginations, dreams and experiences of plebeian Jamaicans,
Rastafari and reggae have historically represented a radical
oppositional politics that have helped to fill the political and
cultural void left by official state politics.[55]

Dread-Rastafari, then, represents a profound reworking of
traditional Christianity – drawing on biblical lore and the dia-
lectical struggle for freedom that weaves through the Bible, but
tailored to the needs of Jamaica's black dispossessed – and a fun-
damental critique of capitalism and imperialism. Reggae artists
often invoke the language and parables of the Bible, and this
prophetic 'dread dub poetry' speaks of the sufferers that Johnson
described in 'Come Wi Goh Dung Deh', 'Problems' and 'Song
of Blood', three poems that are said to have been written about
Jamaica following the poet's visit in the 1970s.[56] In 'Come Wi
Goh Dung Deh' we learn that 'di people dem a bawl' for food,

work, shelter and mercy and 'dem a fite' against one another, against oppression and for their lives down below, but all to no avail, and so the speaker exhorts us to 'goh dung deh' among 'di people' in order to breach the divide between the haves and the have nots.[57] The anaphoric 'Come wi goh dung deh' not only provides sonic and rhythmic pace in the poem, but also emphasizes a dread politics that is linked to the fortunes of the 'sufferah', and the 'wi' in particular implores the outsider who is peering in and from above to go down among the people, much like Walter Rodney did among the Rastas during the 'groundings' in Jamaica in the late 1960s. But while Johnson may have been a natty dread of sorts, he was never a full-fledged Rasta and he delved as spiritually and ideologically deep into the religion as he could before abandoning it altogether.[58] The dread poet identified with the anti-colonial stance and the alluring spirituality and worldview of Rastafari that rejects Eurocentrism, but he could not come to terms with the idea of repatriation to Africa or the claim of the divinity of Selassie.[59]

Rastafari is a modern religion that nonetheless has deep ancestral roots in biblical lore that can perhaps tell us something about the genesis of earlier religions, if we are willing to take it seriously. The Palestinian American critic and theorist Edward Said dismissed Rastafari in what he described as its 'compelling but demagogic assertions about a native past'.[60] But as Hill has argued, when we assess its origins 'from *within* their evolutionary process, both the content and the context of the early Rastafari phenomenon take on a rather different perspective from the reductionist interpretation, since, first and last, they produce their own criteria of investigation' as opposed to external standards of evaluation.[61] For Sylvia Wynter, Rastafari represents a new vision and a reimagination of the world that confronts the 'epistemological imperialism'[62] tied to the legacy of formal colonialism in the post-colonial present.[63] Walter Rodney had a good deal of contact with Rastas when he taught in Jamaica in the late 1950s. Speaking in 1968 following his ban from Jamaica, he said:

In our epoch the Rastafari have represented the leading force of this expression of black consciousness. They have rejected this philistine white West Indian society. They have sought their cultural and spiritual roots in Ethiopia and Africa. So that, whether there is a big flare up or not, there is always the constant activity of the black people who perceive that the system has nothing in it for them, except suppression and oppression.

Referring to the wisdom he gained from his discussions among them, Rodney wrote, 'You have to speak to Jamaican Rastas and you have to listen to him ... and then you will hear him tell you about the Word. And ... you can go back and read *Muntu*, an academic text, and read about *Nomo*, an African concept for Word, and you say, "Goodness! The Rastas know this".' The same was true of their conception of cosmic power.[64]

In Johnson's particular case, he perhaps prematurely proscribed an appreciation of the symbolic significance of Selassie, in opposition to the British monarchy and imperialism. As Colin Wright has argued, the political potency of the symbol of Selassie as God incarnate helped to cultivate and canalize a 'shared consciousness and militancy' among Rastas and non-Rastas who otherwise rejected the idea of Selassie as God.[65] But despite his denunciation of religion in general in the 1970s, Johnson summoned biblical allegory in his 1991 socialist poems, *Tings an' Times*, invoking the symbol of Moses as the wise old shepherd leading his flock across the sea (see Chapter 5 and 6). His use of biblical lore and metaphor to express socialist ideals is not intended to be ironic[66] or as a 'capitulation' to religion in the face of socialist malaise, but instead reflects the symbolic role that the Bible has played in his consciousness despite the fact that he is an atheist.[67]

The cultural and political impact of dread on Johnson is also evident in his post-Poet and the Roots recordings 'Reggae Sounds', 'Bass Culture' and 'Street 66',[68] a trio that poetically and rhythmically embody the poet's expression of reggae as an experiential music that reflects and shapes the communal and material experience of dread. 'Reggae Sounds'[69] literally describes the tension within the blood pulsing, thumping heartbeat sound of reggae as an expression of the anger and anxiety of the dispossessed, but also the love and the power that confronts the wicked like an erupting volcano or a tropical storm, breaking down or at least pushing against the walls of Babylon. The musical accompaniment is not simply, or at least not only, entertainment. As a source of pleasure and joy it threatens to overwhelm the poet's voice even as it broadens his audience; but it also echoes or complements the ominous sense of dread and resistance in his voice, a voice that remains dubbed with dread and the reggae rhythm, even as it is divorced from the music,[70] although the poet reserves the right to revise the tenor, tone and rhythm of his poems in public readings. The music 'speaks' its own language, which, amplified by echo and reverb, both mirrors and enhances the poet's description of reggae as a pulsating, rhythmic and blood-boiling storm.

'Bass Culture',[71] which is dedicated to the reggae chanter, Big Youth, evokes similar images through onomatopoeic sounds combined with the thumping beat of the bass drum as timekeeper accompanied by the organ and trumpet that imitates the rhythm of a tropical storm, anticipating the erupting volcano and the time for bombs and burning, the violent outbursts that will erupt when the tension and the pain proves to be too much to bear. Bass culture represents the reggae bass, the dread beat that pushes against the walls of Babylon, a bass that cannot be contained within the walls of dancehalls; it is about the base culture of the music, that is to say music that comes from down below, from the sufferer's pain and woe; it is a base culture as in bad, that is to say good – it is dread culture. Along with 'Reggae Sounds', the description of reggae music in 'Bass Culture' complements the poet's poetic-prose essay 'Jamaican Rebel Music' as well as his description of internecine violence in the blues dances and dancehalls in 'Dread Beat an' Blood' and 'Five Nights of Bleeding', among others.

'Street 66'[72] also bears the markings of apocalyptic violence and foreboding in what John McLeod describes as the 'fiery apocalyptic urbanscape' of London, and in Brixton in particular,[73] but rooted in the spirit of Rastafari and the subsoil of the Caribbean 'rock steady Blue-beat, ska and reggae music', all of which, in the words of Kamau Brathwaite, 'combined to provide a new vocabulary and syntax of rebellion' in the streets of the Caribbean,[74] but also in Babylonian London. This spirit is typified in the serene and slightly surreal sensibility of the music as the narrator paints the scene of a mystical space that is sanctified by the reggae poet I-Roy's voice and the sacred smoke of sensimilla. The ominous sound of the harmonica is the tone setter, the drumbeat the pacesetter, and as the reggae revellers skank in the space to the dread reggae rhythm our sense of the place and foreboding is amplified by the poet's momentary pauses. But the atmosphere is breached when the police, Babylon, knock on the door. The officer is invited to step inside, but not so that he can profane the sacred space with sacrilege, but in order that he may be administered some 'righteous raas klaat licks | ... hole heap a kicks'.[75] While 'Bass Culture' and 'Reggae Sounds' are obvious examples of the reggae aesthetic that find echoes in Kwame Dawes's 1997 poem 'New Sounds',[76] Johnson's 'Street 66' captures the spirit of this aesthetic and the culture of dread in multiple dimensions and in its cultural complexity. Rather than simply riding the rhythm, the poet's words linger within the beats and his characteristic pauses and deft delivery evoke a spirit of dramatic dread, and a sense of pace and place that complements the meditative and mystic mode of the music in what is ultimately a message of resistance.

Revelation/Revolution

Johnson's relationship with Rastafari and dread is perhaps best expressed in his writing about Jamaica's most famous dreadlocks Rasta, Robert Nesta Marley. Some of his early writing, including music reviews, engaged the 'enigma' of Bob Marley, the Rasta prophet-poet who emerged as a Kingston ghetto youth to become a global musical and political icon and, without even a hint of exaggeration, one of most influential recording artists of all time. Johnson's critical analysis of Marley's music and message not only highlighted the singer's poetic prowess, the contradictions embedded in the music industry and the positions of the socialist-atheist Johnson and the pan-African black nationalist-Rastafarian Marley (these are clearly not divisions to be taken too literally), but also Johnson's ability in this instance to resist the temptation of fixed positions and to evolve over time and with reflection.

It is impossible to speak about the combination of music, poetry and politics without mentioning Marley (perhaps in much the same way as it impossible to do so without mentioning the other Bob – Dylan). No individual has done more to promote the philosophy of Rastafari and reggae music than Marley, and although his larger-than-life stature has overshadowed the music of other great Jamaican reggae artists, he represents the preeminent example of how the poetics of reggae and Rastafari have translated politically. There are several obvious points of convergence between Johnson and Marley: both spent their early years in rural Jamaica and emerged on the world stage in the 1970s; both were signed to Island Records label, which carried their messages around the world; both articulate compelling political ideas through the medium of reggae; both were inspired by W.E.B. Du Bois;[77] and they were both involved in African solidarity work in one form or another. Marley is a global legend, but Johnson also has a loyal following in Africa, the Caribbean, Europe and North America. Lastly, despite his denunciation of religion, we have seen that Johnson, like Marley, has been profoundly influenced by the language, parables and apocalyptic sensibilities of the Bible. But when Marley asked Johnson why he was not a Rasta, the poet replied that he had renounced Christianity and Islam because both religions had been implicated in the enslavement of Africans.[78] When an interviewer asked Marley if he agreed with Johnson's position on religion, Marley emphatically declared that there is no struggle without God,[79] and as the political theorist Richard Iton has suggested, Marley's title track on the album *Survival*[80] is a response to Johnson's 'Reality Poem' which is widely understood as a critique of Rastafari, according to Iton,[81] and perhaps even Bob Marley ('dis is di age of science an teknalagy | ... so le wi leggo religian').[82] In Paul Gilroy's assessment, the dread lyricist's ongoing popularity is the result of the marshalling of the 'universal power of a language that was both simultaneously and inextricably both poetic and political', a language whose roots rest in the lives of slaves who had been reduced to modernity's commodities that were bought and sold on the global market, commodities with tongues that reclaimed the gift of language which, when conjoined with the lore of the Bible, produced this unique music that would traverse the globe.[83] Gilroy is describing Marley, but his description equally applies, though on a lesser scale, to Johnson, whose global reach as a poet rivals that of many renowned reggae singers.

'Reality Poem' is perhaps also a denunciation of a particular brand of cultural nationalism that has historically been prominent in Afro diasporic communities and that is embodied in some of the poetry of Rastafarian Mutabaruka who became a Rasta during the Black Power period of the 1960s in Jamaica. But while Black Power offered a political response to black dispossession, for Mutabaruka it lacked an all-important spiritual element that has been a crucial part of the experience of African peoples as both material and spiritual beings: 'Rasta shows you a sense of being, as a spirit, as a spiritual person. ... I couldn't just manoeuvre myself politically, because I am not only a material man, but I am also a spiritual man, and that was necessary to complete the whole cycle of man and himself.'[84] In addition to his embrace of the divinity of Haile Selassie, Mutabaruka also celebrates ancient African kings and queens as part of the heritage of the African diaspora.[85] Asked to share his thoughts on the Afrocentric movement, Johnson on the other hand once responded, 'Once you know that black people were part of an ancient civilization in Africa and that African civilization has contributed a lot to [the] world, what next? That's my position. Where do we go from there?'[86] Pressed further on the question, he responded: 'You can't tell the children that all of us were kings and queens because if there were kings and queens then they must have ruled over somebody else.'[87] Moreover, 'who wants to identify with absolute rulers?'[88] Critic Albert Murray raised the same question about simplistic analyses of Africa in the US context – a kind of romanticization without research and documentation[89] – but Paul Gilroy was slightly more generous in his criticism, suggesting that the study of ancient African history 'may be useful in developing communal discipline and individual self-worth and even in galvanizing black communities to resist the encroachment of crack cocaine, but ... supplies a poor basis for the writing of cultural history and the calculation of political choices'.[90] But, as the Senegalese physicist, historian and anthropologist Cheikh Anta Diop demonstrated by focusing on a failed rebellion in Memphis during the sixth dynasty (*c.* 2345–2181 BC), the first popular uprising in ancient Egypt and perhaps the first working-class rebellion in recorded history, African antiquity can also be read from below in ways that inform our understanding of politics and struggles from the position of the sufferer in our times.[91]

Johnson's critique of Afrocentricity parallels his assessment of Rastafari and Marley, but while his perspective on Afrocentricity might be described as an anti-nativist critique of Afrocentricity's exaltation of a romanticized African past, it was the 'modern' additions to Marley's music that once troubled the poet. As reggae grew in stature in the 1970s, the poet came to the conclusion that its most widely recognized artist was not the 'musical messiah' that the rock music industry had been waiting for since the death of Jimi Hendrix and the decline in stature of Bob Dylan. He expressed his appreciation for Marley's 'lyrical excellence', but for the poet, the singer's success was ultimately 'the realisation of a commercial dream/a capitalist scheme' orchestrated by Chris Blackwell, the 'descendent of slave masters and owner of Island Records, continuing the tradition of his white ancestors'.[92] Island and Virgin record labels have been tied to the international commercialization of reggae and 'world music' which combined to appropriate ownership of local music forms around the world.[93] For Johnson, writing in 1975, Blackwell and Island were guilty of commodifying Marley's revolutionary spirit and exploiting the image of Rastafari's rebellious roots while capitalizing on his mixed African and English ancestry to make him palatable to a worldwide audience that was more likely to embrace him given his fair complexion.[94] In the process the dread in his music was replaced with a 'howling rock guitar and the funky rhythm' as the enigma of roots and rock in Marley's music distorted reggae's revolutionary verve, taking flight into the world of capitalist marketing.[95] Johnson's issue with Marley's transformation into a rock sensation was not simply that capital was capitalizing on Rasta's rebellious spirit, but that it was recreating Marley's image as if it were adapting a commodity to the demands of the market. In the process, 'capital created idolatry in order to make big money'.[96]

A year later, the poet reiterated that reggae was going through a transformation via commercialization and that in the aftermath of Bob Marley and the Wailers' album *Catch a Fire*, the style of reggae in Jamaica 'has been revolutionized by external markets' and that the music is no longer 'rooted in local feelings and tensions' but rather 'transcends social/historical conditioning, a more impersonal kind of reggae' for a wider market. Again the poet's target was Island – the record label to which he would eventually sign after producing his first album with Virgin in 1978. But in an apparent volte-face, the poet conceded to the inevitability of commercialization, arguing that British reggae consumers, including British-born blacks, couldn't 'relate to the violence, power and tension in Jamaican music because it's a kind of experience which is alien to them'.[97]

Marley's universal appeal cannot simply be credited to Blackwell's marketing, no matter how much Island Records laboured to tightly package his music for international consumption. Cultural historian Michael Denning argues that music played on the gramophone, or what he describes as the 'disruptive noise' that confronted colonial norms of harmony and tone – music that was often circulated by Garveyite sailors on ships – was an important catalyst for anti-colonial struggle and frequently provoked violent responses from colonial authorities when what he calls 'vernacular recording artists' allied themselves with anti-colonial movements.[98] This phenomenon is part of the experiential history of reggae, and the reception of Marley's political-poetics represents a cogent example of this phenomenon in the post-colonial dependency era. Is there another song that is more compelling and emotive, one that reflects the spirit and experience of Afro Caribbean people and, in many ways, Afro diasporic communities in the Americas in general, than the folksy ballad 'Redemption Song'?

My own experience is perhaps a good example of the cultural-political weight of Marley's music, and that of reggae artists in general. During a 1997 visit to Cuba I found myself in the midst of people from across the world who, like me, were attending the International Festival of Youth and Students, a historic gathering that brought together people from across the world to discuss contemporary global politics and to demonstrate solidarity with the Cuban Revolution. In our spare time we were treated to artistic and musical exhibitions in which delegates from Latin America performed folk songs of resistance and struggle. Listening to them sing along to the sound of an acoustic guitar, I could not help asking myself in the midst of this rich cultural display, where are the Caribbean folk songs and songs of resistance? But my lapse was only temporary. 'Redemption Song' came to mind, and as a child of Jamaican parents born in England, it later dawned upon me that our freedom songs have been universalized to the point that we often do not embrace them as autochthonous cultural productions that are borne out of Afro diasporic experiences and, in this case, the peculiar experiences of Jamaica. The song's international popularity also defies ethno-racial, national and class divisions as I was recently reminded when a diverse group of colleagues sang the song at a retirement party. And yet it was the song's compelling cultural-political allure, partially rooted in the Afro diasporic experience, that led to its commercial success as part of the phenomenon in which Jamaican popular music and culture became a component part of a global aesthetic associated with the struggle against exploitation, human degradation and domination.[99]

If as Anthony Bogues suggests, Marley sits comfortably within what, with some hesitation, we can refer to as the black radical political tradition,[100] and if his revolutionary music represents a form of '*symbolic insurgency*',[101] I would add that from his point of departure in Jamaica he 'conquered' the world with the weapon of poetry and music, and that he represents a quintessential example of how an artist can speak to the world from his particular place and set of experiences – experiences that of course are not fixed. He committed his life to Jamaican, Caribbean and pan-African struggles and the overall liberation of the world's sufferers, and at great personal risk. Although in death a great deal has been done to commercialize his legacy through branding (we can now purchase commercial Marley merchandise including shoes, shirts, headphones and beverages), the fact remains that his music was revolutionary to the bone in terms of tenor, message and tone. How else can the apocalyptic lyricism from his 1975 song, 'Revolution', be described? In this fierce reggae-blues poem revelation and revolution are collapsed together as an expression of his political and religious convictions and a call for radical change. The compelling lyrics of 'Revolution' and 'Redemption Song' continue to inspire people concerned with social justice all over the world. As Carolyn Cooper has written, 'Bob Marley's song, like all great local literature which we come to call "universal", speaks first to the particular circumstances of his own time and place; its meaning expands in ever-widening circles of compassion, levelling barriers of race, class, gender and geography. Bob Marley lives in the rich legacy of song he has bequeathed us. Give thanks!'[102]

Johnson joined Marley on Chris Blackwell's Island Records in 1979 after leaving Virgin Records. From his own account, he left the burgeoning Virgin label because of what he has described as its 'colonialist mentality'.[103] Despite the apparent millions that Blackwell was willing to spend promoting him as a reggae artist, the poet produced three albums for Island between 1980 and 1984 before leaving the company behind to establish his own independent label, LKJ Records. One hallmark of a creative mind is intellectual agility and the ability to adopt and adapt new perspectives and styles. In his June 1977 *Race Today* article Johnson repeated an earlier point that the Wailers' debut album, *Catch a Fire*, sparked a revolution in Jamaican music, but this time he not only celebrated the album, but also the Wailers' overall contribution to internationalizing reggae music, and he acknowledged the fact that Marley and the Wailers, notwithstanding 'concessions and compromises, contradictions and ambiguities', were 'breaking down the rock barrier and penetrating the international rock music market'. In this revised view, the Wailers achieved the remarkable feat of developing 'a sound that transcends the local, national limitations of popular Jamaican music, taking it into the mainstream of the popular music of Europe and North America'.[104] While we might query the poet's apparent conflation of the local with the parochial, his revised appreciation of Marley's music was laudable, and when questioned years later about his earlier criticism of Marley Johnson he replied, 'I'm afraid I'll have to live with that statement. That was when I was in my more furious frame of mind. But I regret having said that because it's not really true. I believe that the music was internationalized to reach a greater audience, but I don't think it affected his message in any way.'[105] Here, the important distinction is between the medium and the message. To this day, Johnson still believes that his analysis of Island's Marley marketing method 'was more or less correct', adding, but without explanation, 'even though the sentiments were misplaced'.[106]

Language and Power

Rasta symbolism and the biblical language of Rastafari was a crucial part of Johnson's early poetry. This 'dread talk' might be described as a 'dialect of a dialect', in so far as Jamaica's vernacular language can be described as a dialect. But historically the word 'dialect' has conferred an inferior, non-literate status in relation to the hegemonic English, mirroring the sense of European superiority that is rooted in the Caribbean's colonial history. This negative connotation persists despite the knowledge that a dialect that is dismissed and derided today can acquire full language status tomorrow.[107]

Kamau Brathwaite introduced the term 'nation language' – 'English which is not the standard, imported, educated English, but that of the submerged, surrealist experience and sensibility, which has always been there' – in order to sidestep the stigma associated with dialect,[108] but the term has come under derision for its imprecision[109] and as 'an unnecessary neologism'.[110] Beyond the actual term, for Brathwaite the use of nation language in literature represents an act of resistance because it signals a rejection of the imposition of the literary and linguistic imperial standards of English while embracing the idea that Caribbean languages contain their own musicality that is embedded in their orality.[111] It is perhaps in this sense that we can appreciate the mento-inflected language of Louise Bennett and the language of reggae artists who have been closely connected to Rastafari. Like reggae singers, those whom Johnson described as dub poets have historically interwoven intermediate forms of their native tongue with English in their poetry, and the dread poet himself has drawn from this same linguistic well.

Taking the lead from sociolinguist Mervyn Alleyne, I refer to Jamaica's popular language as Jamaican,[112] a language that has deep roots in Twi-Asante, the dominant language spoken by the Akan in present-day Ghana as well as in parts of the Ivory Coast, Togo and Burkina Faso. The dominant influence of Twi in Jamaica reflects the cultural-linguistic dominance of the Akan among slaves during the early days of slavery in Jamaica.[113] However, English was the language of dominance and power, and as Twi-Asante speakers increasingly absorbed English words into the language the English lexicon became dominant, although the language retained Twi-Asante continuities in terms of vocabulary, syntax, and grammar in general, a persistence that reflects both the resistance to English assimilation as well as the reality of it.[114]

Vernacular, or everyday language, has long been recognized for its creative possibilities and for asserting the national identity of a people. In the case of Scottish poet Hugh MacDiarmid's verse, he deployed a synthesis of Scots and English to express both nationalist and international socialist ideals.[115] In much the same way Johnson deploys Jamaican in relation to black British and Jamaican politics and socialism. Despite the significant difference between the two languages, Jamaican and English are syntactically, phonetically and orthographically close enough to be at least partly understood on the page by non-Jamaican speakers. But again, the use of the Jamaican language in poetry is not simply a convenient form of expression for Jamaicans who want to communicate in their native tongue, or even an act of resistance to the linguistic dominance of English. Refusing to submit to English also permits poets to draw upon linguistic resources that are not available in the English language. It is perhaps not surprising that while the Jamaican poet-critic Mervyn Morris has made arguments in favour of standardization of Jamaican for the sake of clarity and accessibility,[116] Édouard Glissant expressed concern that, in the transition from its oral to its written form, the Creole language becomes vulgarized in the process.[117] In his own inimical way, the French playwright and critic Antonin Artaud expressed the same concern as Glissant when he argued that poetry becomes dead once it is committed to the page, and that it is in the theatre and in the orality of the performance that poetry sustains and revives life and meaning.[118] Among other things, this suggests that, in terms of the creative process, when the poem is transcribed from the mind's voice to the page there is always the possibility that creative meaning will be lost in the transition from thinking in a language to its translated form on the page. It might also suggest that the so-called performance poet and 'dub poets' are closer to an authentic poetic voice that is more closely tied to the poetics of conversation, and affirms Kwame Dawes's and Mervyn Morris's views that there is a need to critically assess so-called oral poetry in ways that take it as seriously as its more scribal form while acknowledging the differences, that is to say the continuum between the two, and dismantling the hierarchy that posits one at the expense of the other.[119] This is no doubt what Fred Moten has in mind in relation to music when he discusses how 'Adorno's valorisation of the auditory phonographic relation to the literary experience of the score displaces the effects and affects of sensuous visuality that seemed an inescapable by-product of musical performance', essentially rendering the measure of music quality less about affect and more to do with its representation on the page.[120]

At issue here is what makes a language a language, including the aesthetics of language, and it is perhaps not surprising that this issue surfaced when a collection of Johnson's poetry was published in 2002 in the Penguin Modern Classics series under the tile *Mi Revalueshanary Fren*. As only the second living poet to be published in this series, some welcomed the publication, but during a BBC broadcast a critic argued that, while Johnson's poetry might convey feeling, it does not necessarily qualify as serious literary work. Another critic, perhaps fearful that the canon's walls were being breached or were about to be exploded by an unorthodox poet who for the most part does not even write in English, attempted to dismiss Johnson as an oddity or novel curiosity rather than a serious poet. Whatever the motivations of these critics, Johnson's poetic language, style and message do not generally elicit the appreciation of the literary establishment and, despite being published by Penguin Books, he remains a longstanding member of the British and European alternative poetry scene in the fight for social justice.[121]

It is impossible to speak about Jamaican language and poetry without mentioning the name Claude McKay. McKay was the first Jamaican to publish poetry in Jamaican, laying the foundation for poets such as Jean Binta Breeze, Michael Smith and of course Johnson. When we consider this fact alongside other parallels between McKay and Johnson, such as their rural backgrounds in Clarendon, Jamaica[122] and their socialist politics, it is more than surprising that McKay is rarely mentioned as a precursor to Johnson (Johnson recalls reading McKay in an anthology of black poetry, but does not elaborate).[123] Moreover, his poem 'England'[124] might be read as a precursor to Johnson's 'England is a Bitch'. 'England' is a bitter verse about the England he encountered between December 1919 and January 1921, and its tone is markedly different to fellow Jamaican poet Una Marson's more positive depiction in 'Quashie Comes to London' (1937). In McKay's England he was denied long-term lodgings, insulted while in the company of a white woman and physically attacked, all of which left him constantly on guard and bitter towards white racists.[125] But he also developed a critique of England's small black middle class that anticipates Johnson's poem 'Di Black Petty Booshwah',[126] and like Johnson, McKay became a staunch opponent of British racism.[127] As a poet and novelist, McKay crossed and blurred the boundaries of black politics and socialism. He was an important figure in the Harlem Renaissance who also visited and wrote about Russia in the aftermath of the Russian Revolution in the early 1920s, and he was actively involved in socialist debates in the first half of the twentieth century. Moreover his fiction inspired Aimé Césaire and Léopold Sédar Senghor,[128] two poets whose writing (especially Césaire's) would significantly influence Johnson's early work. Like Johnson, McKay's poetry was acutely concerned with the plight of the oppressed, and this preoccupation is obvious in his early work – that is to say before he travelled to the United States and Europe. As a free-thinking Afro Jamaican Fabian socialist who would later embrace Bolshevism, race, colonialism and class politics were embedded in his early writing. These poems that were published in Jamaica before he left the island in 1912 convey an acute appreciation of the plight of agricultural workers whose labour produced wealth for Jamaican landowners, a keen awareness of the conditions of the urban underclass in Jamaica's capital, and sympathy for the circumstances of urban and rural women.[129] I emphasize the importance of McKay's early poetry here because, as Winston James argues, analyses of McKay's work tend to overlook the importance of the Jamaica years for his artistic and political development. While Mervyn Morris has argued that his Jamaican poems suffer from 'remembered rhythms' and the influence of Victorian verse,[130] McKay nonetheless laid a foundation for the work of future generations of Jamaicans to produce verse in their national language.

McKay's verse inspired the figure that is most responsible for promoting use of Jamaican in poetry and the performing arts –

Louise Bennett, the legendary poet, folklorist and actor. In some ways she is Johnson's poetic progenitor, and more than any other figure it was Bennett ('Miss Lou') who helped to legitimize Jamaican as a literary medium of expression decades before he was born. Her work has helped to reduce the stigma and friction associated with Jamaican diction that is still derisively described as 'broken English' in many quarters. As the Jamaican Canadian poet Lillian Allen has written, 'the language of the people | is the language of life',[131] and it was Bennett who gave 'wings to the silenced'.[132] As both an oral-scribal poet, her best poetry stands up on the page, but comes vividly to life on the stage, combining for what critic Susan Gingell describes as 'see-hear' poetry. Bennett took her readers beyond the mind's ear towards 'oralizing' or 'reoralizing' the text by resorting to non-standard spelling that ultimately situated her poetry within its particular cultural-linguistic context.[133]

Bennett's 1944 poem 'Bans a Killin' is a bold, satirical and ultimately scathing critique of the dominance of the English language, in which the poet dismisses the hierarchy that separates English as the language of respectability and creativity from Jamaican 'dialect'. If Jamaican is a dialect, so too is English, and if the authorities intend to destroy dialect, Bennett wonders what would happen to dialect spoken by Geoffrey Chaucer, Robert Burns, Lady Grizel Baillie and even William Shakespeare. If Jamaican deserves to die, so too does Scots, Cockney and the dialects spoken in Lancashire and Ireland.[134] Notwithstanding the fact that the focus on preserving the 'dialect' seems to undermine its capacity to grow and change,[135] her incessant use of the word kill in the poem emphasizes that the death of a language signals the death of people's culture, a point that she echoes in her monologue 'Jamaica Language' where the narrator, referring to the opinion of her wise Aunty Roachy, reasons that if Jamaican is a corrupt version of English, then it is also logically a corruption of Twi, and then English, according to Aunty Roachy's reasoning, is also a corruption of Norman French and Latin.[136]

Kamau Brathwaite has argued that T.S. Eliot, originally from Missouri, brought a blues-inflected style to English poetry along with the 'notion of the speaking voice; and the conversational tone' that was important for Brathwaite's generation of Caribbean poets.[137] It could perhaps be said that the Jamaican poet Michael Smith did the same for Jamaican poetry, as is evident in his ingenious poem, 'Mi Cyaan Believe It'. Like Louise Bennett, Smith rejected English poetic standards and 'Mi Cyaan Believe It', along with 'Mi Feel It, Yuh See', 'I and I Alone' and 'Trainer', are remarkable in their capturing of the colourful and poetic everyday speech of Jamaicans, including dread talk, in ways that cannot be fully appreciated when reading the poem on the printed page. Perhaps with the exception of Jean Binta Breeze, Smith was unmatched among his generation in terms of his dynamic and creative poetic use of the Jamaican idiom. With his unique intonation, variation of voice, rhythmic rhyming and adept timing his poetry breaks new ground while often sounding as if he is recounting a conversation or gossip overheard while shopping in a street market.

Like Oku Onuora, Smith consistently acknowledged his debt to Bennett, as he did during a humorous exchange with C.L.R. James during which Linton Kwesi Johnson asked Smith to discuss the impact of Wordsworth and Shakespeare on him. The discussion, which aired in the 1982 BBC documentary film *Upon Westminster Bridge*,[138] highlights fundamental differences between James and the younger poets, but especially Smith. During the conversation Smith mischievously asked James how to pronounce Wordsworth, dragging out the sound of the name, to which the irritated James replied there is no pronunciation, but simply Wordsworth. Smith then cheekily pronounced Shakespeare as 'Shaka Spear', to which James immediately responded, to the obvious amusement of Johnson and Smith, that nowhere in the world is the bard's name pronounced that way. But as James acknowledged during the conversation, both Smith and Johnson were beneficiaries of a Caribbean poetic tradition that did not exist when James came of age in Trinidad in the first quarter of the twentieth century. For Smith, the symbols and sounds of English poetry were an oddity and Bennett embodied an alternative that rejected the primacy of the English canon, even if, as Johnson suggested during the exchange, Bennett was limited by an outmoded iambic form (Mervyn Morris has argued the opposite: that it is Bennett's neglect of iambic stresses that has permitted her 'to follow the contours of Jamaican speech and to point each line for meaning and for dramatic effect').[139] For Smith, then, Bennett was an anti-establishment revolutionary whose poetry emerged out of the Caribbean nationalist and labour protests of the 1930s. Johnson too argued that she was revolutionary, but only in so far as she broke with the dominance of the English language. James's discomfort with the reference to Bennett as a revolutionary is obvious during the exchange, and he makes a sharp distinction between the dialectical poetry of Smith and Johnson and Bennett's humorous nationalistic 'dialect' poetry. For James, and for Johnson, the word revolutionary possessed a specific connotation and the 'folkloric' Bennett could not have been more removed from their conception of the term.

But the word folk, like its Germanic derivative *Volk*, means common people, bringing us closer to a conception of the everyday lives and struggles that, in their own ways, James and Johnson have highlighted in their work. Of course, not only did Bennett possess the gift of wit, satire and humour, and an elaborate understanding of Jamaican folklore, but her talents were frequently deployed towards what were clearly political ends. The poem 'Dutty Tuff', for example, describes the impact of hard economic times on the poor and working class, including the impact of the high price of food:

> Sun a shine but tings no brite;
> Doah pot a bwile, bickle no nuff;
> River flood but water scarce, yaw;
> Rain a fall but dutty tough.[140]

As reggae historian Klive Walker suggests, there are obvious parallels between Bennett's poem and Bob Marley's 'Them Belly Full (But We Hungry)',[141] although critic Belinda Edmondson suggests that Marley, like Bennett, may also have drawn inspiration for the song from Jamaican folklore.[142] However, as a Marxist theorist and socialist it was the Russian Revolution, Lenin and the Bolsheviks that served as the quintessential revolutionary model for James, and given this revolutionary point of reference it was essentially impossible for James to see Bennett in revolutionary terms. For him, she was more closely associated with 'pre-modern' folkloric aesthetics, and despite his appreciation for Jamaican folklore and children's songs, Johnson appears to have downplayed the revolutionary possibilities in her humour, in the joy that is often found within the pain, and Bennett's capacity to subvert dominant colonial cultural and political attitudes.[143]

Bennett's 'Bans o' Ooman!' draws on a meeting of the Jamaica Federation of Women in order to subtly disclose Jamaican class divisions. The speaker is astonished to see the blending of classes in the meeting: 'Me never se such different grade | Kine o' ooman from me bawn'.[144] The laudable event is celebrated but the narrator's shock that women of all classes have been brought together – 'High and low, miggle, suspended, | Every different kine o' class'[145] – underscores the social divisions in Jamaican society. Gender is central here, not only in terms of the issues that Bennett and other female poets have engaged with in their poetry, but also in how these issues have been addressed. As Carolyn Cooper suggests, Bennett is in many ways prototypically feminist as her work captured a range of experiences and behaviours of Jamaican women in terms of class and caste.[146] But whereas the female Jamaican poets who have inherited her legacy have asserted the need to discuss gender and sexuality in their art, their male counterparts, including Johnson, have been relatively silent on and largely ignore issues that directly affect women, as well as on issues related to eroticism and sensuality.[147]

Canadian-based poets such as Lillian Allen, Afua Cooper, ahdri zhina mandiela and d'bi young anitafrika have been at the forefront of injecting gender and sexuality into an otherwise masculine genre,[148] expanding 'dub's repertoire to include familial and women's concerns. Some have done so with a feminist stamp. Sexism, women's oppression, and liberation have all been made central to dub poetry's discourse by its female poets. These poets', continues Afua Cooper, 'have expanded the definition of the term "political" to include personal, private, and domestic matters. Women dubbists also write about love, sex, sexuality; spirituality, healing, and women's inner life.'[149]

Jean Binta Breeze, who lived as a Rasta in rural Jamaica before migrating to England, is the most widely recognized woman within the dub poetry genre and yet, as the critic-theorist Shalini Puri suggests, Breeze has been marginalized within the movement and, we might add, omitted from its founding narrative, a fact that she partly attributes to Breeze's 'quieter Creole' compared to Johnson's and Smith's 'masculine militancy' (admittedly, my own initial appreciation for Johnson and Smith is in part tied to the brand of militancy to which Puri refers, and for which Puri is also not unsympathetic) and to what she describes as a 'critical *deafness*' in analyses of their work.[150] While I would suggest that, while Johnson's stage performance aesthetic is essentially immobile, asensual and even asexual, Breeze proudly expresses her sexuality through sensual dance moves, allowing her body to 'sing' while on stage, despite criticism from her male counterparts.[151]

Carolyn Cooper reminds us that when we consider the complicated but ultimately conservative codes of respectability in both Jamaican and British society, the political and cultural significance of sensuality and sexuality in performance and Jamaican popular music should not be minimized in terms of how it challenges the dominant cultural mould.[152] Like other women within the dub poetry movement, and in the spirit of Bennett who deployed a combination of parody, wit, sarcasm, satire and clever wordplay in order to highlight a range of issues,[153] Breeze has gone beyond the limitations of her male counterparts' avid emphasis on racial and class oppression and deep into themes of love, sexuality, women's labour and joy. For Puri, Breeze's 'poetic energies in some ways are directed toward an effort of the imagination to produce precisely the outside that the austerely realist aesthetic of Johnson's poetry refuses, to reclaim a sustaining lyricism. ... In Breeze's work these sources of spiritual and psychological strength are also reserves that enable materialist struggles.'[154] While Johnson's most recent poetry (late 1990s) integrates themes such as love, life and mortality, and is infused with a more spiritual sensibility, gender dynamics have never occupied a significant place in his poetry. For Breeze, on the other hand, gender has been central, leading Puri to query why critics have paid more attention to spectacular expressions of militancy than to the more mundane but essential work that women do every day:

> Breeze's own poetic concern, like that of many women writers, is not only radical activism in the public sphere but also the dilemma of how to represent women's labor – as she puts it, to 'find a way of making doing the laundry revolutionary.' My question, thus, is where does our critical preference for spectacular transgression leave her project and that quiet, ordinary, daily sustaining labor? How well is it able to probe the tensions between women's desires for transgression and release and the support they find in religious, rural, or familial sensibilities, as well as in humor?[155]

Puri questions the dominant conception of politics as well as the kind of political labour that is valued, or not. While we tend to valorize the more glamorous public work that, when the stars are aligned, can produce spectacular political leaps, politics – at least grassroots popular politics – is an incremental, assiduous process of grounding, reasoning, organizing and building that cannot be reduced to public pronouncements and declarations; and the more private, that is to say behind the scenes, political work and organizing is often carried out by women. It is not only literary critics that have failed to recognize this in their analysis of dub poetry, but also theorists, sociologists and historians in the study of social movements and radical politics.

This said, Puri makes the point that an emphasis on militant dissonant voices both fails to acknowledge subtlety and nuance in Johnson's and Smith's poetry and occludes the implicit politics in the work of Breeze, who invests her personae with the every-dayness of life:

> If Jean Binta Breeze argues that the beat in dub poetry disci-plines and punishes experimentation, I contend that current critical practice aggravates that tendency, reifying a living form, creating monotony from subtle and stunning performances of tonal contrast, hearing only the steady, flat beat of anger, not its crescendos and diminuendos, its shifts in pace or volume. The critical strategy that makes revolutionary consciousness a precondition for gaining entry into the canon silences signifi-cant aspects of Smith's and Johnson's poetry, not least the long octave that spans resignation and refusal. It ignores the very processes – artistic, social, political – through which despair and defiance fold out of one another. And it leaves the speaker (poet and narrator alike) of 'Ordinary Mawning' in the cold.[156]

The beauty in Breeze's 'Ordinary Mawning' lies in its simplicity and the ease with which the poet illustrates how poetry can convey a sense of the extraordinary in the seemingly ordinary. In this case, it is not only the poet's understated language, but how she uses it to describe the seemingly mundane domestic activities of a poverty-stricken single mother and the superlative efforts required in order to raise children and make ends meet, essentially by making bread out of stone. This extraordinary labour is tied to seemingly innocuous daily news items in the poem – two people being shot dead and someone being hit by a truck – and more dramatic events such as the Palestinian and South African anti-apartheid struggles. In the poem, all of these phenomena are ultimately extraordinary, despite the fact that we have become desensitized to tragedy through overexposure and distraction. In the case of the poem's persona, it is only at the end of the poem, when she sees her frock hanging on the clothes-line, that she has an epiphany and becomes fully conscious of the burden that she habitually carries, causing her to break down in tears.[157]

Female dub poets have projected their share of expressive militancy too, often in forms that are less explicit and more attuned to life's complexities in comparison to their male counterparts. This is true of the work of Breeze, Lillian Allen and many others, and in more recent times, the poetry of the Jamaican cum Canadian poet and celebrated stage actor and playwright d'bi anitafrika, or simply d'bi traces her roots back to the work of Breeze, Onuora, Smith, Johnson and especially her mother, Anita Stewart, who also studied and performed at the Jamaica School of Drama. She watched her mother perform as a child in Jamaica[158] and her mother served as a model for d'bi as she was developing her own style.[159]

d'bi is a gifted performer who was also mentored by Toronto-based playwright ahdri zhina mandiela, a pioneer in the dub theatre aesthetic,[160] and when in character on stage, either as a poet or actress, d'bi frequently leaves her audiences dazed, speechless or in tears as she transitions from one poem or character to another. d'bi is also one of the few poets who not only dares to perform Michael Smith's remarkable poem, 'Mi Cyaan Believe It' (not to be confused with poet Devon Haughton's 'Mi Caan't Believe It'), and do it justice (Johnson has read this poem in public on at least one occasion but there does not appear to be an available recording of it). Her poetic style is closer to Breeze and Smith than Johnson, but her irreverence and fearless expression of her sexuality is more reminiscent of the Jamaican model, actor and singer Grace Jones. Several of her poems are both inspired by and represent a critique of the invisibility of women and the absence of the themes of love, sensuality and sexuality in Johnson's early work, and if we take her poems 'Dear Mama', 'Blood' and 'Revolushan I' together it is obvious that d'bi is engaged in a conversation with Johnson in which gender is at the centre of the dialogue for her. d'bi is certainly a feminist, or perhaps more accurately what she describes as a 'wombanist', and yet the fact that 'Dear Mama' is inspired by 'Sonny's Lettah' and dedicated to Johnson does not inherently imply a critique, at least not necessarily a conscious one, of the absence of a female voice in that particular poem, as it could be argued that Johnson is writing through his experience as a black male who came of age in the 1960s and 1970s, and that it is quite natural for him to focus on male subjects in his poetry. And yet, as a woman, d'bi steps into and outside of her immediate experience in her poetry and drama, and extends herself to incorporate a range of interconnected emotions and experiences related to revolutionary politics, race, gender, sexuality and class in ways that, as we shall see, have largely been outside Johnson's purview.

* * *

If, as I have argued, Linton Kwesi Johnson was/is a dread poet, it is his earliest poems recorded under the title *Dread Beat an' Blood* and initially published under the same name that most justify this description. The poems conjoin the dread dialectics and apocalyptic tenor of reggae and the spiritual sensibility of Rastafari devoid of ecumenical sentiment, alongside Frantz Fanon's phenomenological poetic-prose of violence and Aimé Césaire's particular brand of surrealism. These combine to produce some of Johnson's best poetry, despite representing his earliest work. They are dread poems of blood which, when considered in the context that produced them, provide that peculiar poetic insight into a moment in British society that presaged the urban rebellions that gripped England in the early 1980s when black British youth found the oppression in Babylon too much to bear.

Chapter 3

DREAD POETRY AND FREEDOM

Madness shall be on the people, ghastly jealousies arise;
Brother's blood shall cry on brother up the dead and empty skies.

William Vaughn Moody

Dead are the living; deep-dead the dead.
Dying are the earth's unborn –
…
In this dreaded night
Writhe and shriek and choke and die
This long ghost-night –
While thou art dumb.

W.E.B. Du Bois

When History sleeps, it speaks in dreams: on the forehead of the sleeping people, the poem is a constellation of blood.

Octavio Paz

A SIGN hitched on a fence warns against selling, consuming or enquiring about 'Indian hemp' or any other drug on or near the premises. This is the first image that we see in *Dread Beat an' Blood*, the 1979 documentary on Linton Kwesi Johnson. Then we hear the echo of what sounds like a church organ, then a voice, a young poet, head crowned in a red, black and green knitted cap, the colours of black nationalism. In the future he will exchange the tuque for his trademark trilby, or is it a fedora? He is in a dark recording studio, which seems fitting to the mood, wearing headphones, a horizontally-striped multicoloured seventies sweater draped over a large-collared, light-coloured shirt. The poet's choreographed gestures are carefully synchronized with the bass line and the breaks in music as lyrical poetry is orated through his haunting baritone voice. He sets the stage – a blues dance where young brothers and sisters rock to a pulsating dread beat and thumping bass.

The scene then goes underground, to the subway, but we still hear the music-poetry. A train emerges from a dark tunnel into the light, it stops, and the poet steps on board. By now he is wearing a dark trench coat and beige flared pants – we are in the seventies, after all – and the same knitted hat. The poet resurfaces at Brixton Underground station, the heart of London's Caribbean community, a vibrating cultural hub that has somehow managed to reproduce Caribbean life despite (or should we say as a result of?) the hostile English setting. He walks the streets of Brixton with a confident, comfortable strut, almost a skank. He is among the people, his people, the inspiration for his verse. As the bass rises to a crescendo, his voice describes blood-boiling anger resulting in the harrowing act of fraternal bloodletting, the theme that characterized many of his early poems.

The poet explains his method. It involves writing the poem through the music that he hears in his head; the music, which comes to him in the form of a bass line, is embedded in the poem and the instrumentals are then integrated with the poem in the studio. Later, and quite remarkably, the poet argues that poetry doesn't change anything, but simply reflects the changes that are already taking place within the society as a result of material struggles: 'You could write a thousand songs depicting the most terrifying conditions of human existence. That won't bring about the revolution. It's people's actual material struggle to change conditions that brings about political change.' It's perhaps a strange closing statement for a film about a poet who is now globally renowned for his political-poetics.

The poet performs 'Time Come' at the Railton Road Community Centre. The dim and intimate setting amplifies the ominous tone of the poem. 'Time Come' is prophetic. It warns Babylon that the rebellion is coming: 'it too late now | I did warn you'. Babylon has failed to heed the warning to put an end to its Babylonian ways. Too much black blood has been spilled, and Babylon must now suffer the consequences. We then hear the poem 'Come Wi Goh Dung Deh', which, he explains, was written in 1974 when he returned from his first visit to Jamaica since joining his mother in London in 1963. The conditions in Jamaica were the same, or even worse than when he left, he offers, but he doesn't elaborate. He instead describes how growing up in Brixton was like growing up in Jamaica in terms of the cultural feel and the availability of Caribbean foodstuffs. We see an image of the Hip City record shop as we hear the inimitable voice of the reggae don Burning Spear (aka Winston Rodney). As the poet walks through the market we see images of Caribbean women wearing colourful head wraps, but their coats and the presence of a white skin-headed male cuts through the Caribbean aesthetic, as do the signature black cabs. This is England, and the poet is at least as English as he is Jamaican.

Now the poet is reading the poem 'Double Scank' in a radio studio, perhaps at the BBC. The studio is dark and intimate and the poet's sonorous voice adds to the effect. There is a curious energy between the poet and his white female host. Their body gestures are playful, her eyes and smile flirtatious, and her voice inviting. The poet is at ease. He has earned his place there. When and why did you start writing poetry? Do you plan to return to England? Obvious, perhaps even trite questions, but maybe this is what the audience wants to know. The scene then switches to a domino game, a trademark Caribbean recreational activity. The players violently slam the domino pieces on the table in good jest as the poet's voice describes black struggles against fascist tendencies and Thatcherism in Britain. Blacks in Britain are not leaving. England is home and the people of the Caribbean have brought their history and culture to bear on English society, and this has sustained them in their adopted home, says the poet.

Big Youth, U-Roy and others, these are the reggae deejays whose lyricism, backed by reggae music, influenced the poet, but he reminds us once again that for him, the music and poetry come together, that is to say that the music is embedded in his words and is an essential part of his creative writing process. He then performs his signature poem, 'Five Nights of Bleeding', to the nyabinghi drums of Rasta Love and the riveting sound of a bass guitar. As he chants, he also dances, a feature he would later more or less abandon. Suddenly he is reading the same poem a cappella. The difference is obvious. Less animated by the music, he enunciates in a lower register. Then, in the next scene, we hear a clip from the BBC news: Beirut and the UN Security Council; Rhodesia's Ian Smith in the US and a visit to the UK imminent; the Leonid Brezhnev/Jimmy Carter Soviet-US summit; a bombing in Blackpool that injures a woman; Syrian troops battling a right-wing Christian militia as families of UN soldiers head for the Israeli border. From Bristol to Babylon, this is part of the global context within which the poet's words are crafted.

The poet reads 'Doun de Road' to students at his old high school, and then responds to a question about his apparent pre-occupation with violence – the whole world is violent, Brixton is violent, school and pubs are violent, Jamaica is violent, and things even get hot from time to time in Parliament, he says, with a touch of humour. Back in the studio, we hear the poem 'Song of Blood' as the poet joins producer and musician Dennis Bovell behind the control board. He later dialogues with black youth in the Keskidee Arts Centre where he runs a library and coordinates programmes. The youth speak a combination of English, cockney and Jamaican. A young man describes being arrested by the police under the much-reviled suspicion charges. We then see images of the 1976 Notting Hill Riots during which blacks and the police battled for control of the streets. As we watch these scenes unfold, the voice of the poet wails in the background, 'All Wi Doin is Defendin', a poem that anticipated these confrontations. He then reads from 'Yout Rebels', another poem that captures the angst, anomie, but also positive motion of young blacks (blood risin surely | carvin a new path | movin fahwod to freedom'. But it is also an anti-capitalist poem ('sayin to capital nevva | movin forwud hevva').[1]

As the documentary comes to a close, the poet talks about his involvement in the Race Today Collective, a political organization that is at the forefront of Afro and Asian working-class struggles in Britain. It is these struggles, he informs us, that animate his poetry and as we hear the poet's voice reading 'It Dread inna Inglan' – the poem that denounces Margaret Thatcher's 'racist show', declares 'but a she haffi go' and announces that 'African | Asian | West Indian | and Black British | stan firm inna Inglan' – we also witness the poet in a protest in support of George Lindo, a black man from Bradford who was falsely arrested by the police. The scenes switch between the poet reading the poem in the studio and in front of a police station. The message is clear: he is a political poet and his poetry only has meaning in so far as it gives voice to the struggle for freedom, even if he believes that poetry does not, in and of itself, bring about change. The poet has to be actively involved. That is the poet's stance.

* * *

Franco Rosso's 1979 film, *Dread, Beat, and Blood*, announced Linton Kwesi Johnson as a fresh voice on the British scene who not only wrote poetry, but also recorded his poems to music. The release of the film followed the release of the album *Dread Beat and Blood* the year before, which followed the release of a book by the same title three years earlier, all of which announced that a genuine political voice had emerged, a poet whose lyricism captured the thoughts, feelings and aspirations of the youth of his generation. It was in London that he discovered the British Black Panther Movement, New Beacon Books and writers John La Rose and Andrew Salkey, and it was in this diasporic cultural and political hub, in the heart of Babylon, that he discovered W.E.B. Du Bois and a number of other writers and poets of African descent. But it was the prophetic prose and poetics of Frantz Fanon and the searing surrealist poetry of Aimé Césaire that had the most compelling and dramatic impact on the aspiring poet. In England during the 1970s, young blacks confronted systemic racial exclusion, police brutality and harassment, but a new generation of seemingly fearless black rebellious youth began to vent their anger and frustrations. Their anguish resulted in both conscious acts of rebellion and autodestructive forms of violence, and as the poet attempted to give voice to this experience, Frantz Fanon's *The Wretched of the Earth* became a central book for him. As he recalls, it

> had a big impact on me and shaped my thinking on the theme of violence in the process of de-colonisation to my particular situation here, seeing a lot of internecine warfare going on between the youths of my generation. A lot of it had to do with sound systems, a lot of it had to do with neighbourhoods and so on. And, of course, that was happening on the one hand, and at the same time we were being brutalised by the police and framed and criminalised.[2]

In another interview he recalls that he 'was captivated by his analysis of the anti-colonial struggle and the role of violence in the anti-colonial struggle and how the oppressed internalize the violence that is meted out against them and sometimes channelled as violence against themselves. Hence my dealing with the theme of fratricidal violence in some of my early poetry.'[3]

Very little has been written about the place of Fanon in Johnson's verse, perhaps because some may be put off by his apparent obsession with violence. Critic Rebecca Dyer suggests this in her comparison between the poet's early work and the 'lighter tone' of novelist Samuel Selvon, author of *The Lonely Londoners*.[4] But the slight attention paid to Fanon in analyses of Johnson's work could also be linked to the fact that critics have generally tended to downplay the dramatic tension and poetics in Fanon's work, ignoring both the literary tenor of his writing and how this might have been attractive to the young Johnson.

Linton Kwesi Johnson is also recognized as an authority on reggae music, a reputation that stems largely from interviews conducted with him, music reviews that he has published in *Melody Maker* magazine and other forums, his ten-part 1983 BBC documentary, *From Mento to Lovers Rock*, which the poet also researched, wrote and narrated,[5] the 1975 essay 'The Politics of the Lyrics of Reggae Music' and the 1976 essay 'Jamaican Rebel Music'. As we have seen, 'Jamaican Rebel Music' theorizes Jamaican popular music, lyricism and dance in the post-independent era. Drawing on Fanon, the poet argues that Jamaican music – both the music itself and the lyrics of the songs – is 'experiential music', because not only do Jamaicans experience the music, but it also shapes and reflects their experience of suffering, woe and the violence associated with the history and legacy of slavery and colonialism. The music is largely produced by Jamaican sufferers in Kingston's ghettos.[6] It is a cathartic music that conjures up and canalizes the pent-up anger and frustration that the sufferer feels, but in this case catharsis erupts into fraternal fury in the dancehall. Here the internalization of colonization is externalized when the physical and psychological violence inflicted by Babylon proves too much to bear:[7]

> The music invokes what Fanon calls the 'emotional sensitivity' of the oppressed and gives vent to it through dance. As Fanon puts it: 'The native's relaxation takes precisely the form of muscular orgy in which the most acute aggressivity and the most impelling violence are transformed and conjured away'. 'There are no limits – for in reality your purpose in coming together is to allow the accumulated libido, the hampered aggressivity to dissolve as in a volcanic eruption. Symbolic killings, fantastic rites, imaginary mass murders – all must be brought out.'
>
> But it so happens that, at times, the catharsis does not come through dance, for the violence that the music carries is turned inwards and personalized, so that for no apparent reason, the dance halls and yards often explode into fratricidal violence and general pandemonium. Whenever two rival sound systems meet, violence often erupts between the rival

supporters, so the dj is often both the musical pace setter and the musical peacekeeper.[8]

The poet's prose prophesies an ultimate confrontation between the sufferers and the Babylonian tyrants when the sufferer's pent-up anger and anguish proves too much to bear, but at this stage, the fratricidal stage, the violence and rage is expressed inwardly and within the same group. For Fanon: 'Where individuals are concerned, a positive negation of common sense is evident.' For, while on the one hand, 'the settler or the policeman has the right the live-long day to strike the native, to insult him and to make him crawl to them', on the other hand, the colonized reach for their knives 'at the slightest hostile or aggressive glance cast on him by another native; for the last resort of the native is to defend his personality vis-à-vis his brother. Tribal feuds', Fanon writes, 'only serve to perpetuate old grudges buried deep in the memory. By throwing himself with all his force into the vendetta the native tries to persuade himself that colonialism does not exist, that everything is going on as before, that history continues',[9] permitting the colonized 'to ignore the obstacle, and to put off till later the choice, nevertheless inevitable, which opens up the question of armed resistance to colonialism. Thus collective auto-destruction in a very concrete form is one of the ways in which the native's muscular tension is set free.'[10] Here Fanon captures the ways in which colonized natives exorcise their anger and anxiety through violence. Unable to at this stage strike against the master, the native resorts, for the slightest insult or that apparent hostile glance from the corner of another's eye, to his knife, unleashing repressed anger and frustration. Through this internecine violence – which Fanon notes proves in the eyes of the settler that the colonized are not human beings and justifies the settlers' superior existence – the sufferer tries to ignore the reality of colonial oppression, the very reality that engenders this violence. Fanon stresses the role that the psycho-social and political environment plays in conditioning violent behaviour. It is the violence of colonialism that produces the broad phenomenon of violence among the colonized – and by extension, among groups that are oppressed, marginalized and alienated from themselves and the wider society by the power elite. Violence is a way of venting pent-up frustrations and anger within the limited means that are at the colonials' disposal. Unable to directly confront its enemy in a coherent and organized way, the sufferers turn on themselves for muscular and psychological release.[11]

Johnson creatively adopts Fanon's trenchant, poetic analysis of violence in his sociology of Jamaican popular music and society and then adapts it to the experiences of black British youth in *Dread Beat an' Blood*. Fanon's poetic-dramatic language left an indelible imprint on Johnson's early dread poems.[12] His impact on Johnson is evident in the poem 'Dread Beat an' Blood' where we witness the echoes of his eloquent description of the colonial condition in Johnson's depiction of internecine violence in Babylonian Britain. The poet sets the scene in which brothers and sisters move and shake and rock to a reggae rhythm in a blues dance. The music's upbeat tempo mirrors the raging hearts of the party revellers, as the tension and rage erupts in an act of patriarchal violence in which a 'him' hits a 'her' after which another 'him' flashes a blade, resulting in a bloodletting ritual of violence:

> an a fist curled in anger reaches a her
> then a flash of a blade from another to a him
> leaps out for a dig of a flesh of a piece of skin[13]

The blues dances (house parties) that Johnson describes in a surrealist tone in 'Dread Beat an' Blood' and 'Five Nights of Bleeding' are the equivalent of Fanon's ritual dances[14] Dance and religious rites also serve to purge accumulated anxiety while avoiding the ultimate conflict with the colonizer as 'the psyche shrinks back, obliterates itself and finds outlet in muscular demonstrations which have caused certain very wise men to say that the native is a hysterical type. This sensitive emotionalism', as Fanon describes it, 'will find its fulfillment through eroticism in the driving forces behind the dissolution of the crisis'[15] – in other words, exorcism as eroticism helps to purge the mind of its neuroticism, releasing the body's accumulated libido and muscular and psychological tension. But this 'seemingly unorganized pantomime' is, in reality, 'extremely systematic'[16] as 'By various means – shakes of the head, bending of the spinal column, throwing of the whole body backwards' a community seeks 'to exorcise itself, to liberate itself, to explain itself'.[17] Anxiety and anger are conjured away during these ritual ceremonies, but as historians of slavery in the Americas would know, such ceremonies were often the prelude to mass rebellion. For Fanon, 'there are no limits – for in reality your purpose in coming together is to allow the accumulated libido, the hampered aggressivity to dissolve as in a volcanic eruption',[18] and for this to occur, 'Symbolic killings, fantastic rites, imaginary mass murders – all must be brought out.'[19] Fanon's graphic description conjures images of hysteria that reverberate into reggae dancehalls where young revellers meet in order to exorcise their demons and momentarily purge their frustrations and anxieties. Often hands are raised in a gun-like fashion, with the corollary sound effects, with the rapid beat of the music echoing the deadly sound of rapid machine gun fire that is all too common in the garrison quarters of Kingston, Jamaica. But these political conflicts disguise deeper, inner woes and anxieties, whose roots lie in abject poverty combined with political manipulation and the social alienation of the population. 'The dances complement the popular music – the ska, the rock steady, the reggae, the scank, and the chucky – and are at once erotic and sensual, violent, aggressive and cathartic',[20] according to Johnson, but 'the catharsis does not come through dance, for the violence that the music carries is turned inwards so that for no apparent reason the dance halls and yards often explode into fratricidal violence and general pandemonium'.[21] Violence spills onto the dancehall or blues parties in Jamaica or England (and the United States and Canada) and a real gun is often brought out and ceremonially fired into air, and far too often the guns are turned towards live targets, the victim's final words written in a pool of blood. In Johnson's England, the black dispossessed are substituted for Fanon's colonial subjects and Césaire's Rebel, and referring to the relationship between anti-colonial struggles in the Caribbean and black struggles in Britain, Johnson argued in 1986 that 'the struggle we've been waging in the fifties and sixties and so on in Britain is a continuation of those anti-colonial struggles, because we found ourselves in the same colonial situation in Britain, living under colonial conditions'.[22] But if, for the poet, Fanon's analysis of violent phenomena captures the spirit of colonialism in Britain, at what stage and in what form does the actual internecine violence transition into an anti-colonial or anti-oppressive struggle? Ritualistic blood-letting permits the 'native' to forestall armed resistance,[23] but as conditions for change emerge on an ever-widening scale, or the social conditions become so extreme that they can either improve or descend into utter chaos and anarchy (of course things can also, more or less, remain the same), this implosive, internalized fraternal violence is externalized in another way, this time redirected towards the oppressor as 'armed resistance to colonialism begins'.[24]

Césairealism

Fanon analysis of violence had a profound impact on Johnson, but it was the combination of Fanonmenology, Césairealism and the reggae aesthetic that lent shape to Johnson's early verse. Great emphasis has been placed on Jean-Paul Sartre's connection to Fanon, justified in part by the decision to include an incendiary introduction by Sartre to *The Wretched of the Earth*, but as Christian Lapoussinière shows in his detailed, almost forensic comparison of Césaire's work and Fanon's early writing,[25] Césaire was the most direct and sustained political-literary influence on Fanon.[26] The lives of Fanon and Césaire were intricately enmeshed. Fanon was, in a sense, Césaire's spiritual son in much the same way that Walter Rodney was C.L.R. James's – with the attendant disagreements that characterized the relationships within each pair. It was Césaire, that remarkable poet, playwright and co-founder of the Negritude movement, who set the French language on fire in *Notebook of a Return to My*

Native Land, his seething description of the colonial condition in Martinique. As Fanon would write, up until 1940 Martiniquans did not see themselves as 'Negro', but fresh from his studies in France, Césaire's presence in Martinique and his declaration that 'it was fine and good to be a Negro' began to change this attitude. The sheer madness of such a statement within a colonial context, coming from a learned teacher, captured Fanon's imagination and disturbed the racial logic of colonialism in Martinique, where whiteness had been elevated to an idyllic status.[27] When leukaemia claimed Fanon's life in 1961, Césaire elegized him in both verse and prose. This is how he described Fanon in the poem 'Flint Warrior Through All Words': 'you scratch the iron | you scratch the bars of the jail | you scratch the gaze of the torturer | flint warrior | vomited | through the mangrove swamp serpent's snout'.[28] In his prose tribute, Césaire assessed and contextualized Fanon's legacy and his apparent preoccupation with violence: 'A violent one, they said. And it is true that Fanon instituted himself as a theorist of violence, the only arm of the colonized that can be used against colonialist barbarity.' However, for Césaire, Fanon's violence 'was that of the non-violent ... the violence of justice, of purity and intransigence' and 'his revolt was ethical, and his endeavor generous', as in 'him resided the absoluteness of passion'. Fanon's theorizing of violence owes a great deal to Césaire, but as Césaire insists, Fanon was an exacting and assiduous thinker who believed that thought should be translated into action and who hated both compromise and cowardice.[29] Ultimately, Fanon was attempting to free humankind from itself as he implored us from his deathbed to create a new and more complete human, to invent and discover in order to move beyond the morass of madness that has hampered humankind. This, for Césaire, was Fanon's lasting legacy.[30]

For fellow Martiniquan writer Patrick Chamoiseau, Césaire's impact on Fanon is expressed in terms of the latter's *radicalité*, that is to say his radical critique of capitalism, his incessant questioning and calling into question anything that perverts the goal of genuine freedom,[31] and in his '*connaissance poétique*' or what loosely translates as poetic consciousness – a reference to Césaire's famous essay 'Poetry and Knowledge' – and '*le choc d'un langage ... habité par le verbe et par le rhétorique césairienne*'.[32] That said, these features in Fanon's work sit in stark contrast to Césaire's other, more silent presence in *The Wretched of the Earth*, whose critique of bourgeois nationalist leaders, it has been suggested, represents a coded critique of Césaire, among others.[33]

The most direct indication of Césaire's impact on Fanon's conception of violence appears in *The Wretched of the Earth* where he cites passages from Césaire's *And the Dogs Were Silent* (*Et les chiens se taisaient*). This is a dramatic poem that was later adapted for stage production, and Johnson would have been exposed to the poem in his reading of Fanon, if not before. For Fanon, violence takes on prophetic significance in Césaire's work.[34] Césaire's Rebel recounts to his mother (this brings Johnson's 'Sonny's Lettah' to mind) the circumstances that led to him killing his master. Prompted by the master's suggestion that the Rebel's newborn child would make a good chain gang captain – a slave who enforces the enslavement of other slaves – the Rebel takes his master's life.[35] The Rebel's reference to himself and his fellow rebels as 'madmen' would later be expressed in an echo in the first lines of Johnson's poem 'Five Nights of Bleeding' ('madness ... madness ... | madness tight on the heads of the rebels'),[36] and it is not lost to us that Fanon dealt with 'madness' as an occupation:

> We were running like madmen; shots rang out ... We were striking. Blood and sweat cooled and refreshed us. We were striking where the shouts came from, and the shouts became more strident and a great clamor rose from the east: it was the outhouses burning and the flames flickered sweetly on our cheeks.[37]

In citing Césaire's surreal poem in *The Wretched of the Earth*, Fanon asserts that freedom comes at a price, and the Rebel's actions, his 'counter-violence violence', is a direct response to

the violence inflicted by the colonizer.[38] While the Rebel is
eventually executed for his transgression, his martyrdom will
serve as an enduring example, his blood-like seeds buried in the
soil that will bring new life.

Césairealism represents Césaire's unique contribution to
surrealism, which Johnson would later adopt and then adapt in
his early poetry while invoking the aesthetic of reggae culture
– the music, chanting, singing, style and stance associated with
reggae. But what exactly is surrealism? And what peculiar con-
tribution did Césaire and other Afro diasporic artists make
to the movement that Johnson inherited? Surrealism is often
described as a purely European artistic movement, but it would
be a mistake to read Césaire's surrealism as a derivative of its
European counterpart. As Césaire recalled in an interview with
the Haitian poet René Depestre during the 1967/8 Cultural
Congress in Havana, by the time that he embraced surrealism
he was already in the process of forging his own conception of
it. Reading French surrealists affirmed an aesthetic and political
approach that he had been shifting towards on his own, but he
had already been writing in the spirit of the movement, and
when he discovered it, it simply affirmed what he was already
doing. Although he drew inspiration from the same authors as
his French surrealist counterparts, for him surrealism involved
a process of disalienation by delving into his African ancestry.[39]
In this spirit, it has been argued that Césaire's poetry surpassed
surrealism in so far as it not only worked against capitalism and
colonialism, but simultaneously against racism[40] (the same could
be said of Johnson's surrealistic poetry). Césaire was part of a
movement in Martinique whose aim, according to the Marti-
niquan poet and theorist Suzanne Césaire (née Roussi), was to
'explore and express systematically the forbidden zones of the
human mind in order to neutralize them'.[41] Sylvia Wynter's
analysis of the literary tradition that was spawned by Césaire
and that is exemplified by Édouard Glissant's work suggests
that, beginning with the surrealism of *Notebook of a Return to My
Native Land*, this tradition represents a revolt against the secular
humanism and universalism that began with Columbus's landing

in the Americas. For Wynter, Césaire, Fanon and Glissant enact what she describes as an 'anti-Universal' or a 'countertheme of specificity' of the Caribbean landscape and the Creole languages and poetics that the region spawned in terms of 'their syntax, sound, and poetic rhythm' and their orality in opposition to the scribal nature of the European languages that the Caribbean had inherited.[42]

For Richard Iton, the early and mid-twentieth-century surrealist movements and the broad neosurrealist tradition that attempted 'to fuse the dream worlds and everyday practices and bridge the politics/culture divide' are tied to the notion of the 'black fantastic', those 'minor-key sensibilities generated from the experiences of the underground, the vagabond, and those constituencies marked as deviant – notions of being that are inevitably aligned within, in conversation with, against, and articulated beyond the boundaries of the modern'. In this spirit, and given its outrageously outlawed status, it could be argued that 'representations of blackness are always surreal'.[43] Robin D.G. Kelley argues that surrealism embodied freedom aspirations, social justice and the aesthetic-political spirit of revolt, or what he describes as a 'living, mutable, creative vision of a world where love, play, human dignity, an end to poverty and want and imagination are the pillars of freedom',[44] and in this sense, the work of the Cuban painter Wifredo Lam is exemplary of surrealism and the poetics of imagery. Lam was introduced to the Surrealist Group in Paris by Pablo Picasso, in whom he discovered a continuity between the Spaniard's interest in African art and his own childhood memories of art in the home of his Cuban godmother, Mantonica Wilson.[45] In invoking this symbolism in his work, Lam produced surrealist imagery that, rooted in his Afro Caribbean experience, revolted against traditional artistic norms and represented a revolt against Western forms of aesthetic and political domination that continues to dazzle and confound us. His painting *El Tercer Mundo* (*Third World*) may well be understood as the Third World counterpart to Picasso's depiction of the inhumanity and wanton destruction of war in Europe that is depicted in *Guernica*, almost as if he felt compelled to say, this is what has happened in the Global South, too. Césaire attempted to capture the evocative spiritual essence of Lam's art in his poem 'Wifredo Lam ... ' when he wrote: 'nothing less than | the kingdom under siege | the sky precarious | relief imminent and legitimate', describing Lam as a 'diviner of purple entrails and destiny | reciter of macumbas', before asking, 'my brother | what are you looking for through these forests | of horns of hoofs of wings of horses'?[46] Césaire's ekphrasis describes the metaphysical character of Lam's artwork, demonstrating the poet's ability to create images in our minds – in much the same way that Lam creates images with his hands and brush – but in this case the images invoke the spirit of Lam himself who has been described as the visual 'poet of the mythical'.[47]

Early jazz musicians also embodied this spirit, long before it had been named surrealism, and Césaire himself has alluded to the importance of jazz for the emergent black consciousness of the 1920s and 1930s.[48] While surrealism's spiritual progenitor, André Breton, was late to recognize the spirit of surrealism in jazz, many of Europe's early surrealists expressed their appreciation for jazz music.[49] Kelley reminds us that Thelonious Monk – with whom Johnson shares some resemblance in his signature picture profile[50] – would later become a heroic figure within the surrealist movement and part of the surrealist discovery of the Marvellous: 'Monk's music appealed especially to the surrealists' struggle for complete freedom and the overthrow of bourgeois concepts of beauty and art. He made music that destroyed many Western ideas about music making, turning conventional rules of composition, harmony, and rhythm on their heads. He stripped romantic ballads of their romanticism and took his listeners on wild harmonic rides filled with surprising dissonances.'[51]

The Toronto-based Clifton Joseph is one the early dub poets whose poetry has musically extended beyond the reggae aesthetic. Joseph directly invokes Monk's music in 'A Chant for Monk', elegiacally combining scatting, onomatopoeic verse and lyricism that, in announcing Monk's death, in effect bring the piano virtuoso's spirit back to life.[52] He also invokes jazz and surrealism in his Dizzy Gillespie bee-bop-inspired 'Night in Tunisia', in which – accompanied, on one version, by a sparse and understated jazz piano, an overstated drumbeat and a howling rock guitar – he denounces the 'monsoon of inequalities' and the 'disguises of lies' of business and government. There is also his wholly onomatopoeic 'Poem for Coltrane', in which his *sans mots* voice becomes the musical instrument that speaks in the tenor of a saxophone.[53]

While Johnson does not invoke Monk explicitly, the musical accompaniment to 'Two Sides of Silence', for example, is grounded in the jazz aesthetic. The poem betrays reggae's jazz-inflected roots via ska by setting the poem to a jagged-sounding jazz saxophone[54] that was inspired by the poet's appreciation of great musicians such as Pharaoh Sanders and John Coltrane;[55] but the poem also evokes Britain's own tradition of jazz and the spirit of saxophonist Joe Harriott – the graduate from Jamaica's famed Alpha Boys School who is considered one of the few jazz geniuses to emerge outside of the US context (Don Drummond, one of the architects of ska music, also attended Alpha Boys, and although not strictly a jazz musician he was considered one the world's best trombonists) – and St Vincent's Ellsworth McGranahan 'Shake' Keane, the trumpeter and flugelhorn player in Harriott's 1950s–1960s quintet, with whom Johnson was well acquainted personally, while anticipating the work of Courtney Pine and Sons of Kemet's Shabaka Hutchings.[56]

In 'Two Sides of Silence', W.E.B. Du Bois's double consciousness is transmuted to a double side of silence in which the muted aims and aspirations of blacks who, brutalized by slavery and the ravages of racial colonialism, are also stifled by systemic social and political exclusion in the form of state-sanctioned violence, eclipsed dreams and the absence of peace and calm. However, the appearance of extinguished hopes is a ruse, the quiet before the storm, and the tranquillity is an illusion. As the poem's narrator inquires,

How indeed can there be silence
when our hearts beat out a sonorous beat

meeting the beating drums of an African past;
when our eyes shed solid tears of iron blood
that falls on CONCRETE GROUND?[57]

The contrast between hearts beating like drums of an African past and the 'solid tears of iron blood' falling to the concrete implies a world of apparent contradictions that must, in one form or another, be resolved as the cries of misery and 'erupting thoughts of rebellion' forebode tumultuous times. Indeed, as the poet rhetorically asks, 'How can there be calm when the storm is yet to come?'[58]

Surrealism, then, has deep roots among Afro diasporic and Caribbean artists and as Kelley suggests, revolts and struggles for cultural freedom in the colonial world served as an inspiration for Western surrealists who 'discovered in the cultures of Africa, Oceania, and Native America a road into the Marvelous and confirmation of their most fundamental ideas'.[59] It is not difficult to imagine a young Johnson's reaction upon reading Césaire's poignant lines, perhaps for the first time in *The Wretched of the Earth*. Césaire's verse, along with Fanon's poetics, infused his own, adopted and adapted to a political context that was far removed from the one that Césaire had described. The poet experienced the emotional pull of Césaire's dramatic poetry directly from the source when he read *Notebook of a Return to My Native Land*, whose surrealism echoes in Johnson's early poetry.[60]

Notebook has been criticized for both its overindulgence in the Western European heroic form and paternalistically romantic conceptions of women as the embodiment of unreason and devoid of autonomy and human agency.[61] Notwithstanding these criticisms, the poem stretches and bends the French language to the poet's will and in ways that reflect his seemingly boundless imagination and command of the French language, his vision of Martinique's geography and topography, and the global economic and political forces that have been brought to bear on the island. *Notebook* is not written in Creole, and unlike Johnson and Glissant, Césaire, it has been suggested, was less than enthusiastic about the use of Creole in literature as a conduit for complex thought. But perhaps it is more accurate to suggest, as the Martiniquan critic Malik Noël-Ferdinand has, that what Césaire was doing, ultimately, was recasting the French language while drawing on the Creole resources of Martinique.[62] To say that Césaire draws on Creole resources is not to say that the poem is written in Creole, but the poem does invoke Creole words. It is more in tenor and tone that Creole is present, and as Derek Walcott argued, 'For all the complexity of its surrealism, its sometimes invented words, it sounds, to at least one listener familiar with French Patois, like a poem written tonally in Creole.'[63] The surrealism to which Walcott refers is surreal by name and not by tradition, that is to say the tradition that emerged from France in the early 1920s. Césaire's 'surrealism' is best referred to as Césairealism because, while it creates a similar effect and affect in the reader as its French equivalent, it draws on Martiniquan and Antillean resources, and not solely on the body of French literature that Césaire was so fond of. It is this peculiar poetic vantage point that so poignantly struck André Breton. This is to say that, as is the case with Wifredo Lam in relation to Picasso, we must resist the temptation to subsume Césairealism to French surrealism, despite the parallels between them. Moreover, to the extent that we can refer to Césaire's poetry as surrealist, it is more of a descriptor that captures a mood or sensibility created in his particular context, not France. In other words, surrealism and Césairealism should be read in counterpoint – or contrapuntally, to draw on Edward Said's musical analogy.

French surrealist poet André Breton referred to the poem in 1943 as 'nothing less than the greatest lyrical monument of our time',[64] but his statement is diminished by overstating Césaire's blackness on the one hand and his suggestion that Césaire's achievement is partly based on his ability to transcend black anguish on the other.[65] In other words, his universality, his humanity, exists outside and beyond his being as opposed to through it or as a result of it. Fanon has gone further on this point, lamenting the fact that Breton thought it necessary to describe Césaire as a black poet who handles the French language as no Frenchman can, as if to suggest there is some sort of paradox between being a great poet who writes in French and being black.[66] In contrast, John Berger described Césaire as someone who 'uses magic as a metaphor', metaphorically becoming a magician in order to 'speak for and to the Negro world at the deepest level of its experience and memories' while claiming 'humanity for his own people' and accusing 'of savagery – without any nobility at all – those who exploit and repress them'. Unlike Picasso, whose art, according to Berger, had become static in the post-Second World War period, the significance of Césaire's work was constantly being affirmed by world events because Césaire spoke through the experience of his people.[67]

Perhaps more than anyone else of his and subsequent generations, his poetic portraits captured the stultifying socio-economic reality as he attempted to rupture the 'colonization of the cultural Imaginary'.[68] *Notebook* is about violence, the violence of colonization in the aftermath of slavery. It is about a pestilent and disease-ridden colony of dashed hopes and dead aspirations, a dying sun that has set on his native land and a shadow that has been cast over the moon; it is about severed blood ties and the blood of Africans shed in the Americas. However, the poem is also about revolt – a sounding of the alarm and a clarion call of freedom that anticipates the *rendez-vous* of victory. The colonized's social position serves as a reminder of the human condition at its very worst and the reality that the world is in dire need of dramatic change. Words flow like blood in the biblical Nile in the poem, exposing open wounds that need to be healed.

But the point here is not simply that there is a direct link between Fanon and Césaire, but that this connection threads through the poetry of Linton Kwesi Johnson whose blood poems represent a creative combination of Fanonmenology and Césairealism and a prophetic-poetic dramatization of black (largely male) lives in England.

On Violence

On the surface it would appear that Johnson, via Césaire and Fanon, is a zealous advocate of wanton acts of violence. But I would suggest that, while there is a realism to Johnson's characterization of violence that is rooted in internecine conflict and police brutality, it also represents a dramatic poetics of violence that finds expression in Fanon's writing in which he iterates and recants his initial statements as part of an overall dialectical analysis of violence among the colonized and dispossessed, as well as treatise on the dynamics of liberation. Failure to appreciate this has led to misreadings of Fanon's penchant for taking poetic licence, a practice that is tied to Césairealism and Césaire's dramatic oeuvre. It is also easy to misread Johnson in the same way.

In his 2004 foreword to *The Wretched of the Earth*, critic Homi Bhabha describes Fanon as 'a poet of the vicissitudes of violence'.[69] But for Bhabha, the 'poetic justice' of violence, even in the name of liberty, is questionable,[70] a point that brings to mind David Macey's question: how would our conception of the violent phenomena that Fanon describes shift if we were to describe it as armed resistance instead of the more generic and abstract term violence?[71] (It also recalls the *faux débat* between Malcolm X and his opponents on violence/non-violence in which it was implied that even defending oneself against acts of violence was equivalent to the violence of the aggressor.) However, what at face value appears to be a prescription of violence as cathartic release actually has far deeper roots and more profound meaning. The philosopher Tsenay Serequeberhan describes Fanon's conception of violence as a reactive violence, a 'dialectic of violence and counter-violence' that confronts the inherent violence of colonialism and colonial power.[72] Serequeberhan also challenges the intellectual hypocrisy that acknowledges the discourses of violence expressed by Rousseau, Hobbes, Hegel, Heidegger and even Marx, but fails to appreciate its significance in the specific and very violent colonial context that Fanon describes.[73] Serequeberhan is particularly critical of Hannah Arendt, who acknowledges the merits of armed struggle or organized armed resistance in response to Nazism, but minimizes or dismisses the same practice of resistance and freedom by the damned and condemned of the 'Third World'.[74]

I would like to suggest here that Fanon's meditation on violence is at once metaphysical, metaphorical and materialist, drawing on the concrete experience of the colonized and their reaction to the violence of the colonizer, a 'dialectic of experience' that Fanon describes in both real and surreal terms. His writing is infused with 'an organic poise and poetry'[75] that dramatizes the colonial condition on the global stage in what Ato Sekyi-Otu describes in *Fanon's Dialectic of Experience* as Fanon's 'epic imagination and tragic sense of racial destiny' as he 'marshals empirical detail, poetic language, and theoretical engagement with major metanarratives of human bondage and freedom to fashion a critical account of the colonial and post-colonial condition'.[76] The case for Fanon as a dramatist and poetic writer is enhanced by the recent publication of two of his plays, *L'Œil se noie* and *Les Mains parallèles* (he apparently wrote a third, *La Conspiration*, that has been lost), which were written in 1949,[77] but Sekyi-Otu's creative assessment warns against reading Fanon too literally. Fanon's work represents a 'dramatic dialectical narrative' and, despite the resolute tone of his political convictions, some of his statements are not absolute and definitive, but rather complex and provisional or 'a strategic and self-serving act'.[78] Fanon makes what we might describe as an Anancy move, named after the spider in Jamaican folklore who uses guile and trickery, 'playing fool fi catch wise', in order to get the upper hand, leading us into a particular logic or reasoning only for us to realize that we have been misled into a direction that is not final. Sekyi-Otu challenges the 'the unwarranted conflation of what Fanon enacts, dramatizes, and narrates' in his writing, as Fanon often makes seemingly definitive pronouncements only to renounce them, or exaggerates reality in his poetic prose, and then recants or at least qualifies his initial statements.[79] In other words, dialectical dramatization suggests that there is tension and even deliberate contradiction in Fanon's critical remarks, as they advance an interpretation of the colonial experience that is fixed and settled, only to qualify, revise or reverse the same logic or absolute in relation to colonialism, nationalism, race and violence. In concrete terms, Fanon's notion of violence is not merely a description of violent phenomena and it is not an endorsement of wanton, autodestructive behaviour; nor is it solely an analysis of actual anti-colonial violence; rather, it serves as a generalized, though somewhat teleological and symbolic, representation of the various stages in the process of social change.

War Doun de Road

Fanon's framework – his analysis of the violence of oppression (alienation, exploitation and brute force), internecine violence as cathartic release, and oppositional violence as an act of liberation – is creatively adapted by Johnson in what he describes as the phases of violence. Johnson's 'first phase' is characterized by a period of internal doubt, confusion and apprehension on the part of the rebels. Their indirection, frustration and anxiety take the form of violent outbursts among themselves, but the violence is symptomatic of a deeper, more profound feeling of displacement, powerlessness and acute alienation. This includes alienation from one's self, alienation from the society in which one lives, alienation from the product of one's labour and a general feeling of alienation from the various sources of social, political and economic power.

In 'Five Nights of Bleeding', Fanon's dramatic dialectic of desired hope and experience is represented as a teleological process devoid of divergences, distractions and regressions. But as in any social process, there are trials, tribulations and defeats. On the fourth night of Johnson's 'Five Nights of Bleeding', the night after the Babylonian tyrants were wounded by the rebels, violence erupts at a dance, ending in a near fatality as 'Leroy bleeds near death at a blues dance'. Here the poem assumes a specific elegiac reference to Leroy Harris, who was a living victim of internecine violence, but to the extent that the poem probes the Fanonmenology of violence through the prism of black lives its entirety can be read as an elegy to those who have fallen to both internecine and police violence. Not surprisingly, on the fifth night, 'vengeance walked through the doors' and Leroy's stabbing is avenged, and the seemingly never-ending pantomime of violence continues unabated.

The poet's invocation of war and blood in 'Five Nights of Bleeding' is rooted in the experience of black youth, and particularly black males in 1960s and 1970s England, and there are virtually no female subjects in his poetry. One of the few instances of a woman's presence comes in the form of a victim when a 'fist curled in anger reaches a her', to which another male responds by stabbing the 'him'. In other words – with the notable exception of the poem 'Reggae fi May Ayim' and his humorous love song 'Lorraine' – women are conspicuously absent as autonomous actors. Writing more than 25 years later the actor, playwright and poet d'bi young anitafrika also invokes 'five nights of bleeding' in her poetry, but with a distinctly feminist or 'wombanist' vision. In d'bi's 'Blood', the five nights represent a woman's menstrual cycle, and she irreverently invokes the Jamaican curse *blood claat* that literally means blood cloth (it is sometimes mistaken for a blood clot), a reference to a cloth that was historically used to dam a woman's menstrual bleeding. The words *blood claat* are repeated in the poem's inaugural line, highlighting the fact that one of Jamaica's strongest expletives is negatively tied to a woman's natural bleeding process. By throwing the term in our faces, d'bi co-opts its inherent meaning in irreverent indignation and makes it her own while forcing us to engage with the term in relation to women's bodies and to consider how we might understand the 'blood cloth' and a women's blood as transgressive, positive and life-affirming. Whereas Johnson thematizes bloodletting associated with black male oppression, d'bi emphasizes how the psychological warfare associated with menstruation – 'manufactured shame | designed to keep me inna chains'[80] – is manipulated and marketed by corporations to sell sanitary products (she calls out corporations such as Cotex, Tampax, Always and Maxi) to women in ways that reinforce patriarchal norms.[81] Unlike other d'bi poems ('Dear Mama' and 'Revolushun I', for example), she does not indicate that 'Blood' is inspired by Johnson, but if we were to have any doubts, the connection is made obvious in her reference to 'five nights of bleeding' and to the 'brixton/ railton road/rainbow/blues-dance/telegraph',[82] all of which are direct allusions to lines in 'Five Nights of Bleeding'. Moreover, as she has remarked, the idea to write a 'wombanist/feminist version' of Johnson's blood poems emerged while she was living in Havana, Cuba.[83] For her, blood connotes women's 'creashun', 'celebrahun', 'libarashun' and 'revolushun',[84] rhythmic allusions that are juxtaposed with her denunciation of both the tampon/ sanitary pad industry and the shame attached to women's natural bleeding. d'bi's blood is about manufactured menstrual shame and gendered blame; about ritual, though not the 'rituals of blood' invoked in 'Five Nights of Bleeding', but ancestral rites associated with the transition to womanhood and that foreground the experiences of women, and particularly black women.[85] Despite her respect for his work, 'Blood' makes an explicit statement about womanhood and its relative absence in Johnson's oeuvre.

d'bi is not oblivious to the violence to which Johnson's poetry alludes. In the play *blood.claat* she conjoins the theme of menstrual bleeding and internecine violence when Mudgu, the play's lead character, is shamed by her grandmother for soiling her bed sheets with her menstrual blood, and when the bus conductor, Stamma, brandishes a cutlass, causing violent havoc on a bus for what he interprets as ridicule of his stuttering. In another scene, Mudgu's boyfriend, Njoni, of the Black Bird sound system is shot dead when he refuses to sell weed for local dealers. In yet another harrowing scene, Mudgu, a victim of incest, severs the hand of the perpetrator, her uncle. *blood.claat* also shifts in time and space: from Jamaica to Canada and from the days of slavery to contemporary Jamaica, and it is written in a female voice that is rooted in the harsh realities of Kingston's urban underclass as opposed to London.

Mudgu does not find strength and solace in cathartic violence or a direct confrontation with Babylon, but in the ancestral blood ties that bind several generations of Jamaican women, whose resistance stems back to Queen Nanny, a leader of Jamaica's rebellious maroons, former slaves who fought against the British and established autonomous settlements on the island.[86] By embracing the cycle of life, death, rebirth and the love and resistance that has sustained generations of women, Mudgu is able to find a sense of peace and hope, despite becoming pregnant while still in secondary school. In fact, the newborn child symbolizes hope, possibilities[87] and continuity as part of the eternal struggle to attain the good life.

The mytho-poetics of *blood.claat* incorporates African and Afro Caribbean religion, drawing on the spirit of Ogun, the Yoruba warrior god of iron and metal work and the machete, who occupies a central place within Cuba's Santería, Brazil's Condomblé, Haiti's Voudou and Trinidad's Orisha, among other religions (the spirit of the Yoruba goddess of the sea, Yemoja, is invoked in 'Blood' as well as d'bi's 'The Orisha Letters').[88] In this sense *blood.claat* parallels Johnson's *Voices of the Living and the Dead* (1974), which is often described as a poem but is perhaps best characterized as a short surrealist verse play, or what Amor Kohli describes as 'an extended dramaturgic experiment'.[89] It was first performed before an audience at the Keskidee Youth Club where Johnson once worked.

Drawing on Early Modern English idiom and the apoc- alyptic language of the Bible, Johnson's early poetry often combined a sparse, economic use of language and vivid and evocative imagery rooted in his native rural Jamaican culture, his childhood familiarity with the Bible and duppy stories, and his intimate knowledge of reggae music and Rastafari, which he encountered in the concrete jungle of London. Many of these elements are evident in *Voices of the Living and the Dead*. The verse play is replete with repetitive images of blood and violence as the voices of the living converse with the exalted voices of the martyred, whose blood serves as the earth's fertilizer, renewing life and setting the stage for the coming struggle. To give one's life is the ultimate sacrifice because in life's cycle death and life are intricately tied together. The play's narrator conflates 'circle of love in the sky' with a 'circle of blood in the sky'[90] as love, life, death and sacrifice are interconnected and, just like in Jamaica's duppy stories, life and death represent a continuum in which the dead haunt the living in lieu of a proper burial or until they can find peace in the afterlife. Just as in Césaire's *And the Dogs Were Silent*, Johnson's Echo reminds us that the voices of the dead reverberate among the living as the dead's voices break the night's sombre silence, adding to the ominous tone and apocalyptic tenor of the play. The duppies have unfinished business and they cannot find peace until the living exact vengeance for the martyred, until ' ... the banks of the river exploded ... | then the blood began to flow'.[91]

The play is surreal and apocalyptic: 'death must clear the way | for the first new-born flame',[92] and death is 'ecstasy' and 'sweet', all of which suggests that the death of the martyr sows the seeds of future rebellions with drops of his blood. In this spirit the bullets that bless the flesh are like 'Three piercing pollens of love'.[93]

Voices of the Living and the Dead echoes the magical-realism/ surrealist poem 'Song of Blood', in which Vivian Weathers' ominous falsetto is reminiscent of a young Bunny Livingstone (Wailer), Curtis Mayfield and Junior Murvin, who is famous for his rendition of Lee 'Scratch' Perry's classic reggae song 'Police and Thieves' (also covered by the punk group The Clash). Weather's voice also echoes in the Nazarenes' angelic voices of love and rebellion in 'Song of Judgement Day', 'Song of Righteous Life', 'Song of Consoling' and 'Rebel Soul', among others. In 'Song of Blood' Weathers' otherworldly voice is juxtaposed with Johnson's haunting monotone baritone. Weathers' singing symbolizing hopes and possibilities that take us an octave beyond the sky's limits, while Johnson's intonation brings us back down to earth, grounded in the concrete reality of Babylonian dread as guns of war blaze among the sufferers below.

Life and death are part of a continuum in Fanon's work, as they are with Johnson, where he argues that the native, resigned to fatalism under colonialism, finds belief in God's will as an escape from the colonial reality. The native's world is associated with maleficent spirits, magic and zombies, the living dead who perhaps symbolize the liminal status of the native whose living hell is contrasted with the colonizer's heaven on earth.[94] In this spirit, *Voices of the Living and the Dead* echoes George A. Romero's dystopic 1968 flick *Night of the Living Dead*, the classic horror film in which radiation-infected zombies prey on the flesh of the living in a grotesque carnivalesque parade of death. The film's female characters are essentially passive subjects who depend on the protection of their male counterparts, but the lead character, Ben, was played by the African American actor Duane Jones at a time when it was still rare to see black actors in lead roles with a largely white cast. While the initial script did not specify a black actor in the lead role, Jones's presence in the film was nonetheless a significant symbolic gesture. As black audiences have come to anticipate with a sense of resignation, cynicism and humour, Ben eventually dies when he is gunned down as if he too were a zombie, as if to suggest that he too was part of the living dead, although in this case he is the last to die in the film – not the first as has often been the custom – in a not-so-ironic end to a black life at a time when the US was waging war on its black citizens at home as they were being sacrificed at the altar of war in Vietnam.

Zombies represent the bridge between the living and the dead, and as the undead they shed light on social and environmental injustice and the potential for apocalyptic horror. They also underscore the need to overturn imperial orders and restore the faith of believers,[95] in much the way that our poet's resurrected living dead – who occupy a liminal space in society as the citizen/non-citizen, refugee, human/non-human, etc. – confront Babylon in the form of police brutality, Powelism, Thatcherism, neo-fascism, etc. Whereas Romero's zombies – who have been likened to a *lumpenproletariat*[96] – represent a response to industrial decline in Pittsburgh[97] in ways that also anticipate the

Motown to Ghost Town phenomenon (Detroit), the poet's living dead reflect Britain's post-colonial, post-empire malaise; an imperial reordering in which the descendants of Afro Caribbean slaves and Indian indentured workers, along with continental Africans and Indians, have once again been displaced, this time to London in order to fill the jobs that the English were either unwilling or insufficiently qualified to perform, only to become denigrated denizens whose necessary but unwanted presence reinforced their liminal and alien status as the not-quite-English former British colonial subjects. The Apocalypse represents both the ultimate confrontation between good and evil and an eternal battle in which even the heavenly New Jerusalem is not safe.[98] On the other side, the poet's living dead, like their zombie counterparts, are engaged in a battle to achieve the ultimate freedom on earth: to break down the walls of the Babylonian tyrants and construct a new society.

The edict from below that the tyrants must go demonstrates the extent to which biblical lore and metaphor is ingrained in the everyday speech and consciousness of Jamaicans and their diasporic family. Like zombies that freely roam the earth, the poet's black living dead want to be free from state repression that proscribes their freedom of movement, including their right not to move under the guise of anachronistic vagrancy laws that permit the police to stop, search and detain them on the grounds of looking suspicious or loitering, the so-called 'sus' laws.

But the undead in the Apocalypse cannot be contained by heaven's 'cityscape', according to Tina Pippin. They follow Jesus's dictates, literally gorging (his) flesh and ingesting his blood, and yet their presence in the New Jerusalem is transitional and provisional and they are destined to endlessly roam.[99] This too is true for the poet's rebellious living dead: the dialectic of freedom is an eternal one without absolute resolution as freedom is relative, conditional and part of a continuous struggle. *Voices of the Living and the Dead* strikes a note of cautious, even morbid optimism. The living assure the dead that 'Our singers will sing songs about you | Our poets will write poems about you in memoriam | Flowers will bloom on your graves'.[100] Death

becomes the price for freedom, and it is through poetry that
the rebels will be remembered and the seeds of future struggles
passed on from one generation to the next.

Like his 'blood poems', *Voices of the Living and the Dead* was
published when Johnson was in his early twenties, and the short
play's strength is also its weakness. If surrealism exaggerates and
dramatizes reality in order to both bring us closer to understand-
ing the spirit and essence of that reality, and the possibilities of
transcending it, Johnson perhaps stretches the boundaries that
separate the real and the surreal too far. (Is it in fact possible to
set boundaries on the surreal, and if so, who decides how far
is too far?) The dichotomous coupling of night/light and the
dead/the living; the raised voices and the images of bloodletting,
fire, cracked skulls, anger, fury, pain and suffering; flesh-piercing
bullets, shotguns, blades, stones and sticks; along with his use of
repetition for rhythmic and dramatic effect at times overwhelm
the play's overarching narrative in an apparent never-ending
carnival of blood. This said, the play also complements Johnson's
poem 'Doun de Road', where we discover hope in what we might
describe as the post-fratricide stage in which the colonized and
the dispossessed lash out against their oppressors. The poet once
again refers to the stop-and-search procedures that, refined in
Ulster by British armed forces stationed in Northern Ireland,[101]
were also reminiscent of the repression and harassment that
black South Africans endured under apartheid. The net result
of these procedures speaks for itself,[102] and as the poet recalls,
'even Christians whose children' were going 'home from Sunday
School would find themselves in police stations being charged
with "attempting to steal from persons unknown."'[103] The word
'even' emphasizes that no black Briton was immune from the
long hand of the law and how broadly 'suspicious' activity was
interpreted. This is the context in which Johnson's early poetry
was penned.

Alienation, it has been suggested, can 'release a spirit of
revolt',[104] and in the next phase of struggle, the dispossessed
repossess themselves, almost as if they are in fact possessed.
Rather than seeking recognition and affirmation from their

oppressor, they assert their humanity, their being, and the right to be – freedom. Though this process can, and often does, manifest itself in the form of violent action, at its deep structure this phenomenon represents the need for individuals and the group to command their destiny and assume their place in society, or to contribute to a necessary radical social change towards the building of the new society. This represents an attempt to turn a negative position into a positive condition through an assertion of the right of freedom of expression, not in the narrow sense of the term, but in terms of the freedom to create and realize one's potential as a human being, and to collectively organize for change. (The otherwise insightful Arendt misses this point completely and, as a result, she reduces Fanon's analysis to a celebration of wanton violence.)[105]

In the fourth stanza of 'Five Nights of Bleeding' we discover young rebels who have been left in the cold outside a blues dance while others revel in the music of James Brown inside. This London is reminiscent of William Blake's 'London', written 200 years before about a city of dread, of faces marked by 'weakness' and 'woe' and 'fear' where the chimney sweeper cries, 'And the hapless Soldier's sigh | Runs in blood down palace walls'.[106] Blake's use of biblical language and his vivid proto-surrealist poetic style[107] perhaps invite other parallels between him and Johnson, but in sharp contrast to Blake's black skin/white soul allusion in the poem 'The Little Black Boy', Johnson's London rebels do not apologize for, qualify or negotiate their existence, but fight for it. As they peer in upon the blues dance, bobbies (the police) descend and pounce upon them and 'the bile of oppression was vomited | an two policemen wounded | righteous righteous war'.[108] It's a familiar scene – youth are accosted by the police. Frustrated and enraged, the rebels unleash their anger on the 'babylonian tyrants'. For the speaker, the reaction of the rebels is part of a 'righteous righteous war' as the pouncing by the police was unjustified and the rebels' actions, in defence of themselves, were therefore a legitimate act of 'war' and self-preservation.

In 'Doun de Road' the raconteur speaks of Powell 'prophesying a black ... conquest',[109] which is a reference to Enoch

Powell, the former British parliamentarian who heightened
social tensions that would reverberate throughout the 1960s and
1970s when he suggested that if the British government did not
act to stem the tide of immigration of people of African and
Asian descent these newcomers would swarm over society like
bees and their presence would result in bloody racial confronta-
tions. In addition to the racist 'sus' laws and Powell's apocalyptic
proselytizing, the National Front, the violent British neofascist
organization, ' … is on the rampage | making fire bombs fe burn
we'. It is ' … in the heat | of the anguish'[110] of the moment
that the brothers turn on each other and unleash their frustra-
tion, with predictable consequences. However, at some point the
violence turns outward, or, as the poet puts it,

> but when you see your brother blood jus flow;
> futile fighting; then you know
> that the first phase must come to an end
> and time for the second phase to show.[111]

This second phase, as the poet's echo-like voice chants in 'All Wi
Doin is Defendin', is war. Here the narrator speaks directly to
the oppressors, warning them of the battles to come. The days
of oppression are numbered and will soon come to an end as 'all
oppression | can do is bring | passion to di heights of eruption |
an songs of fire wi will sing'.[112] For the police and the oppressor,
it is too late to run and hide. Now is the time for war as the bitter
taste of oppression causes the oppressed and colonized to lash
out against their enemy. In a stanza that anticipates the riots and
protests that gripped England in 1980 and 1981, the narrator
exhorts the rebels to 'choose yu weapon dem | quick! | all wi
need is bakkles an bricks an sticks | wi hav fists | wi hav feet |
wi carry dandamite in wi teeth'.[113] In these few lines the poet
articulates the thoughts, feelings and emotions of his generation
in the 1970s, capturing the sense of dread and dispossession that
possessed the hearts and minds of many young blacks. These
lines convey an immanent sense of imminent dread that evokes

another Johnson poem, 'Time Come', in which Babylon is warned that it is too late and that:

> Fruit soon ripe
> Fi tek wi bite,
> Strength soon come fi fling wi mite.[114]

The poet then proceeds to list a number of brutal police transgressions that have brought the situation to a tipping point – imprisonment, police brutality, the killing of the Nigerian vagrant David Oluwale and the brutal beating of the Jamaican labourer Joshua Francis, both in Leeds, as well as the abuse of members of the Black Panther Movement – all of which now presages a violent rebellion in retaliation.

'Time Come' also recalls Michael Smith's later poem, 'It a Come', in which he warns Margaret Thatcher that her days of reckoning are nigh:

> It a come
> fire a go bun
> blood a go run
> it going go teck you
> it going go teck you.[115]

Ultimately, for Johnson, the next phase in the struggle is the shift to violent struggle, to 'war' against the oppressor, in this case the Special Patrol of the British police force, the penultimate symbol of Babylon. But here, the Special Patrol, National Front, and Enoch Powell's declarations have symbolic significance. They are synonymous with state oppression, institutionalized racism and exclusion, class exploitation and the sense of humiliation that comes with being alienated, subjugated and physically and psychologically scarred, and Johnson's declaration of war epitomizes the conscious acts that the colonized and oppressed undertake in the exercise of freedom as they exorcise their demons. His point is obvious: people make change and change often comes about when we believe it to be least possible, at times when social conditions appear to be at their worst, or actually are. It is often at this point that we see the self-activity and creativity of people, the capacity to adapt to conditions and circumstances as they present themselves, to take action in order to tangibly transform negative conditions into positive possibilities. In this sense, Johnson's blood poems represent an important step in our journey down this revolutionary road, mapped and motivated by our resident poet. But elegies have also been an important part of the poet's oeuvre, and in Chapter 4 we explore the theory and practice of political transformation through the prism of another Johnson poem, 'Reggae fi Radni', written in memory of Walter Rodney who, like Fanon, committed his life to African and Caribbean liberation and international socialism.

Chapter 4

POLITICS AND MOURNING IN 'REGGAE FI RADNI'

Some of our finest comrades will fall, have fallen, in struggle, and we don't set about to get the best of our workers and revolutionaries killed just so that we can write poetry to celebrate them subsequently. When they are lost, they are lost, it's an irreparable loss and may in fact qualitatively affect the development of struggle in another phase. And even for those whom we might not remember in poetry and song, what about their lives, their decision to risk all? As materialists we have to say that they are risking all. If we had some other philosophical belief we could say that they are going to a better life, but from a materialist point of view we say that they are prepared to end this particular material existence with no compensation except their own feeling that the society which they are recreating will hasten towards socialism.

Walter Rodney

When History wakes, image becomes act, the poem happens; poetry moves into action.

Octavio Paz

We must understand that we are still locked in struggle, and we are saying we are ready to proceed. We are moving forward, we are not intimidated, we recognize the pressures but are far from bending under those pressures.

Walter Rodney

'**R**EGGAE FI RADNI' was first published in *Race Today* and then appeared on Linton Kwesi Johnson's 1984 LP *Making History*. It is a political elegy, and one of his most poignant mediations of the demands of revolutionary struggle. Johnson has written a number of elegies over the years. In fact, it is fair to say that elegies have been a central part of his oeuvre, and even his 'blood poems' deal with death, even when it is a kind of collective death of sorts, in ways that might be described as elegiac. So what, then, makes 'Reggae fi Radni' unique? The answer lies in Walter Rodney's biography. He was a singular figure, a remarkable intellectual and political voice whose ideas and actions influenced his generation in the Caribbean and its diaspora, in Africa, and among Afro diasporic peoples in general. He was also a powerful voice for socialism and was internationally recognized as a historian and political thinker. In other words, because Rodney was such an exceptional historical figure, the gravity of his death still lingers in the present. His life and work continue to capture our imaginations, and his ghost still haunts us because the revolution that he anticipated and to which he committed himself remains unfinished in Guyana, the Caribbean, Africa and the world at large.

Johnson's earlier work largely invoked the anti-colonial poetics of Fanon and Césaire, and the conjoined themes of fratricide and rebellion, as a way of expressing the violence and frustrated life chances of black youth in England. It also meditated on 'bass culture' and the experiential nature of reggae. In some respects, *Making History* continues the theme of the poem 'Independent Intavenshan', in which the poet promoted the necessity of an autonomous black movement that is free from undue external influence.[1] But it also represents an explicit shift in consciousness or, perhaps more accurately, towards a conscious expression of autonomous socialist-inflected international poetics that is influenced, at least in part, by C.L.R. James, who at this stage was in his eighties and living in London above the offices of the Race Today Collective. In a full-page *Race Today* advert for the LP the poet appears solemn-looking and contemplative in his trademark trilby and wide-framed glasses while draped in a trench coat as he stares into the distance. On the album cover the brown hand of the faceless human profile holds a brown book with gold engraving entitled *Making History*. The image of the book and the title hint that history is a deliberate, deliberative and creative process in which people engage, but it also hints at Walter Rodney's vocation as a historian who did not simply write history, but understood that history was made, that is to say constructed into a narrative by conscious human action. For Rodney, 'History was not an inert set of documents gathering dust on the shelves of archives', says Alissa Trotz, because Rodney 'was interested in a living history, in the ways in which it could offer us insights that could transform our contemporary condition'.[2] As Trotz points out, while gender was not central to Rodney's work, the feminist and Marxist Selma James was an important influence on him, along with his wife Patricia Rodney. History was about movement and possibility for Rodney as it was for James Baldwin, who described a process in which a weary history emerges from the terror of the times as 'A slow, syncopated | relentless music begins'.[3]

In his historical writing about his native Guyana, Rodney attempted to capture those moments in which women exercised self-activity through protest by withdrawing their labour from the fields or in their involvement in the 1905 urban riots.[4] Rodney did not write history as someone who was concerned about history for history's sake or as a mere academic exercise; nor was he solely preoccupied with revolutionary theory. He was a historian who took his craft seriously, but ultimately he was concerned with revolutionary change as an active participant in the making of history.

While hegemonic histories are manufactured by the power elite and conservative intellectuals, *Making History* is a counter-history that in part celebrates the creative capacity of 'ordinary' people to do the extraordinary within the context of the anti-colonial, and the post-colonial Cold War Reagan–Thatcherite reality. *Making History* not only historicizes the 'crises in Black Britain',[5] but also reflects a politics of solidarity, or what Édouard Glissant has described as a relation between different regions of the world, and what Johnson in conversation with Glissant has called a global consciousness.[6]

'Di Eagle an' di Bear' captures the indifference that many felt towards the threat of apocalyptic nuclear attack – their lives already constituted a dystopian nightmare – and 'Wat about di Workin' Claas?' describes the crushing weight of the Cold War and the stifling of human creativity under both official communist and capitalist rule. In the upbeat 'Di Great Insohreckshan' and 'Making History', history is celebrated in terms of insurrection, rebellion, protest and change in an effort to forge what John McLeod describes as a communal 'black' solidarity movement, particularly between Afro and Asian Britons[7] – despite what Paul Gilroy had identified by 1987 as a shift away from a definition of 'black' that embraced Afro-Asian solidarity[8] – and gives voice to the experience of Afro Britons, whereas the last two poems, 'Reggae fi Dada' and 'New Craas Massahkah', grapple with tragic death. In the case of the first poem, Dada's death becomes a metaphor for a decaying Jamaican society that had become a microcosm of Cold War ideological politics that, as Marlon James's *A Brief History of Seven Killings* vividly illustrates, had deadly consequences for the island's people. In 'New Craas Massahkah' the speaker attempts to derive meaning from a tragic fire: what was widely believed to have been a racist-motivated arson attack that killed 13 young people during a birthday party in New Cross, London (a survivor also committing suicide in the aftermath). Johnson's sombre elegiac meditation on Rodney's life and assassination as well as on the exigencies of political transformation is sandwiched between the two poems on the album and in it Rodney's life and death become a metaphor for deferred dreams within a post-colonial nightmare, but are also a reflection of the horizon of possibilities for the people of Guyana and, by extension, humanity as a whole.

Kindred Souls

In 'Reggae fi Radni', arguably Johnson's most political elegy (we will discuss the elegiac form a little later), the poet captures the tragic implications related to this seminal figure's death, a death that, like his life, deserves to be considered alongside the likes of Frantz Fanon, Malcolm X and other political figures whose lives were cut short early. The lives of Johnson and Rodney intersected in various ways, almost as if the poet was destined to elegize the historian. Their connections speak to an informal but deeply embedded network of writers-artists-intellectuals, channels of communication and affiliation through which political ideas and art are exchanged in mutual appreciation and critical reflection.

The poet and the historian were part of a shared political and artistic circle and Johnson admired Rodney's politics, convictions and eloquence.[9] Moreover, while Johnson was very familiar with Rodney's work, there is a particular link between James and Johnson's elegy: 'Reggae fi Radni' is in part a versification of James's posthumous presentation on Rodney's life and work in much the same way that Johnson's 'blood poems' poeticize the poetics of Fanon's phenomenology of violence. This is not to say that the poem does not reflect the poet's independent assessment of Rodney or the conversations that Johnson would have contributed to in Caribbean and pan-African circles in London following Rodney's death,[10] nor does this view diminish the originality of the poem in any way. Rather, the point is to highlight the interplay between his poetry, Rodney's politics and James's assessment of Rodney's praxis – intriguing connections that help to situate a poem in which Rodney's life becomes a political metaphor for the exigencies of revolutionary politics.

Rodney and Johnson were active in the same informal political circles. Both moved to London from Jamaica in 1963 (Johnson to join his mother and Rodney to pursue a PhD). Though not dreadlocks Rastas, both had been closely associated with Rastafari – Rodney with the dispossessed Rastafarians of Jamaica and Johnson in London where he performed with the group Rasta Love. Both were preoccupied with African liberation solidarity work and, despite their appreciation of African and Caribbean history, both eschewed the great king and queen's syndrome, that is to say that they avoided those romantic representations of an African past in lieu of confront-

ing the weight of contemporary challenges.[11] Both admired the
Guyanese poet and politician, Martin Carter, whom Johnson
declared 'the political poet par excellence'[12] and whose *Poems
of Succession* he described as 'the finest poetic response to
historical change in the English speaking Caribbean' – poems
that 'were born out of, and reflect, Carter's own involvement
in the struggle of the Guyanese people for national sovereignty
and the thwarted efforts to forge a socialist path'. Carter was
once an ally of Rodney's nemesis, Forbes Burnham, but he later
became Burnham's staunch opponent, and as Johnson suggests,
the poems written between 1951 and 1975 illustrate the shift in
Carter's consciousness over time as the 'defiant, resolute mood
of the earlier poems are counterpointed by the more philosoph-
ical, brooding, skeptical tone of later poems'.[13]

Carter remains underappreciated within the pantheon of
Caribbean poets, a reality that Johnson partially remedied in his
recording of 'Shape and Motion One', Carter's meditation on
the dialectic of non-being, being and becoming, a soul-searching
poem on eclipsed dreams and unfulfilled aspirations:

> I was wondering if I could find myself
> all that I am in all I could be.
> If all the population of stars
> would be less than the things I could utter
> And the challenge of space in my soul
> be filled by the shape I become.[14]

For Rodney, Carter was an individual who stood out during the
nationalist period in Guyana as someone who was 'extremely
creative and extremely revolutionary'.[15] Although he was not
a poet, Rodney's appreciation for poetry mirror's Johnson's
appreciation for the making of history and this is obvious
from the poems by Carter, along with poems by Edgar Mit-
telholzer, Edward Brathwaite, A.J. Seymor, Aimé Césaire and
David Campbell that inaugurate the chapters of the histori-
an's posthumous book, *A History of the Guyanese Working People,
1881–1905*. Among the Carter poems that Rodney cites is the

first five lines of 'I Come from the Nigger Yard', a poem about self-loathing and colonial dispossession in Guyana in the 1950s:

> I come from the nigger yard of yesterday
> leaping from the oppressors hate
> and the scorn of myself;
> from the agony of the dark hut in the shadow
> and the hurt of things;[16]

But the poem is also about the repossession of the spirit, once again emanating from the tension between non-being, being and becoming:

> I take again my nigger life, my scorn
> and fling it in the face of those who hate me.
> It is me the nigger boy turning to manhood
> linking my fingers, welding my flesh to freedom.[17]

Rodney's appreciation of literature extended beyond poetry and into fiction, and the Barbadian novelist George Lamming was perhaps the writer he most appreciated (it was Lamming whom Rodney requested to write the introduction to *A History of the Guyanese Working People*). In his lectures on the Russian Revolution, Rodney stressed the importance of pre-revolution Russian literature, and especially the writing of Tolstoy and Dostoyevsky, who in their various ways challenged Russia's ruling elite and in the process helped lay the foundation for the Russian Revolution.[18]

Unlike their Caribbean predecessors, Rodney and Johnson benefited from a large body of Caribbean literature (fiction, poetry and prose) that helped to shape their political perspectives, and they were both significantly influenced by C.L.R. James's work and were directly connected to him (Rodney was part of a study group with James in the 1960s[19] and Johnson was linked to James through the Race Today Collective and served as a caregiver for James in his waning days). Dating back to his student days in Jamaica, there were two books in particular that profoundly influenced the aspiring historian – and also Johnson – as he began to think about politics and history. Eric Williams's *Capitalism and Slavery* (and Rodney makes an effort not to confuse Williams the historian with Williams the 'sometime-ish', perhaps to say at times irreverent and taciturn, politician). Rodney described Williams's history as a book in which he 'could recognize one's self' and 'feel with it',[20] a response that was even more pronounced with *The Black Jacobins*, a book about 'black people involved in revolution, involved in making choices, involved in real movements of history, in which there were splits and some people fell by the wayside', but which, nonetheless, 'also possessed a tremendous underlying strength and represented a real achievement',[21] though it was not until later that he came to understand that James employed a Marxist methodology in *The Black Jacobins*, which raised 'its quality over and above that of several other attempted formulations on the revolution'.[22] James was a model for Rodney as someone who stood out in the Caribbean and in England as the individual that fully recognized the necessity of breaking with the colonial past in order to forge a new future.[23]

James's speech, *Walter Rodney and the Question of Power*, was circulated as a Race Today Collective pamphlet, and as if the stars could not be any more aligned, an advert for Johnson's *Voices of the Living and the Dead*, also published in *Race Today*, appeared beside an advert for the pamphlet's publication of James's speech in a 1983 issue of the journal.[24] Johnson was obviously very familiar with Rodney's work, and both the poet and the historian had also been published by Bogle-L'Ouverture (Rodney's *The Grounding with My Brothers* and Johnson's *Voices of the Living and the Dead*). In 1976 *Race Today* also covered Rodney's visit to London as a representative of the Working People's Alliance (WPA) in order to galvanize support for the organization's work among Afro and Indo Guyanese workers and farmers in opposition to Burnham's repressive rule.[25] As early as 1975, Johnson wrote a review for *Race Today* of Salkey's novel, *Joey Tyson*, a fictional account of the political climate that anticipated and ensued after Rodney's expulsion from Jamaica in 1968. In his characteristically colourful prose the poet describes the book as 'a brilliantly simple revelation of the stark realities of the political environment in which young people in the Caribbean grow, gain experience and mature early'. For the poet, the novel not only captures the history of the historian's expulsion, but also the prevailing social climate: the 'Political corruption; the omnipresent threat to the political elite of the soundings of the revolutionary knell; their fear and consequential ruthlessness; the violence of oppression and the violence born of oppression.'[26]

Not surprisingly, Salkey would pay tribute to Rodney in the introduction to an anthology of poetry that included Johnson's 'Reggae fi Radni', in which he described the 'lingering feeling of scissored dislocation and icy shock' and a 'spiking of a nerve in the back of my neck!' as he watched a report of his friend's murder.[27]

Rodney's Revolutionary Road

Walter Rodney sits high among Caribbean and African political-intellectual figures that have left their mark on humanity. For many he represented the quintessential example of political and intellectual integrity, someone who was unwilling to compromise for the sake of expedience and who ultimately sacrificed his life for his convictions. He first came to international attention when he was banned from Jamaica in October 1968,[28] and since his death in 1980 he has attained legendary status. Despite the brevity of his life, Rodney captured the imagination and helped to shape the political conscious-ness of a whole generation of women and men concerned with African and Caribbean liberation and black struggles for human freedom in Europe and North America. He broke new ground as a young historian and political thinker and as I have already hinted, he should be considered, with Fanon, one of the most important post-Second World War intellectual-political figures of his generation. For writer George Lamming, 'Walter Rodney had achieved at an early age, the special distinction of being a permanent part of a unique tradition of intellectual leadership among Africans and people of African descent in the Americas. He belongs to the same order of importance as Marcus Garvey and W.E.B. Du Bois, George Padmore and C.L.R. James. Products of various doctrines of imperialism, they had initiated through their work, as writers and orators of distinction, a profound reversal of values. It is not possible to have a comprehensive view of all the ramifications of Africa's encounter with Europe without reference to these men.'[29] Of course, Lamming's list is not exhaustive and it is hard to imagine that Claudia Jones, Elma Francois, Amy Ashwood Garvey or Angela Davis, as examples, do not deserve a seat at this table. That said, Rodney's influence extended across the globe and, more than 35 years after his death, and in part as a result of the circumstances surrounding it, his work and the struggles of his life still reverberate in political and academic circles.

Rodney authored several important books, including *A History of the Upper Guinea Coast: 1545–1800* and *A History of the Guyanese Working People: 1801–1905*, and numerous influential articles and lectures on African and Caribbean history and politics. However, his *The Groundings with My Brothers* and *How Europe Underdeveloped Africa* were revelations in that his conception of history, race and class, and his appreciation of the philosophy and creativity of Jamaica's Rastafarians in *Groundings* overturned the dominant order of knowledge production in favour of the dispossessed. Moreover, *How Europe Underdeveloped Africa* enlightened his readers about an African continent that was, according to G.W.F. Hegel, overshadowed by darkness and the absence of reason while Europe was portrayed as the beacon enlightenment.[30]

Groundings also captures the spirit of Rodney's pedagogy in Jamaica where he 'grounded' and reasoned with Rastas, sometimes engaging with 200–300 people during informal Sunday conversations. This was not a prophetic shepherd-figure engaging his flock or a professor pontificating to the minions or holding court. He engaged in these dialogues among equals according to historian Robert Hill, who also participated in these groundings, and from Rodney's own admission he learned more from Jamaica's sufferers than they did from him.[31] Applying his own brand of what the Brazilian theorist Paulo Freire describes as the dialogical approach,[32] Rodney developed a critical pedagogy long before the term became popular in academic circles. These groundings helped to lay the groundwork for a popular movement, and when Rodney was expelled from the country out of fear that his off-campus activities were contributing to political ferment in the country, protest against his expulsion unleashed the anger and frustration of a population whose post-colonial reality had proven to be an extension of the old colonial order. If, as Hill justly suggests, Caribbean history can be divided into the pre-October 1968 Rodney-inspired protests and the period after them[33] – events that not only spawned a movement in Jamaica in the form of the group Abeng, but inaugurated various new left groups in the Caribbean – then Rodney's impact in the region has been understated in studies of Caribbean history.

As a student of African history Rodney reminded us that Africans have made their own contributions to what is far too loosely termed civilization (indeed, he also questioned the very idea of civilization and its antithesis, so-called primitive society) and that these societies were undermined and eventually under-developed by Europe, but with the collusion of African elites who benefited from the misfortune of those who were caught in the tidal wave of the slave trade and the advent of European colonial rule. Another significant feature of *How Europe Under-developed Africa* is Rodney's keen sense of historical process, a feature of his work that has not been given sufficient attention. In the face of those who would describe African independence as an utter sham, Rodney took a more mature, reasoned and dialec-tical view in suggesting that the absence of direct colonial rule and the removal of its symbols (flags, anthems, military, judiciary, etc.) was a necessary part of the process of developing genuine economic, social and political alternatives.[34] He was neither defeatist or celebratory in his analysis of independence, and while he refused to conflate formal independence with economic independence and genuine freedom, he argued that 'the removal of overt foreign rule actually cleared the way towards a more fundamental appreciation of exploitation and imperialism' and gave the people a conscious sense of their 'ability to make their own history' in the process of 'grappling with the heritage of objective material conditions and social relations'.[35]

Like Fanon, Rodney questioned the legitimacy of political leaders who betrayed the aspirations of their followers once they assumed power. He believed that the conscious activity of 'ordinary people' would ultimately be the decisive factor and the driving force behind meaningful change, a process he equated with the development of socialism. As a Marxist, Rodney's appreciation of history was shaped by economics, political economy, trade and human geography, which is apparent in his earliest writings on the slave trade and commerce on the Guinea coast. Socialism and Marxism animated his historical writing, and his analysis of class differentiation and trade paralleled the work of Karl Polanyi on Africa and the slave trade.[36] His work echoes Fanon and, as I have suggested elsewhere, Amilcar Cabral in terms of class, culture and politics.[37] Rodney blurred the lines that have historically separated the disciplines of history, politics and economics as history was for him a process, a struggle between the power elite and the dispossessed, and was not simply reducible to race or ethnicity, even when race and ethnicity were central to it. History was not static for Rodney, but a process in motion, representing movement, one hoped, towards a more progressive and egalitarian society through conscious and deliberate actions, and it is precisely this sense of historical movement, and 'from below', that Johnson engages with, chronicles and reflects upon in the poems on the album *Making History*.

Rodney was deeply preoccupied with the role of ordinary people in shaping politics and society, and as a professor in Jamaica in the late 1960s he dared to go 'down below' to reason with Jamaica's most dispossessed, Rastafarians and the sufferers in general, and to exchange with and learn from them. His actions were a poignant expression of his broader belief that the most fundamental change and expressions of creativity would emanate from the dispossessed as opposed to the established economic and political elite. The significance of Rodney's groundings in Jamaica's highly stratified and colour-coded society should not be underestimated. As a university professor, he committed the crime of breaking with established caste and class codes that separated the brown middle and upper classes in Jamaica from the country's largely black dispossessed. These were divisions according to socio-economic status and skin complexion, with skin colour being both a constituent and constitutive marker of class. Rodney's breach of these norms earned him respect and admiration among Jamaican sufferers while raising the ire of Jamaican government officials. The groundings, along with his criticisms of the Jamaican political establishment led to the government's decision to expel him from the country for alleged subversive activity.[38] After his expulsion from Jamaica, Rodney was immortalized in 'Dr. Rodney (Black Power)', released as a single by the renowned ska-reggae vocalist Prince Buster, an important poetic and musical influence on Johnson who was outspoken in his criticism of the government's ban of Rodney (as a result, his record shop was raided by the police).[39] As he chants in the sparsely worded salute to Rodney and Black Power, to be black and ambitious in Jamaica is dangerous.[40] The Rasta elder and mentor to Bob and Rita Marley, Mortimo Planno, also appears to have written a poem about Rodney and the events of 1968,[41] and during the days of protest that ensued after Rodney's expulsion, reggae great Peter Tosh registered his anger by commandeering a bus, which he then drove into a department store in Kingston. Once the store was looted he drove the bus crammed with luxury goods to the district of Trench Town where he received a hero's welcome.[42] Rodney had now entered the realm of popular culture, contributing to what would emerge as a kind of legendary status that for Lamming as well as reggae historian Lloyd Bradley evokes comparisons with the larger-than-life pan-African figure-cum-prophet of the Rastafarian faith, Marcus Mosiah Garvey.[43]

Rodney's Return

In 1974 Walter Rodney returned to Guyana to assume a teaching position at the University of Guyana. He had spent the previous five years in Tanzania teaching and was highly respected by his peers for both his historical work and his political convictions. But he felt it was now time to directly participate in the political development of his country, the place where he could lay roots and be politically engaged as a son of the soil in an environment that was intimately familiar to him.[44] He returned to a Guyana clouded by fear and political intrigue. The People's National Congress (PNC) under Forbes Burnham, the country's maximum leader, used violent repression, intimidation and manipulation while stoking the fires of racial tension to win, and where that was not possible, to steal votes in order to maintain his hold on power. Irregularities during political elections were a matter of course; newspapers were banned and constitutional reforms were enshrined in order to further entrench his power. As the situation in Guyana deteriorated, violence towards dissenters and opposition leaders became more pronounced and acute, and included assassination. Burnham had become a dictator who used extra-governmental and illegal means to maintain his hold on power, a phenomenon that James anticipated in 1967 when, with a group of young Caribbean students in Montreal, he discussed the potential for fascism and totalitarianism to take root in the Caribbean.[45] This sense of anomie, dread and despair, the feeling of chaos and nothingness that Rodney encountered upon his return, is eloquently expressed, as only a poem can, in Martin Carter's 1970s poem, 'There is No Riot', in which he describes the sense of desolation in that moment, ' ... But everywhere | empty and broken bottles gleam like ruin'.[46]

'There is No Riot' captures the sense of disillusionment and dejection, the negation of the self and shattered dreams and hopelessness. Rodney was acutely attuned to this, as he was to Guyana's history of class struggle and the deliberate attempts to divide African workers from their Indian counterparts in the post-emancipation period. His posthumously published book,

A History of the Guyanese Working Class,[47] is a nuanced analysis of the complex dynamics of race and class in which he demonstrates his penchant for simplicity and clarity when he describes the situation in Guyana in terms of 'real or imagined conflict, of real and potential conflict, between two racial or ethnic groups of African and Indian ancestry'. But the roots of this conflict lay in European racism towards Africans in Guyana under plantation slavery, which later facilitated intra-class conflict between people of African and Indian descent, generated and encouraged by the ruling class in the post-slavery indentured and 'free' labour context. This conflict found expression in racial stereotypes associated with 'Quashie', a creolization of the Akan (Ghana) name *Kwesi* (born on Sunday), the equivalent of Sambo in the US, that represents the lazy, docile Africans who are somehow prone to acts of resistance;[48] and 'Sammy', derived from the Indian word *swamy*, which refers to a Hindu with religious training. Among other things, Sammy represented the cunning, idle, but also hard-working, violent, thievish, frugal, deceitful 'coolie' who undermined the value of African labour.[49] These stereotypes were rooted in the plantation economy and capitalist development, and served to entrench racial division and undermine worker solidarity. Even Guyanese of Portuguese descent who, like Indians, had initially been brought to Guyana as indentured workers in the post-emancipation period were considered a separate 'race' from other Europeans, a fact that further suggests that racial status was at least in part tied to class as opposed to purely biological notions of race.[50] The 'real' that Rodney refers to reflects the lived reality of racial division in the country, while the 'imagined' suggests that the basis of the schism is not preordained or rooted in pre-existing divisions between the two groups. The 'potential' of the conflict suggests that it can get worse, but also implies that the conflict, as its core, is only an appearance – the illusion of an apparent natural division – that has been fostered by the ruling class dating back to the post-slavery period in order to upset the potential unity of workers across ethno-racial lines. However, the fact that the real and imagined conflict is an appearance suggests that these contradictions and conflicts can be overcome. Rodney's analysis challenges Marxist orthodoxy by emphasizing the twin demons of race and class, as opposed to reducing race to a derivative of class. In this sense, and to borrow from, and slightly distort, Carole Boyce Davies in reference to Claudia Jones, Rodney was left of Marxism[51] in so far as the combination of his reading of history and life experience taught him that an overdetermined analysis of class that dismissed race as residual to it could not account for the lived reality of Guyana and the Caribbean.

Rodney became a leading member of the socialist Working People's Alliance, a popular organization that attempted to go beyond racial divisions. The WPA, which gained prominence among working-class Guyanese, transcended the racial divide that separated people of Indian and African descent and the two longstanding rival parties, the People's Progressive Party (PPP) and the PNC, both of which self-described as socialist or, in the case of the PPP, communist. Rodney's presence in Guyana within the WPA represented a significant threat to Burnham's political tenure, and from the outset steps were taken to diminish his ability to actively participate in Guyanese society and politics, including rescinding his position at the University of Guyana, which effectively limited his capacity to earn a living there, forcing him to take on lecturing stints abroad as he engaged in political work at home. Unlike the PNC and the PPP, the WPA was able to effectively draw support from and connect both Africans and Indians whose division had polarized the country for decades. Rodney and the WPA helped mobilize bauxite and other workers, held rallies and protests, and published the opposition newspaper *Dayclean*. The WPA now had the capacity to mobilize thousands of people, and as it grew in stature with Rodney as its most prominent leader, the Burnham government laid plans to destroy it. Rodney and several other WPA members were accused of and arrested for setting fire to a PNC building. They were later acquitted of the charges but it was clear that Burnham was willing to resort to extreme measures to eliminate his most prominent critic. The conflict in Guyana was escalating to a high pitch and for Burnham, it appears, there was no question about it – Rodney had to go.

Rodney and Burnham appear to have developed a personal political rivalry. Clearly, some of Rodney's later speeches took on a personalized tone, and perhaps even signs of desperation that may not simply be reduced to the poetics of Caribbean partisan politics. In a 1979 speech Rodney suggested, 'Our language must express not only ridicule but anger and disgust. The dictatorship has reduced us all to such a level that the situation can be described only in terms befitting filth, pollution and excrement. ... That is why the WPA repeats the legend of King Midas who was said to have been able to touch anything and turn it to gold. ... Now Guyana has the "Burnham Touch" – anything he touches turns to shit!'[52] In reference to an incident in which Rodney made a speedy retreat away from Burnham's thugs, the prime minister suggested that Rodney be sent to the next Olympics.[53] But the comedic back and forth took on tragic proportions. On 13 June 1980 Rodney was killed in a car by a bomb that exploded on his lap. He was in the process of testing walkie-talkies that he had acquired when the bomb, planted in one of the devices, was detonated. Rodney was only 38 years old.[54] A huge gap, a void, was left with the loss of Rodney, and amid the mourning his followers, friends, comrades and compatriots sought explanations: questions were raised about who was responsible for his death and why he had been killed, but also about the peculiar political circumstances that led to his murder and the thorny question of what, if anything, he could have done to avoid some of the political pitfalls in which he found himself enmeshed and that ultimately resulted in his elimination from Guyana's political scene.

Elegy for Rodney

'Reggae fi Radni' is part of an elegiac tradition that is perhaps as old as poetry itself. Elegy invokes the three m's of melancholy and mourning tied with memory – and in the case of Walter Rodney we might add another, martyrdom – as the living recall the dead as they lived. By choosing to remember them the dead are resurrected, their lives reproduced or reborn in a process of renewal in so far as their spirits are conjured up, fulfilling the living's need to keep the dead alive or to maintain an attachment to the deceased. Elegies are about the mourner's need to heal and feel whole and, in this spirit, they are as much about life and for the living – the mourner – as they are about death and the mourned. Great elegies capture, in J. Edward Chamberlain's words, 'a person's and a people's grief'[55] while setting 'the human imagination up against the overwhelming reality of death, and in so doing they embody both our resistance to it, and our acceptance'.[56] For the poet and theorist Fred Moten, the elegy is tied to tragedy that represents yearning, mourning, lament, a desire for home and a sense of belonging, and a reaction to a tragic state of affairs or a breach or radical interruption of the 'fragile singularity' as well as an invocation of the ghost of totality.[57] As critic Peter M. Sacks has written, in the English poetic tradition elegies frequently shift from darkness into renewal or light, often invoking the life cycle of vegetation as a metaphor for the cycle of life, death and rebirth in general. This is part of a process in which death is naturalized as if it is merely part of a season that has passed, only to return again.[58] For Sacks, elegies also serve to unleash the pent-up anger and frustration that is part of grieving while giving voice to protest and posing questions that shift from the mourner's preoccupations with the deceased to the larger social arena as a way of making sense out of a death, and life.[59] This is precisely what Johnson and the many other Rodney elegists attempt to do.

But Johnson's poem is more consistent with the more recent tendency within the elegiac tradition to offer a critical reflection and even criticism of the deceased,[60] and in this spirit, 'Reggae fi Radni' might also be understood as the poet's internal dialogue or engagement with Rodney, externalized in the form of an elegy. Here the poet meditates on Rodney's life and work from a critical distance in order that the ideals and spirit of Rodney's politics may continue despite what Jacques Derrida refers to as the 'ultimate interruption' of death.[61] In this spirit the poet combines respect, admiration and even celebration of Rodney's life with critical questions about his praxis and the circumstances surrounding his assassination. In the process we encounter Rodney, not simply as a martyr or heroic figure, but a human being, someone who is vulnerable, prone to doubt and even forlorn which, rather than diminishing him in our eyes, brings his struggle closer to us while at the same time elevating his humanity.

'Reggae fi Radni' is part of a larger tradition of elegies and tributes by and/or about Caribbean artists and revolutionary figures,[62] and one of many Rodney elegies that were published in the aftermath of his murder, many of which were collected under the title *Walter Rodney: Poetic Tributes*. Rodney's son Shaka opens the anthology with a harrowing poem in which the narrator-persona tells his mother not to weep if his enemy massacres his body, but, 'Rather be proud | That you gave your country | A son who would not be a slave, | Who preferred the silence | Of the centuries | To a moan produced | By the oppressor's lash'.[63] Both Marina Omowale Maxwell ('what more can they add | to our private panoramic view from the cross?')[64] and John Agard dedicated their poems to Walter's widow Patricia Rodney as they endeavoured to capture the pain that lingered among Rodney's loved ones.[65] Grace Nichols queried the inevitability of Rodney's death: 'But then you became a light | the people saw | And so they had to put you out | Or did they?'[66] In Jan Carew's long elegy for his countryman the narrator invokes the keen insight of his mother, who peers into Rodney's soul and shares in his 'sullen secret' that he was going to die. Recognizing her concern, it is Rodney who assuages her fears with a smile 'behind a curtain of pleasantries' as 'Hungry dogs barked in the alleyways'.[67] Rodney's mother also has an ominous premonition and she exhorts her son to 'Take care, walk well', but when she cannot bear the news of his death she turns to Jesus for mercy. Here Carew resorts to the customary elegiac images of redemption, resurrection and the Christ-like figure while cursing the men 'who pushed this chosen son down slippery trails into an exit of death'.[68] 'Our faith was in abeyance', the speaker tells us, until Rodney 'preached redemption | for all except the meek, | the poor in spirit | or the lumpen elite'.[69] Resorting to elegiac metaphors of plant life and natural phenomena as Rodney lies entombed beneath the earth, the speaker assures him that,

> while you're listening to the sound of roots
> marrying the dark earth,
> and sap flowing in the stems of flowers,
> you'll hear all of a sudden
> the thunder of famished hearts you touched,
> chorusing your words/inheriting the victory that you preached
> with your tongue of fire[70]

Carew's poem ends with a triumphant note, but for Martin Carter who was living with the despair and despoliation of the spirit in Burnham's Guyana, there is no silver lining and no recourse to romance or resurrection as the flesh wound is too fresh. Now is a time of mourning: 'I sit in the presence of rain | in the sky's wild noise' and 'I intend to turn a sky | of tears, for you.[71]

Andrew Salkey goes one step further by graphically depicting Rodney's gruesome murder: 'Though we'll remember you sliced in half, Walter, we'll never, | never, forget you as a beautiful whole!'[72] Clifton Joseph's 'Rites/for Walter Rodney' implores us to fight, but first we must also 'see the promises already evaporated', killed by opponents of freedom and justice, 'but the spirit pulls | as the equinoxes pull | and plants the seeds | in the souls of the dead | and in the wombs of the unborn'.[73] For Kamau Brathwaite, Rodney's life was comparable to the short life of a cereus flower that disappears after flashes of brilliance: 'But darkness spawns | explosions of living | a thousand cereuses | will trumpet their beauty' and 'from the acrid green shoulders | the spiked times | petals unfold | the intricacies of freedom'.[74] Another Brathwaite poem, 'How Europe Underdeveloped Africa', first published in 1987, is much more graphic in its depiction of Rodney's death, recalling the insufferable savagery of his assassination:

> to be blown into fragments. your flesh
> like the islands that you loved
> like the seawall that you wished to heal.[75]

Rodney was killed because he simply wanted to bring dignity to the lives of the people of Guyana, and as the poem's speaker proffers, speaking directly to Rodney, 'but there are stars that burn that murderers do not know I soft diamonds behind the blown to bits I that trackers could not find that bombers could not see' and 'that scavengers will never hide away'; and while 'the Caribbean bleeds near Georgetown prison', a reference to the prison wall in front of which Rodney was killed, 'a widow rushes out & hauls her children free'.[76]

The poems vary considerably in content and style, but many of Rodney's elegies frame him as a martyr or a saviour and lament the loss of someone whose life embodied the aims and aspirations of the people of Guyana and the greater Caribbean and pan-African world. In keeping with the elegiac heroic martyr figure, Rodney is depicted as Jesus Christ, but in the spirit of Pier Paolo Pasolini's cinematic depiction of the revolutionary Jesus in *The Gospel According to St. Matthew*, the Jewish prophet whose radical theology and deeds threatened established Judaism[77] and eventually spawned an entirely new faith. Rodney did not overturn tables of money in temples, but he did preach a radical revolutionary politics and paid the price of freedom with his life – an ordinary human being of exceptional intellect and deep political conviction who lives in the hearts and is remembered in the minds of his friends, comrades and followers, and whose spirit lingers in those who choose to take up his call.

'Reggae fi Radni' is by far the best known of the many Rodney elegies, in part because of Linton Kwesi Johnson's international stature, which is in turn tied to the fact that he combines verse and music, considerably expanding the reach of his art. The poem is sombre, meditative and repetitive, and its use of counterpoint brings to mind Mahmoud Darwish's elegy for his friend and fellow Palestinian, Edward Said. In the poem the Darwish speaker engages in dialogue with his late friend on life, struggle and the future of Palestine, shifting from agreement to disagreement and then ultimately back to agreement.[78] Like Darwish's 'Counterpoint', Johnson's poem goes beyond lament, hagiography and celebration and into the realm of criticism-critique. Instead of opting for valorization by recalling Rodney's many virtues it poeticizes the politics surrounding his death, taking us beyond the romanticism that is so often attached to elegy and memory, beyond Rodney's life and death and into the praxis of revolutionary politics through a meditative reflection on the art of insurrection and social transformation as the poet attempts to glean meaning from the otherwise senseless killing of the revolutionary historian. By drawing on Rodney lore as a metaphor for politics, the poet-speaker muses on the meaning of political struggle as Rodney's life becomes the personification of eclipsed hopes and dreams and untapped potential.

'Reggae fi Radni' is best appreciated phonographically. Its simple monorhyme scheme, coupled with the haunting music of the Dennis Bovell Band that includes the melancholy melody of a mandolin, recalls the mournful music of Francis Ford Coppola's classic film, *The Godfather*. The mandolin sustains the poem's sombre sensibility while the playful tone of the xylophone hints at the possibility that, despite the tragic turn, there is still hope that better days are ahead. Meanwhile, the poem's refrain – the elegiac device of repetition[79] – creates a cyclical sense of continuity between past, present and possible futures in a rhythmic lament that canalizes grief while keeping the mourning in motion as if, over time, it can be purged. Despite the poem's sensibility of sorrow, it is deeply spiritual, but not morose. Rodney's ghost haunts the poem just as duppies – a Jamaican word for ghosts – haunt the living in the Caribbean. The spirit world is omnipresent in the Caribbean and is embodied in the duppiness that is dubbed into the poem in ways that recall W.E.B. Du Bois's famous chapter in *The Souls of Black Folks*, 'Of the Songs of Sorrow'. The chapter captures the elegiac sensibility of 'Negro' spirituals or folk songs, elegiac in the sense that their spirit, the *Geist* which reflects Du Bois's studies in Germany and his engagement with Hegel's dialectic, is conjured up from the same place as mourning, a place of lingering sorrow associated with that liminal space that former slaves occupy between death and the quest for human freedom in what Du Bois describes as the 'rhythmic cry of the slave'.[80] If, as Alexander G. Weheliye suggests, Du Bois was the original deejay dub mixer and *The Souls of Black Folks* the prototype for hip-hop in that it mixes, cuts and collates African American and European American literary and musical genres,[81] then 'Reggae fi Radni' represents a three-dimensional contrapuntal elegiac mix that can only be genuinely appreciated in the totality of its aurality, that is to say in its orality and musicality, without privileging the scribal which is essentially a transcription of voices and soundscapes in our heads.[82] When we hear the poet's monotone baritone mourn and lament in rhythmic harmony with the music his voice haunts and taunts us, beginning with the refrain, 'Yuh no see', a common Caribbeanism that, in this context, both poses a rhetorical question and reinforces the sense that the speaker is searching for answers in the sonic scenarios that the poem presents for its readers and listeners. In short, this mournful poem attempts to derive meaning from Rodney's death – the meaning of social change and the demands of revolutionary politics – and to proffer a politics by raising questions about his political life. It offers a friendly critique, devoid of romanticism and mystique, that ultimately hints that his tragic failure to patiently wait for 'the people' to take the lead in the transformative process in Guyana, to wait for that momentary pause or what Moten refers to as the break, the caesura, which engenders moments of innovation and improvisation, interruptions that are sometimes the result of tragedy which also breeds creativity, novelty and the demand for a fundamental shift or reorientation that represents a cut away from the mundane sense of continuity.[83] Revolution, like poetry, is about rhythm and repetition, that painstaking work which lays the groundwork for the coming movement that emerges out of the ongoing struggle. Like poetry, it is about tempo, timing and the turn, that moment of possibility embedded in the break – and the moment, that poetic-political cut, had yet to present itself in Guyana, it would seem.

In the poem's first stanza, Johnson employs the image of a cloud hovering over a dream 'like a daak silk screen' obscuring the speaker's anticipated vision. He moves in counterpoint with the 'some may say' refrain, juxtaposing various views and perspectives on Rodney's life and death, engaging in what we might call the three d's elegy – dialogue, debate and disagreement – in an effort to derive meaning from Rodney's death. The poet's third-person dialogical approach – 'some may say' and the Jamaicanized 'some wi seh' – facilitates the playful presentation of perspectives without committing to or compromising any of them. He contrasts the 'some' say Rodney 'woz a victim of hate' with the others who say he has 'gaan | through heaven's gate', while still others might say that Rodney 'shoudn tek-up histri weight' and carry it on his back in attempting to expedite the revolutionary process. The poet-speaker's reference to the historian's carrying of history on his back like an anorak is perhaps an allusion to what C.L.R. James described as Rodney's attempt to take history into his own hands through armed struggle before the actual conditions in Guyana were ready for it. In the aftermath of Rodney's killing there was a deluge of commentary on his life, death and politics as people sought answers to why such an important figure had been eliminated. The most prominent voice among those who posed questions and attempted to provide clarity following Rodney's death was James, his old friend and mentor – if it can be said that he was mentored by anyone.

This was not the first time that James made a public intervention on Rodney's behalf. He had sat alongside him in Montreal at Sir George William's University (now Concordia) following Rodney's expulsion from Jamaica in October 1968 where he argued that the Hugh Shearer government's desperate actions were part of the general misgovernment and decline in political leadership in the Caribbean. Rodney is highly respected in London and on the African continent for his scholarship, James told the audience, and he 'is in difficulties because he is telling the people there something about the history of Africa which has been so much neglected'.[84] When Rodney wrote a scathing critique of the African leadership and bourgeoisie as part of his contribution to the Sixth Pan-African Congress in 1974,[85] it was James who sounded the alarm and encouraged Rodney to exercise caution: 'We of the Caribbean cannot go to the Pan-African Congress and be the leading ones in putting forward these ideas. That would be a political blunder of the most primitive type.'[86] It was not that James did not agree with the sentiments outlined in Rodney's essay. He himself had written a critique of the leadership of his old friend Kwame Nkrumah when he came to the conclusion that the president had lost touch with the people of Ghana,[87] and he did not attend the Pan-African Congress because it had been co-opted by state officials who prevented the participation of the non-governmental – not to be confused with NGOs – Caribbean delegation.[88] Moreover, James consistently wrote about and spoke of the active role that the general population can and should play in governing Africa and the Caribbean, in fact in all societies. James was not admonishing Rodney, but making a statement on his tactics: that Rodney, from the Caribbean, was not in a position to lay such a devastating critique of the African petty bourgeoisie in a public forum, particularly given that at that time he was living in Tanzania and might be subjected to undue pressure as a result of his criticisms. James was always looking out for his younger friend.

The next time that James would have occasion to discuss Rodney publically was during a Rodney memorial symposium held at the University of California at Los Angeles where he addressed Rodney's politics and the factors that he believed contributed to his death. It is worth noting that James was living in England, removed from the eventual crime scene as events leading up to Rodney's death unfolded in Guyana. It is also important to consider the intense and incessant pressure that Rodney and other WPA leaders were subjected to by the Burnham government, including the imminent threat of death. That said, James offers an analysis that, whether or not his narrative entirely reflects Rodney's reality in the months, weeks and days leading up to his death, provides several political insights on the dynamics of social change. James's thesis is simple: Walter Rodney did not sufficiently appreciate the exigencies of taking power. In presenting his argument, he cites Lenin's 22 January 1917 lecture on the 1905 Russian Revolution. Speaking to young Swiss workers in Zurich, Lenin stated, 'We of the older generation may not live to see the decisive battles of this coming revolution'. Nonetheless, 'I can, I believe, express the confident hope that the youth which is working so splendidly in the socialist movement of Switzerland, and of the whole world, will be fortunate enough not only to fight, but also to win, in the coming proletarian revolution'.[89] Despite his own confident prediction that he would not see revolution in his time, by March of that same year the Russian Revolution was underway and Lenin was forced to hastily make his way to Moscow to catch up with it. For James, Lenin's speech suggests that you can never tell when the possibilities for change will present themselves. James argued that the role of the revolutionary and the proponent of social change is to lay the groundwork and be prepared to seize opportunities for change when they arise. History is replete with examples of liberation movements that have waged struggles to seize power only to find that, once they have won it, the leadership is ill-prepared to lead. James believed that Rodney should have spent more time grounding with the people of Guyana (perhaps in much the same way that he had grounded with the people of Jamaica before being expelled in 1968), laying a foundation for the moment when political oppor-tunities would arise, opportunities that Rodney's work itself would have helped to create, so that he and his co-conspirators would be well-positioned to make the most of them. By devoting his energies towards solidifying ties with the working class, including agricultural labourers, while helping to develop the political consciousness of his political associates, Rodney and the WPA would have presented a more formidable threat to the Burnham government that could not be so callously crushed.

James believed that, despite the repression of the PNC government, the climate in Guyana was not ready for an immediate and direct insurrectionary challenge for power. Rodney had not exhausted all the political channels available to him and the population was not at a stage at which they would endorse open insurrection and, regardless of the circumstances, he should not have found himself in a position where he was handling an explosive device. For James, 'a revolution is made by the revolutionary spirit of the great mass of the population. And you have to wait' until the people and the social circumstances are ready[90] because revolution 'comes, as Marx says, like a thief in the night'.[91] So again, when the speaker in 'Reggae fi Radni' suggests that Rodney 'shouldn tek-up histri weight' and carry it on his back, he is suggesting that Rodney was attempting to take the struggle in Guyana to a place it was not ready to go; that the people were not prepared for insurrection, yet. In this spirit James argued that, although Rodney was aware of what James described as the lack of revolutionary political experience among the WPA's leadership, he did not spend sufficient time training them in the art of taking power, an art that is rooted in the knowledge that the opposition is preparing to eliminate you.[92] Ultimately James's critique hinges on the view that Rodney lacked the patience and perhaps temperament to build a revolutionary movement in which the population would play the central role.

Once again, the poet-speaker invokes the image of a cloud sitting on top of his dream, but this time the cloud is 'like a shout ar a scream | ar a really ugly scene | dat awake mi fram di dream | an alert mi to di scheme'. The scheme is Rodney – the 'prizinah af fate', which implies that his fate was tragically sealed once he decided to confront Burnham's power – being killed.[93] Again, for 'some', Rodney has gone 'through the heroes gate' while others suggest that he fell victim to the pressures of the moment, 'couldn tek histri weight'.

Deploying a clever rhythmic rhyme scheme, the poet writes: 'soh im tek it awf im back | an goh put it pan im lap | an goh fall in a trap | an soh Burnham get e drap'.[94] Rodney carried the weight of history on his back, but the load, the burden, proved to be too heavy to carry, and so he put it on his lap, which is where the bomb that killed him was detonated. But rather than attempting to carry this weight on his own, the poet-narrator implies, the load should have been shared with the mass of the population in order that they too could make history.

The cloud overshadows the speaker's dream and fore-shadows an untoward scheme – Rodney's death – before the dream reaches its climax, the point where the true protago-nists, 'di people', enter the dream's 'crucial scene'. The dream has a twofold meaning: on the one hand, Walter Rodney is the dream personified, a leader in the people's struggle in Guyana who was physically eliminated by a bomb; on the other hand, the dream represents the struggle itself, which is 'blown to smidahreen', or destroyed, before the people, the workers and peasants, can take their place at the forefront of the struggle. In killing Rodney, an embodiment of the hopes and aspirations of his people, Guyana's dreams of liberation are momentarily extinguished. 'Walter found himself in a car with a member of Burnham's army', says James, 'making some arrangement about some gadget that turned out to be an explosive. *He should never have been there*'.[95] For James this is a case of the road to hell being paved with the best of intentions: 'No political leader had the right to be there', and 'Not only should he never have been there, the people around him should have seen to it that he was not in any such position. That was a fundamental mistake, and it was a political mistake ... because he was doing all sorts of things to show them that a revolutionary is prepared to do anything.' Fully aware that Burnham was prepared to physically destroy his opponent, James says he warned Rodney to beware of assassina-tion, a warning that was not sufficiently heeded.[96] Here James takes his cue from the Russian Revolution where the Bolshevik leaders fled to Finland in order to avoid arrest and persecution, but if he were to take Cuba as the model, Rodney's actions were consistent with those of Fidel Castro and other key leaders of the Cuban Revolution, all of whom were on the front lines of Cuba's revolutionary struggle in the 1950s.

Rodney took the study of revolutionary struggle seriously and he was conscious of the risks, the potential real-life consequences involved in armed struggle. He was young, but he had a history of political involvement in the Caribbean, dating back to his youth in Guyana, where he canvassed for the PPP, and his student days and his groundings in Jamaica as a professor at the University of the West Indies. He was well respected throughout the Caribbean, even by those who did not share his political ideals. With all of these factors working in his favour, he represented a serious challenge to Burnham. At some point, Rodney and other members of the WPA arrived at the conclusion that armed struggle was the only political option available to them, and Rodney was not shy about the potential use of arms as an instrument of politics. As early as 1968, during the Montreal Congress of Black Writers, he pressed psychiatrist Alvin Poussaint on Fanon and the revolutionary nature of violence during an exchange.[97] In his 1969 essay on Black Power he poetically posed the question: 'By what standards can we equate the violence of blacks who have been oppressed, suppressed, depressed and repressed for four centuries with the violence of white fascists. Violence aimed at the recovery of human dignity and at equality cannot be judged by the same yardstick as violence aimed at maintenance of discrimination and oppression.'[98] As he remarked in the spring of 1975, any decision to engage in armed struggle would involve taking stock of the political situation in a given context and arriving at the conclusion that change would not be possible under the leadership of the ruling government.[99]

Rodney went even further in 1976: armed struggle 'is often associated with the greatest revolutionary heights which people have reached', but this is not as a result of some reverence for it or the result of romantic notions of violence, but 'because it is in those contexts that the political struggle has been most highly evolved' because the 'depth and extent of political mobilization which accompanies and precedes armed struggle in so many places, most recently in Angola, Mozambique and Guinea-Bissau, is really what accounts for its success, rather than the fact of arms itself'. This said, the decision to engage in armed struggle can only be made by 'the people already engaged in struggle, because it is really when people have engaged in struggle historically through a variety of forms that they settle upon the most effective' form of struggle, including the possibility of armed struggle.[100] Given the circumstances that led to Rodney's death and his subsequent immortalization in verse, the following dread statement by him sends an eerie echo into the present: 'we don't set about to get the best of our workers and revolutionaries killed just so that we can write poetry to celebrate them subsequently' as the loss of revolutionaries in armed conflict can lead to 'an irreparable loss and may in fact affect the development of struggle in another phase. *And even for those whom we might remember in poetry and song, what about their lives, their decisions to risk all?*' This is why '*people move very slowly and only finally towards armed struggle*', only when other means are exhausted.[101] Armed struggle was not an absolute for Rodney, and he had no romantic illusions about the kind of martyrdom that is expressed in Johnson's verse play *Voices of the Living and the Dead* ('Our singers will sings songs about you | Our poets will write poems about you in memoriam | Flowers will bloom on your graves').[102] He rather expressed his faith that the people of the Caribbean were capable of determining their mode of struggle as they organized against government repression for a more egalitarian society.[103] His philosophically sobering assessment of revolution, martyrdom, death and elegy, as well as his openness to the possibility of armed struggle while cautioning against hasty decisions to engage in it, demonstrate his complex understanding of the dynamics of revolution, which he acquired from both his deep appreciation of revolutionary history and practical experience.

Rodney had followed the Cuban Revolution closely and delivered seminars on it while teaching in Tanzania (he also assisted in seminars on China).[104] While in Tanzania he also began preparations for a manuscript on the Russian Revolution, which he outlined in the form of a series of lectures that demonstrate the depth and breadth of his study of literature on the revolution in general. His familiarity with contemporary Russian literature on the subject is particularly noteworthy, a body of work for which James, the Hegelian Marxist who, going back to his days within the international socialist movement and his association with Leon Trotsky, would have cared little. But in addition to Lenin, Rodney also shows his appreciation of the work of Leon Trotsky, who had been denigrated and discarded by Moscow and official communism, along with Tolstoy and Dostoyevsky.[105] Like George Lamming, Horace Campbell has argued that Rodney and James shared an experience as West Indians who, as a people, were forged out of an encounter between the peoples of Africa, Europe and Asia and the indigenous peoples of the Americas – a worldly, cosmopolitan experience that catapulted figures such as Aimé Césaire, Claude McKay, René Depestre, Frantz Fanon and George Padmore[106] (to which we can add Suzanne Césaire and Claudia Jones, among others) – onto the international arena. However, Rodney came of age after these figures had set a foundation of intellectual-political inquiry and he benefited immensely from his predecessors, a luxury that James's generation did not have. And yet, Rodney was an independent thinker who carved his own political path, and in this sense Rupert Lewis perhaps slightly overstates James's impact on Rodney's appreciation of Marxism in *Walter Rodney's Intellectual and Political Thought*. Like Johnson, Rodney would have been familiar with the Algerian liberation struggle through the work of Fanon and he was attuned to the various revolutionary movements in Africa from his first-hand familiarity with African history and politics.[107] We also know that he was very familiar with the history of the Haitian Revolution through James's *The Black Jacobins*. In other words, and this is important in terms of tempering accusations that he was an adventurist who carelessly and naively attempted to artificially ignite an armed movement, Rodney was well acquainted with revolutionary theory and history and he had put a great deal of thought into the social, political and individual cost of armed struggle, genuinely believing that the working class, 'the people', would come to their own conclusions to take up arms if and when they deemed it necessary. Revolution and armed struggle was not something to play with, and it was only after careful consideration that he reasoned in 1976 that, while 'above-ground struggle' may still be a viable option in much of the Caribbean, this may no longer be possible in Guyana, the obvious implication being that, given the level of repression by Burnham's government, armed struggle was not only inevitable, but imminent.[108]

For Anthony Bogues, James's critical remarks about Rodney failed to appreciate that, by putting his own life on the line, 'Rodney was more *preoccupied* with defining a new kind of revolutionary political leadership' in which 'the gap between the highly educated and the mass of the population would not be reproduced in a political hierarchy where the educated did the thinking about political programs while members of the oppressed class did the doing, the mundane work which sometimes places their lives in danger'.[109] This leadership approach was partly reflected in the WPA's unconventional rotating chair, which essentially meant 'that there was no single leader, and the maximum leader, appointing and disappointing, unaccountable in all essential matters was discarded', according to Tim Hector. Along with the WPA's bi-racial leadership, this approach 'could better represent the society itself and escape the racialism which plagued Guyana's politics. Few things were more novel or more creative in Caribbean politics.'[110] Rodney and the WPA were attempting to do something new in Caribbean politics, and for Bogues, playing with the title of Edward Kamau Brathwaite's 1973 review of *How Europe Underdeveloped Africa*, Rodney endeavoured to integrate 'the local dialect with the dialectic' in his praxis, to flexibly apply Marxist theory to Guyana's local cultural-political realities;[111] and to encourage the leadership to do for 'the people' what the leadership was asking of them. This was the model that was applied during the Cuban Revolution against the Batista regime, and Rodney's respect for what he described as the Cuban Revolution's dynamism in the 1960s outstripped even his admiration for the dynamism of Jamaican society.[112]

For Rupert Roopnarine, who worked closely with Rodney in the WPA, James's analysis was not up to his usual standards and he attributes this lapse to James's deep sense of loss of one of his 'disciples'. Yet he acknowledges that Rodney had grown impatient following his return from Zimbabwe's independence celebrations in the spring of 1980 where he unsuccessfully attempted to acquire assistance from the new southern African government. The movement in Guyana was ebbing at this point and Rodney felt an urgent need to get things moving and to regain momentum in the direction of insurrection,[113] to perhaps 'heighten the contradictions'. This reality may have unduly influenced Rodney's decision-making at the time, but Roopnarine believes that James failed to appreciate the dynamics on the ground in Guyana in relation to the details of the secret efforts to unseat Burnham. He does acknowledge Rodney's desire to demonstrate that he was willing to lead by example, but also that Rodney found himself in the position of acquiring arms because he was trusted, and in a relatively small and close-knit society where news travels fast through informal networks, trust was paramount in order to minimize the danger.[114]

Andaiye, a key figure in WPA, has argued that it was not Burnham that Rodney misread but the so-called 'lumpen' in Guyana. Rodney was drawn to this group and it was an alleged member of this class that handed Rodney the walkie-talkie that killed him.[115] Andaiye's analysis raises pointed issues about the poor, dispossessed and working class, and the often facile and romantic ways in which they are portrayed, ignoring that the dispossessed can also be as conservative or even reactionary as the political elite. In essence she suggests that despite his deep theoretical and historical understanding, in this instance Rodney was perhaps too trusting, even careless, in the political relations he fostered. Her view veers somewhat towards James's and recalls Johnson's refrain 'some may say', which ultimately suggests that Rodney perhaps could have been more cautious and discerning in his political relations in Guyana, particularly given the Burnham government's penchant for violence, and that in taking on Burnham he perhaps 'woz noh shaak fi di sea' (was no shark for the sea) and 'like a fish to di ook' he fell prey to Burnham.

'Reggae fi Radni' ends before the dream reaches its climax, the crucial moment. Rodney's revolutionary aspirations and the hopes of 'the people' are scattered (at least for the time being) when he is eliminated, before the people of Guyana are able to enter the stage and assume their role at the forefront of the struggle. Ultimately, the poem emphasizes the idea that politics is about people, about ordinary people, the 'each and everyone' that is so important to Johnson's later work; without popular participation in which 'the people' mount the stage of the 'theatre of the oppressed', the final scene before the new beginning of the next scene, politics is essentially an empty shell, a ruse in a carnivalesque play in which politicians perform and their constituents passively observe or act as bit-part players as the political parade passes them by.

There is no easy road to freedom and Walter Rodney was clearly operating under very challenging circumstances. The logic and spirit of the circumstances appear to have been carrying him along, and once set in motion, it appears as though the tragic end was inevitable. If it was going to be a choice between Burnham maintaining his grip on power and eliminating the opposition, then Rodney's tragic demise was inevitable, as he himself seems to have come to terms with. In 'Reggae fi Radni', his life becomes a metaphor for the eclipsed dreams of the Caribbean left and the poem itself is a meditation on the demands of social change. The eerie spirit of the poem is only enhanced by the knowledge that, according to Robert Hill, Rodney anticipated his death ('I won't be here'),[117] a point that Jan Carew also hints at in his Rodney elegy. As the Kenyan-Kikyu novelist Ngũgĩ wa Thiongo has written about Rodney, 'in his death, he has come alive as part and parcel of those millions foreseen in one of the poems by Martin Carter, those wretched of the earth in Africa, the West Indies, the Third World, all over the world, "who sleep not to dream, but who are always dreaming to change the world."'[118]

This was Rodney's dream, ultimately beginning and ending with that corner of the world that he knew best – Guyana.

During a 1995 African Liberation Day celebration in Montreal, Patricia Rodney implored us to think about her late husband, 'not just as a political activist, but somebody who was a humanist who loved people, who enjoyed people – and I think that is the reason he was a revolutionary. Because a revolutionary wants to change the lives, the circumstances of people, to make them economically, socially, politically and spiritually better … it is in that context I would like him to be remembered.'[119] Beyond his revolutionary image, 'Reggae fi Radni' humanizes a committed radical intellectual who was cut down in his prime, and seemingly before his time. We are all the wiser for Rodney's experiences and, despite his unseemly death, his work, spirit and, crucially, his life lessons persist in our ongoing struggles to bring about the freedom for which he lived and died. Rather than engage in the romance of martyrdom Johnson pays Rodney the highest tribute, by critically deriving meaning from his politics for posterity.

Chapter 5

THE WISE OLD SHEPHERD

I believe that the distinguishing feature of the civilization of the twentieth century is the fact that the masses have entered upon the stage of history. And those people are most successful as individual artists, political leaders, etc., who recognize this.

C.L.R. James

Everything that lives, not vegetative alone, emerges from darkness and, however strong its natural tendency to thrust itself into the light, it nevertheless needs the security of darkness to grow at all.

Hannah Arendt

*T*ING*S AN' T*IMES is 'as far a cry as you could wish for from the narcissistic, untranslatable, apolitical and gutless "Martian-Masterclass" school that rules the roost of official English verse. As on the album's predecessors, LKJ's succinctly measured deep-voiced syllable sculptures are swathed in a wondrously audible sunlight by the shimmering modulations and unfaltering group-feel of Bovell and his virtuosi.' Michael Horovitz's review is one of the few to capture the tenor and tone of *Ting an' Times*, poems that superficially appear to be a departure from his usual form and content, but that are in fact continuous with his earlier work: 'While he explores continuing repression and acknowledges the ruthless enemies of liberation, the recording's impact is one of sustained uplift, as rhythmically and spiritually compelling as it is enjoyable thought.'[1] What this one-page review lacks in details is more than compensated for by the way that it concisely captures the spirit, rhythm and tone of the poems and their musical accompaniment.

It is hard to discern why so little critical attention has been devoted to Johnson's socialist poems,[2] but when they have received consideration the critics generally tend to ignore or downplay the politics that are embedded in his poetics. For example, in his assessment of 'Mi Revalueshanary Fren' and 'Di Good Life', Roberto Masone's textual-linguistic analysis reduces the former poem to a celebration of the collapse of the Soviet bloc and the latter to what he describes as sarcastic praise for socialism.[3] Yes, it is true that the poet celebrates the collapse of totalitarianism in Eastern Europe in 'Mi Revalueshanary Fren', but only in so far as it opens up the space for the genuine socialism that he describes in 'Di Good Life', and so to separate the sequential and contextual relationship between the two poems is misleading.

Henghameh Saroukhani's intriguing paratextual analysis of 'Mi Revalueshanary Fren' presents a different problem. Her essential argument is that Johnson's inclusion in the exclusive Penguin Modern Classics series not only expanded the poet's audience by virtue of Penguin's vast distribution networks and marketing, but that the organization of his verse in the Penguin selection recontextualizes the poems along transnational lines, in essence going beyond the black protest framework to which his work has historically been associated. In support of her argument she notes that 'Mi Revalueshanary Fren' is included in the 1980s section of the selection despite the fact that it was written in 1990 or 1991, released on the 1991 LP *Tings an' Times*, and published in the eponymous collection by Bloodaxe Books. The inclusion of this 1990s poem under a 1980s banner serves as a bridge between the seemingly timeless socialist poem and 'Di Great Insohreckshan', a poem about mass black mobilization and protest in the early 1980s. By conjoining the poems Penguin created 'inter-poetic attachments between Brixton, Eastern Europe and South Africa' as opposed to 'ossifying the contextual distinctions between the poems or any one specific articulation of revolution, uprising or protest',[4] and in so doing Penguin 'pluralizes the ways in which we have conventionally read his poetry, particularly as a *text*'.[5] Saroukhani's analysis reminds us of the importance of context and how editorial decisions can influence how and where we situate an artist's work. However, although it is true that we can read 'Di Great Insohreckshan' alongside 'Mi Revalueshanary Fren' as an example of textual cosmopolitanism, in which the themes of socialism, apartheid and black struggles are linked together in ways that internationalize black British struggles, doing so raises important issues and questions. The first is whether black struggles in England have already been adopted and universalized by people of African descent and other groups outside of Britain. The answer of course is yes, and Saroukhani acknowledges this in her reference to Johnson's popularity in France,[6] to which we can add the poet's popularity in North America and South Africa, among other places. In other words, despite the tendency of critics to limit the impact of Johnson's poetic-political reach, his work has long extended beyond the boundaries of Britain, although not necessarily as written text.[7]

Second, to the extent that Saroukhani's argument works, it hinges on the idea that the juxtaposition of black liberation and socialism is new to Johnson's poetry, but in actual fact 'Di Great Insohreckshan' was released on the LP *Making History* in 1984 and included three poems that addressed local and international socialist/communist themes – 'Di Eagle an' di Bear', 'Wat About di Working Claas' and 'Reggae fi Radni' – as well as poems about black protests that are socialist-inflected in their own way. With the exception of 'Di Eagle an' di Bear', these poems were also published in 1991 by Bloodaxe Books, a major publisher of poetry, though of course not at the marketing level of Penguin. Even the poem 'Independant Intavenshan' can be understood as a critical engagement with socialism and the white left from the vantage of its black equivalent's stating its need to maintain its autonomy. What I am suggesting here is that despite his longstanding relationship with socialism there is a tendency to limit Johnson's poetic production to 'black struggles', as well as a failure to appreciate the universality and transnationality that is implicit in the particularity of the experiences that he captures in his 'black poems'. It is this porous nationality that theorist

Richard Iton described as 'the capacity to imagine and operate simultaneously within, against, and outside the nation-state', the possibility of challenging racialized exclusion and domination from within the nation-state while transcending its boundaries and limitations.[8] Johnson's poetry has long been transnational and even transracial (though not post-racial) in its appeal, including in England among people of Asian and European descent (and among members of the punk music scene), precisely because it addresses themes specific to black Britons, and because of his belief in the ideals of socialism and social justice.

Walter Benjamin argues that the translation of poetry is a process of creative interpretation as opposed to simply transmitting information from one language into another,[9] but it is also true that criticism is in part a creative process of translation, or more accurately interpretation of *poetic* language. Reading and listening to poetry involves a process of conscious and unconscious decoding. On one level, the truth behind a poem is phenomenological, that is to say it lies with the readers and listeners and what their eyes and ears see and hear in response to what the poet conveys. On another level, poetic language is ontological, that is to say it speaks its own tongue and possesses its own truth that is independent from what we might describe as the poem's inner meaning, which the poem may or may not openly divulge. In its process of becoming, poetic language resuscitates dead language and keeps it alive.[10] This is what both Fred Moten in relation to his own poetry and Jacques Derrida in his analysis of Paul Celan, via Martin Heidegger, refer to as the poem's secret or, in Derrida's words, its 'overabundance of meaning' that conceals itself or presents itself in the form of a mask without revealing the face behind it.[11] Poetry is open to interpretation, and readers and listeners bring their own perspective to bear on a poem that is independent of the poet's intended meaning; and even a poet's presumed meaning is open to question, regardless of her own interpretation of her own work. But this is only true to a point: poems derive meaning from contexts and are shaped by events, precedents and politics and the secret to critically assessing what Emily Taylor Merriman describes as Johnson's demotic form and style as well as the sophisticated political content[12] of his poetry (to which I would add his semantically rich poetics) lies in the contexts and intellectual-political-artistic styles that have shaped its language and meaning. In the spirit of what Amiri Baraka once described as the dialectic of Thelonious Monk's and Karl Marx's 'two is one',[13] in concert with the reflexive I-and-I of Rastafari – and despite Benjamin's view that poets do not write for their audiences[14] – Johnson's poetry reflects in part the Afro diasporic call-and-response phenomenon in terms of how his audience relates to his poems. All of this suggests that too literal a criticism diminishes the poem, and that as far as possible the critic should attempt to imaginatively dwell or linger in a poem long enough to distil its inner meaning. Part of this process involves understanding the context of a poem without wholly reducing the poem to it. It also necessitates an appreciation of the fact that the spontaneous and deliberative creativity that produces poetry is open to creative interpretations that both engage with, but are not beholden to, how poets interpret their own work. But because of poetry's deliberate, deliberative and spontaneous nature it retains its right to be secretive, even deceitful, and can perhaps never be fully grasped, even if poets are willing to give their secrets away, because these secrets have secrets of their own about which even the poet is unaware.

Again, revealing the poem's secrets, to the extent that this is possible, involves dwelling in or inhabiting the poem[15] and pondering its meaning in terms of language and in relation to the moment in which it was written, and the political and aesthetic customs that have touched it. It is precisely in this area that Christian Habekost falls short in *Verbal Riddim: The Politics and Aesthetics of African-Caribbean Dub Poetry*,[16] the first major assessment of the idiom of reggae-inflected poetry. A critical reading of Habekost reveals some troubling trends that, measured within the broader context of literary criticism and critical thought, are part of a larger set of problems associated with writing about art that sits outside of the Western canon.

In the introduction to *Verbal Riddim*, Habekost presents a seemingly innocuous argument: 'The view from the outside can open perspectives and allow insights which insiders tend to ignore. Provided they have done their homework, white critics may well be in a position which is advantageous to the exploration of a known yet foreign territory.'[17] But *if* there is any merit to this claim, *Verbal Riddim* is hardly the best example of an 'outsider's' view. In fact Habekost's analysis is typical of a practice that literary critic June D. Dobbs describes in her study of the poetry of Kamau Brathwaite and Derek Walcott: 'very often critics and theorists, convinced of the superiority of Western literature, and awed by the sanctity of Western literary traditions, impose upon non-European literatures a tradition of Western aesthetics'.[18] These critics are often guilty of being 'shrouded in a mantle of omniscience that results in closed readings of Caribbean texts', and there is a 'very real need of the critic to be aware of the tradition out of which these poets emerge'.[19] Habekost's failure to evaluate Johnson's poetry on its own grounds – poetry that is described by him as being 'devoid of the religious mysticism and nebulous ganja smoke', a distorted reference to reggae music and Rastafari, as he understands it, and 'much closer to a white perspective in politics'[20] – speaks volumes. What exactly is this 'white perspective in politics' that he refers to? His reduction of the relationship between Rastafari and reggae to mysticisms and marijuana brings to mind 'Sense Outa Nansense', Johnson's satirical *Tings an' Times* poem about the absence of critical curiosity. In other words, his critical analysis of the poet's work demonstrates the limitations of a certain kind of criticism on the one hand, and the need for a more critical criticism on the other. It is difficult to discern a critic's motivations, and as Marx once reminded us, the road to hell is paved with good intentions. This said, Habekost's critique of Johnson's poetry, despite its limitations, inadvertently serves as a muse for the contemplation of the poet and of criticism.

Verbal Recidivism

Habekost takes issue with what he describes as Johnson's attempt to resurrect a discredited socialism from the dead via biblical allegory. The poet 'is obviously struggling to maintain and defend his ideological position' in *Tings an' Times* and the poems are 'dominated by indirection and non-referential language, while the actual political discourse is frequently clothed in allegorical constructions and mystical imagery'. For Habekost, 'The title poem suggests an autobiographical background. Having lost his bearings the poet-persona feels a need to reassure himself and his audience of his ideological position.'[21] Conflating alleged changes in political positions with poetic style, Johnson is accused of poetic-political alteration, the most egregious example being the poem 'Di Good Life,' which the critic describes as 'a plea on behalf of socialism'.[22] In short, according to Habekost, the poet has departed from the militancy of his earlier political positions for a deflated socialism couched in biblical lore that is all the more troubling because of the role that the Bible played in the subjugation of people of African descent in the Americas. He is clearly uncomfortable with what he sees as the poet's new departure towards socialism and hints that he would prefer that Johnson stick to what he describes as pugnacious black protest poems. In this sense, he both fails to see how the particular experiences of people of African descent can contribute to our universal appreciation of the world in which we live, and appears to be uncomfortable with the poet weighing in on themes that presumably step beyond the immediate experiences of black Britons.

The socialist poems are also curiously described as 'less rhetorical and more metaphorical'[23] than his previous poems. Although it is true that Johnson has written what might be described as 'protest poems' in the past, they are not characteristic of all of his poetry, and given that poets employ metaphors, among other devices, in order to creatively manipulate language as a means of expression, in what sense would this development be considered a negative? In fact, Habekost also commends the artist for his 'poetic accomplishment', but this ruse is really a muse that permits him to criticize the poet through a feigned give and take. This ultimately leads Habekost to the view that, in his efforts to redefine socialism away from the Soviet model,

Tings an' Times 'fails to meet the high demands made by its author' in terms of separating 'the original ideology of socialism from the state ideology of discredited socialist regimes', instead taking refuge in 'mythological encoding' as 'the sole remaining means to reclaim the pristine dignity of a devalued concept'. In the eyes of the critic, 'The application of socialist ideology by political systems' along with 'its corruption into an instrument of repression and exploitation, and the eventual collapse of the Communist states – all these crucial developments are not accounted for in the poem'.[24] But has so much ever been demanded from a single poem?

Were Habekost to have it his own way, Johnson would be limited to 'militant' and 'pugnacious' 'praise poems' or his 'campaign poems and unveiled political messages'[25] instead of resorting to apt and timely metaphors in 'dialect' to probe the delicate dialectic of socialism and social change in the afterlife of communism. This is a subject that Habekost apparently believes is beyond the Jamaican British poet's purview and, seemingly, unless Johnson is screaming militant epithets or chanting down Babylon from a hilltop, his voice cannot possibly be authentic. To highlight this point, Johnson is contrasted with Benjamin Zephaniah, whose 1990 album *Us an Dem* is dedicated to C.L.R. James. Zephaniah enjoys 'being an entertainer in the best sense of the word' and, compared to Johnson, his 'approach is much more satirical, his style ... much more the comedian about it'. It would seem that the critic is searching for a comic. Johnson, on the other hand, has more of a 'deadly serious didactic attitude' when performing on stage and is 'hampered by ... ideological positions'[26] which are presumably reflected in his understated movements on stage, keeping an 'intellectual distance' between himself and his audience. Moreover, the poet's 'facial expressions and gestures are reduced to a set of repetitive motions' and he 'fails to fill out the space of the stage and his occasional body movements suggest rather than present a response to the powerful music accompanying him'. While he acknowledges that Johnson's inactivity on stage is contrived 'so as not to distract from his words by any superfluous movements or gestures',[27]

Habekost clearly believes that the poet is either too serious or takes himself too seriously.

Johnson is grim and too serious, on the one hand, and lacks pugnacity and militancy on the other. But there is, according to the critic, a modicum of militancy in the 'radical phonetical spelling' in Johnson's poems and 'LKJ's typographical militancy marks one of the few attempts in dub poetry to transfer all the originality of Jamaican creole to the pages'.[28] Here Habekost rightly acknowledges how the poet's writing in Jamaican challenges the linguistic hegemony of English,[29] but in doing so he overstates the case, finding consolation in language in what he perceives as the otherwise absence of politics. Ultimately, it is argued, Johnson's 'allegorical apology for his own ideology sounds like a nostalgic swan song rather than a radical dub version of the Internationale'. But notwithstanding Michael Horovitz's suggestion that the poem 'Di Anfinish Revalueshan' represents a '*new* Internationale',[30] why does Internationale become the barometer that measures the poem's political value? Ultimately, for Habekost, 'Socialism, forced into the garb of LKJ's "wise ole shephad," resembles a retired self-complacent and slightly dotty professor of philosophy' and 'an exiled pensioner with theatrical ambitions who is, however, very unlikely to re-enter the world stage of the late twentieth century. And even the potentiality of a belated breakthrough of "real" socialism is realized only in the form of mythology.'[31]

Such is the critic's clever political conclusion, but he also takes issue with the poet's choice of music which he describes as 'a continuation of its predecessors, although it incorporates an unusual 'ethnopop-stylish' instrumentation (accordion, violin, etc)' and the 'sloppy' production that lacks the ingenuity of his previous albums.[32] While a thorough analysis of the music (Johnson is also a musician and plays an active role in the musical selection along with Dennis Bovell) is beyond the scope of this book – and the limits of my critical abilities – as Michael Horovitz eloquently suggests, the combination of instruments on *Tings an' Times* 'such as accordion, Caribbean-style guitar, and the violin of Johnny T (formerly of the Reggae Philharmonic Orchestra) blend in joyous counterpoint, harmony and unison with the more familiar plush exuberance of flutes, saxes, trumpets, trombones and Afro-Jamaican percussion'.[33] Moreover, critic Robert J. Stewart has argued that the variation in the poet's choices of music represent 'an extension of his prosodic craft' and the internationalist perspective that infuses the poems.[34] This blend of music and poetry is perhaps best expressed in 'Story', a meditative poem that was inspired by a John La Rose poem about 'inner feelings and outer expressions',[35] as well as Johnson's inability to find the inspiration to write:[36]

(it is a aad awt fi mawstah yu know
dis smilin an skinin yu teet
wen yu awt swell-up soh till yu feel it a goh bus
wen yu cyaan fine di rime fi fit di beat
wen yu cyaan fine di ansah fi di puzzle complete)[37]

The speaker's inability to find his poetic rhythm is analogous to a general sense of vulnerability, feeling out of sorts and an inability to 'fine di rime fi fit di beat', an apt analogy as music has been an integral, intricate and, as 'Story' demonstrates, intimate part of Johnson's poetry, both in terms of the music that is embedded in the poetry itself, and the instrumental musical accompaniment to the poetry. The music is part of the poetry's secret, but it also tells its own story.

While the speaker in 'Story' muses on the mask that he wears in order to shield his inner emotions and feelings, protecting himself from the harsh realities of the outer world, Johnny T's introspective and soul-searching violin accompaniment is particularly moving. In the BBC documentary *Shake, Beat, and Dub* about Johnson and the late Vincentian poet and trumpeter Ellsworth McGranahan 'Shake' Keane, the violinist puts on a remarkable performance before a live London audience, demonstrating tremendous emotional depth and remarkable dexterity on his instrument.[38] In both the concert performance and the album, Johnny T's playing produces heart-wrenching wailing sounds as he serenades and soothes the souls of his listeners, at times playing as if he were attempting to stretch each note from each string beyond what the instrument is musically capable of. In some respects, his performance transcends the poem itself. We feel and hear in the music what cannot be expressed in words in a manner that is reminiscent of Billy Bang on the violin, John Coltrane or Courtney Pine on the saxophone, or Jimmy Hendrix on the guitar, as the sheer mournful and emotive power of his playing takes us on a journey into the tormented inner sanctum of the heart and soul that hides behind the *mawga*[39] chest of the 'storyteller'.

'Story' is an intimate, almost spiritual poem, and one of the poet's rare attempts at exploring inner feelings. It also fits neatly with the retrospective tone of the socialist poems of *Tings an' Times*, poems that are also meditatively optimistic about the prospects for social change – a new beginning at the end of official communism. The poet sees socialism as the necessary response to capitalist market forces and state-corporate collusion. There is no post-communism melancholia here, but instead a more upbeat vision of socialism's prospects that is largely influenced by C.L.R. James, and particularly his Hegelian meditation on socialist revolution, *Notes on Dialectics*.

A Note on Dialectics

C.L.R. James's work played an important role in the development of Linton Kwesi Johnson's perspective on socialism. As the poet recalled in a 1999 interview, *Notes on Dialectics* helped him to appreciate that 'what they had in the Soviet Union was not socialism, but was the paramountcy of the one-party state and that is not what Marx was talking about in his various writings; and it was inevitable that that system would eventually implode on itself', adding that 'his clarity about Soviet communism and the one-party state in Eastern Europe – his clarity about that and the need for people's power, I think was the most important legacy he left me personally'.[40] In another interview five years later, Johnson acknowledged that the Soviet Union played a positive role in some anti-colonial movements, but he nonetheless reiterated the impact of *Notes on Dialectics* on his political outlook and how James used the Hegelian dialectic 'to prove that Marx's conception of communism had been turned upside down on it's head'.[41]

Notes on Dialectics was written in the US in 1948 in the form of letters and circulated to members of a small Marxist organization called the Johnson-Forest Tendency, a political group that alternated between the Trotskyist Socialist Workers Party and the Workers Party. As James recalled: 'In 1940 came a crisis in my political life. I rejected the Trotskyist version of Marxism and set about to re-examine and reorganize my view of the world, which was (and remains) essentially a political one. It took more than ten years, but by 1952 I once more felt my feet on solid ground'.[42] It was during this period that James and collaborators Raya Dunayevskaya and Grace Lee developed their theory of Russian state capitalism, the idea that Russia was a capitalist state, disguised as socialist.[43] Written one year before George Orwell's *1984* was published, the Hegelian *Notes on Dialectics* was an important part of James's re-examination of Marxism and international socialism at the height of Stalin's rule in the Soviet Union and the onset of McCarthyism in the US. But while Orwell's ominously dystopian account of totalitarianism struck a doomsday chord, *Notes on Dialectics* presented an anti-statist notion of socialism and the view that a new society will come into being through the self-organization of the working class. While *Notes on Dialectics* might be criticized for being too abstract and mystical, it is precisely because of its theoretical 'mysticism' that James is able to project a new theory of social organization. The result is a synthesis of Hegel's system of logic with his own critique of international socialism and Trotsky's analysis of the Soviet Union, as he guides the reader through historic revolutionary developments in Europe, including the English Civil War, the French and Russian revolutions, the Soviet Union and the US labour movement.[44]

For James, socialism meant the abolition of the labour movement, the single party and the government apparatus as the embodiment of politics or, put another way, the elimination of the contradiction between labour and politics.[45] James argued that the new government formation, the new party structure, will be the labour movement itself, comprised of thousands and millions of workers (in essence, becoming the antithesis of a party). In his view, government bureaucracies and unions alike sacrifice the economic and cultural interests of the workers, and whereas in the Soviet Union and its satellites political and economic power were concentrated in the hands of the single party that was synonymous with the state, in the Western world this power was (and is) increasingly centralized in the hands of fewer and fewer large corporations, with the collusion with national governments. However, in James's schemata people become the caretakers of their own well-being and the architects of their destinies, and it was this dialectical reading of socialism and its shifting political categories that Johnson creatively invoked in *Tings an' Times*.

Notes on Dialectics is not without flaws. It does not account for the roles of women, blacks and other groups, or the history and struggles of colonial peoples and their role in the struggle for a new society. These are significant omissions, and particularly so in the case of the black struggles when we consider James's earlier writings, including *The Black Jacobins*, *A History of Negro Revolt* and his work on the 'Negro Question' in the United States. The end result is a somewhat teleological outline that is limited to working-class efforts in Europe and the United States, excluding groups that, in addition to being an integral part of the working-class movement, also significantly impact society outside of the sphere of labour. Another flaw is the pre-eminence that James accords Europe and the US. The pitfalls of an overdependence on Western historical and philosophical constructs (of course the term 'Western' is problematic as a social and cultural marker but it is used here for the sake of simplicity) should be obvious given Hegel's infamous ideas on the 'primitive' and 'backward' African continent and 'The Negro'.[46] Others have posited alternative philosophical traditions – for example, Paget Henry's groundbreaking *Caliban's Reason: Introducing Afro-Caribbean Philosophy* draws on Akan philosophic constructs and the Akan dialectic[47] – as a way of providing insight into the human condition. Henry's work is part of a larger African and Afro diasporic philosophical tradition that includes, among others, Kwame Gyekye's *An Essay on African Philosophical Thought: The Akan Conceptual Scheme*,[48] as well as Kamau Brathwaite's Akan philosophy-inflected poem 'Masks'.[49]

I am not suggesting that these traditions are mutually exclusive as, read in counterpoint, they might reveal a great deal about the parallels and particularities of philosophies across borders. One book cannot meet all of our expectations, and we should read *Notes on Dialectics* alongside James's other work. Moreover, his ability to project beyond the present, in a flexible and less dogmatic way, separated him from many of his contemporaries. He nurtured his notion of socialism well into his twilight years,[50] and as he observed world developments from the comfort of his Brixton home above the offices of *Race Today*, surrounded by books and papers as world events crossed his television screen in the 1980s, Poland's Solidarity movement signalled the end of the Soviet grip on Central and Eastern Europe and further solidified his belief that the mass formation of the population comprised of thousands and even millions of workers would supplant both the Soviet and Western models. It is easy to argue in retrospect that James overstated the imminence, immanence and even the eminence of socialism at the time; today's world is far removed from the kind of society that he foresaw in 1948, an aspiration that has failed to materialize.

It is James's visionary capacity to inspire us to aspire, to imagine beyond the immediate moment and to dream of freedom that is crucial here in terms of Johnson's socialist poems. For the poet, James possessed 'a very clear analysis of Soviet communism which he saw as being a distortion of the original ideas of Karl Marx, in particular the Stalinist version of communism' which resulted in a dictatorship over the proletariat.[51] When Johnson speaks vicariously through the persona of a revolutionary in the poem 'Mi Revalueshanary Fren' and asserts that all the leaders in Eastern Europe, and their regimes, had to go; and when he speaks of the 'each an evry wan' in 'Di Anfinish Revalueshan', he is communicating in a voice conditioned by his own political involvement and observations in Britain while articulating a tradition of socialist thinking that echoes James's unique critique of the Soviet Union and his vision of a new society.

Black and Red

In the aftermath of the urban rebellions in England in the early 1980s, Paul Gilroy argued that the left has failed to seriously consider the more than six decades of Afro diasporic critical engagement with Marxism, the relationship between race and class, and Afro diasporic critiques of capitalist exploitation.[52] Johnson's socialist poems are also part of this long tradition, a history of Caribbean and Afro diasporic engagement with Russia, socialism and the former Soviet Union that includes a number of artists, beginning with Alexander Pushkin, the Russian playwright, poet, novelist and founder of modern Russian literature (he was the great grandson of the African military engineer and Russian nobleman, Abram Gannibal). The African American Shakespearean actor Ira Aldridge lived in the UK but sojourned in Russia in 1858–9 and between 1861 and 1866, touring the Russian provinces where he introduced Shakespeare to many Russian audiences for the first time.[53]

In more recent times, the Jamaican poet and novelist Claude McKay also visited the Soviet Union in the early 1920s. He participated in the Fourth Congress of the Communist International after which he wrote very favourably about Russia.[54] He also penned the poems 'To "Holy Russia"'[55] and 'Moscow' that exalted the Russian Revolution and Lenin respectively. Aimé Césaire once claimed communism, but eventually renounced it because French communists failed to grapple with the dynamics of colonialism and refused to recognize the 'need to complete Marx' by recognizing the particularities of the 'Negro problem'.[56] The American poet Langston Hughes also visited the Soviet Union in 1932,[57] as did singer Paul Robeson, who embraced communism and settled in the Soviet Union in the

1930s; and the Trinidadian American pioneering communist and feminist political activist and writer Claudia Jones who, among other things, co-founded London's carnival, also visited Russia.[58] Jan Carew studied in Czechoslovakia and he travelled to Russia in the early 1960s as a guest of the Soviet Writer's Union. His *Moscow is Not My Mecca*[59] is a fictional account of the experience of Malcolm, a Guyanese student in Moscow, and the novel attempts to strike the delicate balance between critique of the Soviet leadership and bureaucracy and acknowledgement of the humanity and dignity of the Russian people. In more recent years, black British writers Caryl Phillips and Gary Younge travelled to the Soviet Union (Phillips in 1987 and Younge in 1991, the same year that *Tings an' Times* was released, on the eve of Soviet communism's collapse).[60]

Malcolm X, an oratory artist in his own right, once described capitalism as a 'vulture' that sucked 'the blood of the helpless',[61] a description that presaged Peter Tosh's and Black Uhuru's vampire analogies and that echoed Karl Marx for whom capital was 'dead labour, that vampire-like, only lives by sucking living labour, and lives the more, the more labour it sucks'.[62] On another occasion, when asked to describe his economic position, Malcolm declared that 'all of the countries that are emerging today from under the shackles of colonialism are turning towards socialism. I don't think it's an accident.'[63] However, Johnson's socialist poetic-politics are also in keeping with Amiri Baraka's 'Das Kapital', the Cuban poet Nicolás Guillén's 'Lenin', and Claudia Jones's poems 'Visit to the USSR' and 'Yenan – Cradle of the Revolution',[64] among others. When all is said and done he is a poet, and in *Tings an' Times* he invokes centuries of debate on perhaps the most pressing questions of our time: how do we find sanctuary from the cloud of despair and disillusionment that hovers above our heads? How can we more effectively struggle to bring about a new order, a new day? And what might the desired new society look like?

For Johnson, the collapse of those regimes meant 'now socialism has a real chance to develop and to take root. But what is necessary is that the term needs to be redefined by radical and progressive and humanist thinkers because the term has been discredited by so-called Communism'.[65] This is precisely what the poet set out to do in 'Di Good Life'. Of course, the poem is also dedicated to James in memoriam and is thus a kind of elegy for him as the embodiment of socialism, and Johnson's description of the wise old shepherd/socialism – a bedraggled, thin, bronze-skinned old man with white hair – bears a strong resemblance to the wise old man (James) in his last days.

In the inset to *LKJ A Capella Live*, Johnson tells us that 'Di Anfinish Revalueshan' (and, we might assume other poems of *Tings an' Times*) is 'an antidote to the demoralisation of the revolutionary spirit' and is not 'all doom and gloom by any stretch of the imagination'.[66] While we cautiously accept artists' interpretations of their own work as the gospel truth – artistic creativity works in mysterious ways – there is no logical reason to disagree with Johnson's general assessment of his own work in this instance, particularly when we consider the poems in relation to his earlier work. As he remarked in 1991, he belonged to 'the most advanced section of the black movement' in England that was 'certainly head and shoulders above anybody else' in what they were thinking and advocating for. This same grouping, which was centred around the Race Today Collective and John La Rose, was 'making connections with organisations like Solidarity', organizations that 'were fighting against totalitarianism'. He adds that in '"Wat about di Workin Class" ... I was making connections between the rise of Solidarity, the struggles of workers in Gdansk, and the New Cross massacre, which was a struggle against another type of totalitarianism'.[67] As early as 1984, on the album *Making History*, he explicitly engaged socialism and revolutionary politics in the poems 'Reggae fi Radni', Wat About di Workin' Claas' and 'Di Eagle an' di Bear'. In the last of these poems, both the capitalist system and the Soviet system are described as crisis-ridden societies in which workers contest the exploitation of their labour and the suppression of their freedom.[68]

'Di Good Life' is neither a struggle to defend socialism nor a plea on its behalf. On the contrary, it stands as the poet's affirmation that, in his own words, although 'we still no build di New Jerusalem', yet, 'the socialist ethos is not dead'.[69] The poem is not commemorative, nor does the poet attempt to trace political lineages. 'Mi Revalueshanary Fren' is followed in sequence by 'Di Good Life' on the album, and like the poet's dread blood poems, it is important to view the socialist poems of *Tings an' Times* sequentially, almost as if they are one poem divided into several interrelated parts.[70]

The Wise Old Shepherd

The Bible – its language, lore and poetics – has been a component part of the Caribbean and Afro diasporic literary and political tradition, and as C.L.R. James argued in his 'Letters to Literary Critics', the role of the critic is to understand the 'social and political assumptions of the work he is studying'.[71] As the Guyanese critic Gordon Rohlehr signals, 'At all times in the history of Black Jamaica, culture has had a religious basis', and more importantly for our purposes here, the same has been true for politics, 'and the reaction of people to depredations of politics and politicians has always had a clearly mystical basis. This is why it is difficult today to separate religious music from the music of open rebellion' in Jamaica.[72] While Johnson's conception of the world is not religious, religious symbolism has been a consistent part of his cosmology. In *Tings an' Times* he deftly draws on the biblical shepherd and his flock as a symbol of leaders and their followers, a practice that, according to Northrop Frye in his magisterial classic *Anatomy of Criticism*, has its parallels in other traditions dating back to ancient Egypt.[73] Johnson was nurtured on this biblical spirit as a child and, as a central part of the Western canonical mythos, the Bible is full of the 'metaphorical identification'[74] that Bob Dylan has also been drawn towards in his poetry[75] – and the same can be said of Mahmoud Darwish.[76] We should not, then, be surprised that the German philosopher Martin Heidegger, inspired by his compatriot poet Friedrich Hölderlin, described poets as those who attempt to trace the steps of fugitive gods while speaking the holy and guiding us towards the divine.[77] Poetry is metaphysical and otherworldly in so far as it can imaginatively take us beyond the present and into the promised land, that is to say outside of our immediate material modes of being and into becoming what we and the world can be.

We know that the Bible was historically used both as a tool of liberation and a whip of oppression that was interpreted and tailored to justify the enslavement of Africans in the Americas and to render slaves submissive. But the relationship between the Bible and people of African descent is complex. Adapting the Bible to their specific context, slaves in Jamaica, for example, established black-oriented churches that sowed the seeds of black nationalism and rebellion that struck mortal fear in minds of planters and slave owners.[78] The conjoined phenomenon of Rastafari and reggae has historically been revolutionary, chanting down the Babylonian system, and this is true despite what Carolyn Cooper refers to as 'The unproblematised identification of oppressed Africans in the diaspora with biblical Jews', which 'underscores the incongruities of cross-cultural mythologising'.[79]

By invoking the Bible, Johnson acknowledges the impact of the Good Book and socialist and Marxist ideas on Afro diasporic struggles to transcend the limitations of contemporary capitalist fundamentalism. If, as Derrida argues, poetry is about the revenant that both haunts and returns – not 'in the sense of Christian glory' but in terms 'of resurrection of language'[80] – then Johnson revives the language and lore of the biblical resurrection in order to resuscitate socialism. Amor Kohli, among others, has drawn parallels between Johnson and William Blake, highlighting the keen attention that both poets devote to London's dispossessed. J. Edward Chamberlin has drawn a similar parallel between the poets, and as Johnson himself acknowledges it is likely due to his use of biblical metaphors that he has been compared to Blake.[81] While Blake bears witness to the cries of the underclass, Kohli suggests that it is Johnson who gives them a voice that permits them to speak for themselves.[82] Blake has been referred to as Christianity's 'most radical biblical interpreter',[83] but both poets draw from biblical lore and imagery as metaphors for their respective times. In a 2004 interview the poet described the idea of the New Jerusalem mentioned in his 'Di Anfinish Revalueshan' as a way of restating Blake's idea of a utopian society, arguing that 'if we aim for a utopia we don't believe that we can get utopia, but if we aim that high I think we will get to where we want to go. Call me a middle-aged idealist if you like, but that's my position'.[84] In the same interview the poet also affirmed that his belief is socialism, that 'socialist ideas still pervade society and still offer the best option for working class people to liberate themselves from class oppression'.

In 'Di Good Life' and 'Tings an' Times' socialism assumes an eschatological tone as the atheist poet revisits his biblical roots in order to resurrect socialism. His use of biblical symbolism in the poems reconciles the Bible and Judeo-Christian radical religious tenets with socialism and the writings of Marx whose *Capital* was once referred to as the 'workingman's Bible'. However, as Fred Moten reminds us, unlike the European working class the voices of black slaves are muted in *Capital* as they are not part of Marx's representation of labour and the labourer – the European working class.[85] To state the obvious, slaves too were labourers, the literal and figurative embodiment of labour that played both a constituent and constitutive role in the construction of capitalism, as well as a fundamental role in the struggle against capitalist exploitation of labour.[86]

As Johnson suggests, movements ebb and flow and there are periods 'of intense activity during moments of extreme crisis. And then there's a lull, and then there's another movement and there's another period again', but these moments 'always come again'.[87] His cyclical sense of historical time does not predict with certitude that socialism will resurface, but as someone who was nurtured on the vicissitudes of black/working-class struggles in England and informed by the history of centuries of struggle against slavery, colonization and capitalist exploitation – and for socialism – the poet chooses to see human possibilities as opposed to hopelessness and despair.

So far we have made only indirect references to Johnson's socialist poems, while probing the political-aesthetic traditions and styles that have shaped them. As I have suggested, not only have these poems received very little critical attention, but critical analyses of his work have generally failed to linger in and ponder his socialist poetics-politics. Chapter 6 examines these poems and what they suggest about the prospects for socialism in our time.

Chapter 6

THE GOOD LIFE

We are accustomed to dealing in certainties, with having some clear and reassuring idea of where we are likely to end up. The Left does not much like venturing into uncharted territory. It is filled with suspicion. And yet there is surely something odd about the Left – a political force committed to historical change and to a different future – only feeling comfortable on well trodden ground.

Stuart Hall and Martin Jacques

By calling upon change – what the Africans call *nommo* in the Kongo language – by creating the concept of change, the concept of rebellion, the concept of freedom, you in fact encourage its encompassment.

Kamau Brathwaite

THE EARLY 1990s and the dawn of the twentieth century were in large part defined by two historically connected events that signalled new political moments and possibilities, and also foreclosures. The poems of *Tings an' Times* represent a continuum in which one poem informs the other in an ongoing conversation about the epochal changes in the world in light of the demise of the Eastern European communist states, the imminent collapse of the Soviet Union and the anticipated end of apartheid. This was a moment of deep uncertainty, a moment that engendered a sense of fear and hope that was eloquently captured by the visionary philosopher Cornel West during this shape-shifting time:

The present moment of massive social breakdown in America occurs at a time of epochal change in the Soviet Union and Eastern Europe: the revolutionary shift of authoritarian regimes with command economies. This collapse of bureaucratic elitist forms of communism – encouraged by the courageous visionary Mikhail Gorbachev of the USSR and enacted by the heroic working peoples in these countries – has helped revivify the spirit of the revolution in our day. Yet this epochal change warrants both support and suspicion. It is salutary because it reasserts the autonomy of integrity of civil society (e.g. individual liberties to speak, organize, publish, travel, and worship). It is also frightening in that it rekindles ugly xenophobia (such as anti-Semitism and chauvinistic nationalism) and unleashes harsh 'free market' forces. To put it crudely, the breathtaking anti-communist revolutions of 1989 affirm and accent the libertarian – not egalitarian – aspects of the capitalist revolutions of 1776, 1789, and 1848. Like those revolutions of old – and the present moment of the major capitalist power in the world, the United States – fundamental issues of employment, health care, housing, child care and education for all are being ignored and overlooked.[1]

West was not only conscious of the dangerous dialectic at play, in which communist decline augured both renewed possibilities of freedom or entrenched social and economic degradation and despair, but also the implications these changes could have in Africa, Asia, Latin America and, of course, although he doesn't name it, the Caribbean, including socialist Cuba:

> The profound tragedy of the epochal change in the Soviet Union and Eastern Europe may be a turning away from these fundamental issues – a kind of global erasure of egalitarian and democratic concern for jobs, food, shelter, literacy, and health care for all. This would mean that along with the unleashing of capitalist market forces on a international scale goes an unleashing of despair for those caught within or concerned

about the world's ill-fed, ill-clad, and ill-housed, especially those in 'invisible' Africa, Asia, and Latin America.[2]

West does not mention South Africa specifically, but his remarks anticipate the sense of euphoria and the predictable disappointment that South Africa would come to represent in terms of its neglect of its dispossessed in the post-official apartheid period.

This was the context, the political moment within which Johnson penned the poems of *Tings an' Times*, with four of the poems specifically about socialism and the meaning of freedom. Referring to the political life of a one-time revolutionary, the title poem's speaker describes the sense of demoralization and trauma that gripped many on the left after the collapse of official communism in Europe. The image of Auguste Rodin's thinker comes to mind here, as the persona, mired in an ideological conflict – with himself – attempts to come to terms with the past, and where his efforts and those of his comrades failed. The dejected revolutionary reflects on the deceit, corruption and intrigue that was characteristic of the former socialist states, as well as the failure to understand 'dat an di road to sowshalism | yu could buck-up nepotism | him wife dangerous | him bredda tretcherous | an him kozn very vicious'.[3] In this spirit, the poet deploys the image of light trapped in the dark ('now like a fragile fragment of lite | trapped inna di belly a di daak nite'),[4] perhaps recalling the biblical story of Jonah who was trapped in the belly of the whale for three days and nights (which, in turn parallels the death and resurrection of Christ after three days). It also brings to mind Herman Melville's *Moby Dick* as interpreted by C.L.R. James in his 1953 book *Mariners, Renegades and Castaways: Herman Melville and the World We Live In*, in which Captain Ahab's command of his crew and his obsessive efforts to capture the whale becomes a metaphor for the tendency towards totalitarianism.[5]

The poet's metaphor of a blind man who is 'stupified an dazed' connotes a sense of loss, dislocation and vulnerability as 'Mr. Man' drifts endlessly like flotsam and jetsam with the tide, 'laas inna di labahrint af life | if you like'.[6] The refrain 'if you like', used twice in the same stanza, casts a seed of doubt as to whether the image of a displaced, dejected and drifting revolutionary is real or a ruse, and whether the lost revolutionary will eventually land on solid ground. The perplexing political paralysis runs deep as the seasoned revolutionary licks his wounds and ponders socialism's woeful past. Plagued by doubt, he recalls the days when rebels fought against oppression, for freedom and justice; a time when 'nuff crucial trail did a blaze | tekin di struggle to a highah stage'.[7] Those effervescent days are contrasted with his thoughts on how young rebels of yesterday become old and inactive today ('some sell dem soul | some get lef out in di cowl | some get elevate | some get depreciate'),[8] while others have emerged as part of the middle class and, comfortable in their new-found sanctuary, have left the struggle behind.

Our speaker is not defeated and he acknowledges that gains have been made through previous struggles. Blacks are now in positions of authority and a black middle class has emerged with a presence in the media and other public positions. Nonetheless, he still wonders if there is the need for a messiah, 'anadah moses | fi tek wi craas di sea'[9] and carry the struggle to another stage. The poet's persona also wonders whether the days of the individual leader directing his flock to the promised land are over and whether it is now up to the population as a whole, 'each an evrywan' to rise up 'fi meet di dawnin af a diffrant age?'[10] Seen within the context of the poems of *Tings an' Times* as well as 'Reggae fi Radni', this question is clearly a rhetorical one and there can be little doubt that the speaker-poet believes that in order to bring the struggle to the next phase, each and every person will have to play their part.

The poem ends on an optimistic note. Though dumfounded and dismayed, the revolutionary is not defeated. He pulls himself up, digs deep down into the depths of his soul, and is able to find light in the dark and cling to a positive ray of hope, finally finding solace in the solemn. He consoles himself that out of decay and the ashes of the past new life can emerge as the sense of demoralization and despair are simply 'tings an times | wonders an sines',[11] a direct biblical reference to the supernatural plagues and disasters that were revealed to Moses and his followers in Egypt in the events leading up to the Exodus. Yahweh, god of the Hebrews, performed these 'signs and wonders' (Deuteronomy 7:12, but also mentioned in many parts of Deuteronomy) as a demonstration of the will of God to deliver the Hebrews from bondage. As the signs and wonders in the Bible purportedly augured the deliverance of Hebrews, so too does the pungent odour of decay in our time foreshadow a new day, the metaphoric New Jerusalem that is so prominent in the lore of Afro diasporic peoples. Despite his resort to supernatural biblical metaphors, the speaker cautions the listener/reader to 'noh get mystic | be realistic', returning once again to the mystical/reality dichotomy of 'Reality Poem' and staying faithful to his secular stance. Finally, in a parting word of encouragement, we are told that 'sometimes di pungent owedah af decay | signal seh bran new life di pan di way'.[12]

'Mi Revalueshanary Fren'

Communism, and the fear of it, was a global phenomenon, and while it is easy to acknowledge retrospectively its totalitarian nature in Eastern Europe, it is also true that communist support was instrumental to many liberation struggles around the world, including the struggle against apartheid. It was in part the fear of communist influence in South Africa as negotiations were underway to end apartheid that inspired the assassination of South Africa's communist party leader, Chris Hani, one of many incidents that augured tragedy in the post-apartheid period. As Rob Nixon prophetically wrote in 1991, racial allegiances and divides in South Africa shielded even deeper conflicts in this fragile society. While international attention shifted from the anti-apartheid struggle to the challenges of European unification, leaders of the United Democratic Front and Mass Democratic Movement, among others, were sidelined in favour of longstanding members of the African National Congress. Meanwhile, the apartheid government of F.W. De Klerk attempted to refashion its global image as it simultaneously colluded with Mangosuthu

Buthelezi's Inkatha Freedom Party to further destabilize the fragile state in a game of divide and rule.[13] Significantly, Nixon's article begins with a quote from Johnson's 'Mi Revalueshanary Fren', a poem that was released in the midst of these defining historical moments in South Africa and Eastern Europe; but while he presciently argued that it would be a mistake to misconstrue the end of official racism in South Africa with the end of apartheid itself,[14] he perhaps underestimated how apartheid in South Africa could realign itself along class lines under the rule of a black majority.

'Mi Revalueshanary Fren' assumes the form of a dialogue between two friends: one who probes the significance of the collapse of the communism in Eastern Europe while his Marxist-Leninist 'revalueshanary fren' proffers a standard, stoic and resolute routine response to his friend's musings. Framed by the collapse of the Soviet Union and the Eastern bloc and the impending end of apartheid, the friend insists on his conviction that the deposed leaders of the former communist states in Europe 'ad to go' as apartheid will soon be gone.[15] But rather than simply celebrate 'the fall of Eastern European regimes as a prelude to the revolutionary movement that will cause the fall of South African apartheid',[16] the revolutionary's adamant assertion that these regimes and their leaders all had to go, stated in a detached, distant, determined and declarative voice suggests the inevitability of the fall of the communist wall. While there may be a hint of celebration, the revolutionary conveys more a sense of resignation that these regimes were totalitarian and moribund, that it was obvious that they would collapse, that similar social circumstances prevailed in South Africa and that these conditions would also lead to apartheid's dissolution ('jus like apartied I will av to go').[17] Despite the suggestion that the poem shows 'no relationship between the demise of Eastern bloc socialism and the cause of black liberation',[18] we would have to extend our imaginations beyond reasonable boundaries in order to make this claim, particularly when we consider that Johnson suggests that the dialogue transpires between two aged black revolutionaries.[19] Our interrogator expresses his uncertainty about the consequences and implications of the collapse of Eastern Europe in general and for 'black libahraeshan' in particular, but he does not conclude that there is no connection between them. In a 1991 interview, Johnson recalled that he was part of a political movement since the 1970s that 'always knew that the struggles of the black working class in this country [England] had to build solidarity with other movements in other parts of the world',[20] and as far back as 1982 he was connecting black struggles with socialist and other international movements.[21] Notwithstanding Richard Iton's statement about the 'solidarity blues' associated with black–white collaborations due to the failure of the white left to contend with endemic racial exclusion,[22] these connections not only represent Johnson's views on international solidarity, but align black lives in England with these historic events in Eastern Europe and South Africa.

The dialogue continues as the speaker-interrogator comments on the way in which global geopolitical shifts have contributed to a feeling of insecurity, the same feeling of rootlessness that was expressed in 'Tings an' Times'. While bloodletting is employed metaphorically to provoke a sense of poetic-dramatic tension and movement in his earliest poems, here the poet invokes the image of a changing landscape, an erupting volcano with lava bubbling within, and shifting geological strata.[23] These images convey the idea that society is in a constant state of transition, that the only constant state is permanent change and that, just when it seems as though the struggle has reached its zenith, a new level or stage in the struggle presents itself. Yet the revolutionary, undaunted by his friend's insecurities and sense of dislocation, and still resolute in his convictions, pauses and then repeats the refrain that all the leaders of communist states have to go, as apartheid will eventually be gone.

Pressed for time but still not satisfied with the answers, our interrogator raises questions about Mikhail Gorbachev's glasnost and perestroika reforms in the Soviet Union. Gorbachev shook up the caretakers of the old Soviet regime and opened up the floodgates for much needed reforms:

soh Garby gi di people dem glashnas
an it poze di Stalinist dem plenty prablem
soh Garby leggo peristrika pan dem
canfoundin bureacraetic strategems

Yet, according to our interrogator, 'Garby' also opened up a Pandora's box in which the dialectic inherent in his attempt to reform a seemingly intractable system made it increasingly difficult to separate the predatory wolves from the sheep – those exploiting the new openness for their own selfish ends – and the genuine reformers:[24]

yes, people powah jus a showah evry howah
an eyrybady claim dem demacratic
but some a wolf an some a sheep
an dat is prablematic
noh tings like dat yu woodah call dialectic?[25]

Still unfazed by the interrogator's reflections, the revolutionary insists that all the communist leaders had to go.[26] Notwithstanding his reservations and a confessed lack of understanding of the significance of the changes in Eastern Europe for the West, and with his curiosity not fully satisfied and in the hope of resuming the conversation at another point, the speaker agrees with the revolutionary friend, but with trepidation, repeating the leitmotif that all of the former communist leaders had to go. While we might be tempted to read and hear 'Mi Revalueshanary Fren' as an anti-socialist poem and an appeal to liberal ideals, clearly the revolutionary – in a doctrinaire tone that ironically recalls the resolute convictions that stereotypically characterized communist leadership – suggests that the Eastern bloc leaders had outlived their usefulness and that they had to go in order to open up the possibility of a more genuine socialism. Here the dialectic worked against official communism as opposed to renewing it, its inherent contradictions leading to its demise.

In 'Di Anfinish Revalueshan' the poem's speaker reproaches 'Mistah Man' for his defeatism, reminding him that, despite challenging circumstances, changes have occurred for blacks in England, and that, despite the need to be 'still mindful af di minefields pan di way',[27] future change is possible. The speaker beckons Mistah Man to shed his shell and not dwell in the prison cell of despair, or what he describes as 'di doldrums a di daak nite' now that the 'sun a shine brite'.[28] Despite laying a solid foundation, there still remains a great deal of work to be done 'far wi noh reach mount zion' or the 'new jerusalem' – yet,[29] and the time will come when the speaker and Mistah Man will march again, a time to 'mobilise wi woman an wi fren dem'.[30] However, the poet's unfortunate paternalistic turn of phrase infers that men will lead the movement and bring women, friends and youth into the fold: that women and children are peripheral or external to the movement itself, contradicting Johnson's own suggestion that the black movement, shop stewards' movement and women's movement point the way forward for social change.[31]

It is fair to say that Johnson's last recorded poems (*More Time*, 1998) represents a departure, or perhaps a transition in this respect. As we will see in Chapter 7, the older, more mature poet is far more at ease meditating on love, life and mortality, themes that he has largely ignored in his earlier work. The recording, and his 2002 Penguin publication, includes a poem that elegizes the Afro German feminist poet and activist, May Ayim. But Johnson's allusion to women and children in the 'Di Anfinish Revalueshan' is also part of a larger lack in his poetry, and part of the ambivalence towards feminism that he expressed over 20 years ago. In an obvious allusion to the Wages for Housework Campaign that was initiated by feminist and activist Selma James,[32] Johnson expressed his befuddlement with the idea that women should be paid for housework: 'The whole business of "wages for housework" ... I couldn't really see it. Frankly, I don't see why women should get paid to raise their own children.'[33] He has also described feminism as 'a confused ideology' before qualifying his remark by expressing his appreciation for the work of bell hooks and Toni Morrison:

bell hooks, now she, among feminists, she's one person whose ideas I could relate to. I think, of all the feminist thinkers, she has brought a black dimension to feminism, she seems far more lucid than any of them. I don't particularly care much for Alice Walker's work, but Toni Morrison I think is a brilliant writer. As women, writers like Toni Morrison have broadened the black experience, and the human experience, by bringing a woman's perspective to bear on the core questions of Black Liberation, and individual liberation and freedom.[34]

There is an obvious disjuncture here as, despite his ambivalence towards feminism, the poet's appreciation for hooks's and Morrison's ideas is obvious. For Richard Iton, Johnson's poetry has traditionally placed 'emphasis on the political, cultural, and implicitly collective, and on emotional sobriety' and 'has also generally been linked to an absence of sensuality, sexuality, and female creative agency'.[35]

In yet another poem inspired by Johnson's work, d'bi young anitafrika's 'Revolushun I' is part of an ongoing dialogue with her older male counterpart (the poem's dedication reads 'inspired by LKJ'). Like 'Mi Revalueshanary Fren', the speaker begins with a declarative statement about revolution – 'bwoy mi friend | it look life revolushan come to an end' – within a political context in which 'di left is di right's right-hand man', essentially rendering left and right politics indistinguishable.[36] 'Revolushun I' is about disillusionment, a sense of hopelessness and despair, and the human void that is filled by a long list of American sitcoms and trash television and daytime soaps – *Friends, Seinfeld, Ally McBeal, Geraldo, Jerry Springer, Ricky Lake, All My Children, The Bold and the Beautiful,* and *The Young and Restless.* Television is escapism from the prevailing pessimism and it permits its audience to perpetually ignore daily realities that are far less attractive – poverty, homelessness, sexual exploitation and the sex trade (which the poet humanizes while acknowledging the hardships associated with it), the high dropout rate and the allure of brand names: soda companies, running shoes and brand name clothing as we search for an illusive identity in 'tables of labels'.[37] While 'Mi Revalueshanary Fren' is framed within the context of the collapse of the Soviet Union and the Eastern bloc, 'Revolushun I' draws on a different, though not unrelated set of politics and circumstances, but it is a nonetheless anti-capitalist, and even socialistic, poem in so far as she calls for a new politics and new society rooted in 'the people' who embody the meaning of revolution. While her list of revolutionary figures includes Amilcar Cabral, Frantz Fanon, Che Guevera, Stokely Carmichael and Steve Biko, her emphasis on the spirit of various 'wombanist' revolutionaries such as Queen Nanny, Assata Shakur, Sojourner Truth, Angela Davis and Winnie Mandela, distinguishes her poem from Johnson's. Moreover, while Johnson reminds us that freedom is not an ideology, but a human necessity that depends on the 'each and evry wan', we are still left to ponder on the prominence of women in the struggle for freedom.

Di Good Life

The Italian filmmaker and novelist Pier Paolo Pasolini has been described as 'the greatest poet of his generation'.[38] Like Johnson, he wrote about the failures of communism, and in the poem 'Victory' he laments the Italian communist party's failure to support the armed struggle of thousands of young Italian soldiers in the fight against fascism and Nazism during the Second World War, and later its inability to organize the strike of thousands of young workers in Italian towns.[39] While Johnson adopted C.L.R. James as his primary political influence, Antonio Gramsci was Pasolini's Marxist paragon, and his 'Gramsci's Ashes' perhaps best captures his assessment of communism in the post-Second World War period. On the one hand, Pasolini reconfigures Gramsci's politics in a poetic language that is devoid of the pretence that positions politics as scientific truth while, on the other hand, he values intuition and ambiguity in a manner that, despite his fidelity to Gramsci, recognizes that reason can lead us down the road to totalitarianism.[40] If 'Gramsci's Ashes' is a 'metaphor of melancholic negation' in which 'the Master, the Father of Italian Marxism' and the ideals that he represented appear to have 'dissipated in the dust of History',[41] then it is also possible to understand the scattering of Gramsci's ashes as the embodiment of new points of departure that suggest new realities and possibilities that veer from the constraints of 'History' contrived as destiny.[42] 'Great poetry is always an anticipation, a vision, of the collective future', according to Alain Badiou.[43] In this spirit, the poem's apparent melancholia is comparable to Johnson's elegy for James who died on the cusp of the collapse of official Eastern European communism.

'Di Good Life' represents Johnson's most explicit and succinct poetic expression on the failure of communism, and its afterlife. It is about the birth, death and ultimately the resurrection of socialism underscored by the notion that, as in nature, social phenomena have an immanent rhythm of their own, waxing and waning like the moon and evolving and developing over time. While this rendering of socialism is typically elegiac, it also parallels the poetic-philosophy of Kamau Brathwaite's poem 'Masks', the second part of his classic trilogy *The Arrivants*, a poem that invokes Akan lore and philosophy to explore the universal cycle of life, decay, death and regeneration. Surprisingly, very little attention has been paid to the connection between the two poets,[44] particularly considering that the Barbadian poet is arguably the most important poetic influence on him.[45]

According to critic Maureen Warner-Lewis, *Masks* is about 'the relationship between the conditions of hope and fear at a dawn period in the historical evolution of a people'.[46] 'Since history is a cycle', we are told, 'the sequence of migrations, for instance, will never cease. Men will be forever on the move and forever having to face the challenge of new environments.'[47] 'A cyclic concept of history also tends to lay stress on the rise and fall of nations, so that good times are seen following on from bad ones, and power is seen as containing the seeds of its own destruction'.[48] 'To look back into the past is therefore to learn of both achievements and corruption. This is why an honest look at history frees one from ignorance and self-deception.

It brings pride mellowed with humility, and therefore fosters a sane and balanced national sense of security.'[49] 'History also teaches patience,' Warner-Lewis adds, 'for it demonstrates that stability and achievement are the reward of determination and effort. This is why Brathwaite's poetry, while often analysing certain distressing aspects of human behaviour, in the long run emphasises hope.'[50] In 'Masks', Brathwaite employs the metaphor of a cock and other ritual symbols within the Akan worldview to register, according to Warner-Lewis, 'that after a period of relatively passive incubation during colonisation, the ex-colonials will arise from their dormancy to reassert their active dominance over their own affairs and chart the course of their own historical development'.[51]

Linton Kwesi Johnson appears to draw his sense of hope from the same well as Brathwaite as he imagines social change as cyclical and deploys images of natural phenomena such as droughts and blizzards, brown grass and green pastures, and an ageing shepherd who is well past his prime, all of which mirror Brathwaite's analogies. Like Brathwaite he argues that what is dormant today can be vibrant and full of life spirit tomorrow – that out of ashes, stench and decay can emerge renewed life which, having benefited from history and experience, has the potential to inaugurate brighter and more agreeable times.

Perhaps as an indication of the significance attached to 'Di Good Life' – although it may also be an indication of its presumed marketability at the time – it is the only Johnson poem that has its own music video.[52] In the poem socialism is coterminous with social change personified in the form of a wise old shepherd who survives floods, droughts and blizzards as part of the process of finding a route back into the socialist fold.[53] The poet returns to the 'some wi seh | some may say' of 'Reggae fi Radni',[54] proposing several alternative histories and descriptions of socialism while engaging in an internal debate about its age – whether it began 200 or 70 years ago (referring to the French and Russian revolutions respectively) – and whether it is a ghostly metaphysical phenomenon that haunts us like a duppy that has unfinished business in the material world; or a sage whose wisdom will guide us into uncharted territories.[55]

The duppy reference implies the revenant, that is to say the return of socialism, but in a new form. The spectre that Marx and Engels once wrote about in *The Communist Manifesto* still haunts us, although this ghost does not elicit the fear of totalitarianism, but is a response to it. A date is a spectre that facilitates remembering.[56] Dates, moments and names allow us to trace – to use a word from Derrida that echoes Heidegger – a certain kind of remembering that in turn facilitates commemoration of a moment or moments that are impossible to return to,[57] but that are nonetheless relived as the dates carry us back into the past, however fictitious or contrived, even if that past shows no immediate or likely attachment to the present. Allusions to the French and Russian revolutions in 'Di Good Life' not only imply that they were foundational moments in the making of socialism, but that they haunt our understanding of socialism today – particularly when we consider their internalized violence and totalitarian outcomes. They also haunt our understanding of the possibility or desirability – or undesirability – of reviving their spirits, as new possibilities for socialism and social justice are imagined in the present.

Ultimately these traces are not essential because nobody really knows the sage's age or where socialism began. But so faithful is the shepherd's flock that it clings to socialism/the shepherd whose role is to protect the flock. But now, in a period of political retreat and uncertainty, it is the flock that has to protect the shepherd,[58] which is stretched out and incapacitated on the decaying brown grass – an obvious symbol of imminent death – with 'di white hair pan him branze hed | like a kushan gense di weepin willow tree | lookin bedraggled an tin' (as James did before he died at the age of 88 in 1989) as if bracing himself for death. However, the poet-speaker cautions us to temper our concern for the shepherd/socialism because 'due to di heat a di time' socialism/the shepherd is sleeping 'like likkle bwoy blue' and dreaming 'bout likkle bow peep'.[59] Here the poet collapses the nursery rhymes 'Little Bo-Beep' and 'Boy Blue' as socialism, embodied in Boy Blue, falls asleep while his flock drifts away. In Johnsons' version Boy Blue dreams about the shepherdess Little Bo Peep who also lets her flock stray, leading to her tragic downfall. Bo Peep follows the advice of the Evil Shepherdess who corrupts Bo Peep's 'youthful idealism' that, in 'Di Good Life', embodies the ideal of socialism. Gender bias is inescapable here and, as David J.A. Clines argues, the 'little' in Little Bo Peep symbolizes the belittling patriarchal nature of the poem in which the persona is depicted as negligent for allowing her sheep to go astray, and the Evil Shepherdess embodies the stereotype of a woman as temptress.[60] Bo Peep also symbolizes the innocence – another gendered term – of socialism that, in the poem, has been betrayed and lost its way. But Bo Peep/socialism find their way as the flock returns to show the shepherdess the way forward. Meanwhile, the predatory 'isms' watch askance, attempting to confuse and even consume members of socialism's stray flock, in much the same that a hungry wolf stalks and attacks it prey. However, the imminent death of socialism is just a show, ruse or appearance, foreshadowing its own immanent re-emergence on the political landscape.[61]

As Johnson suggests in the poem 'Tings an' Times', the pungent odour of decay often implies that new possibilities wait on the horizon,[62] and despite the fact that some of the shepherd's flock has drifted away, the shepherd/socialism is just biding its time, presumably until the conditions are ripe for it to resurface. In the next round, however, it is the flock that will safeguard and protect socialism, personified as the shepherd. It is the flock that will 'shephad di sage' or the wise shepherd 'to a highah groun', on through to the next phase in the struggle for socialism. Unlike in the nursery rhymes 'Boy Blue' and 'Little Bo Peep' in which the shepherdess and shepherd remain the ultimate leaders of the flock, in 'Di Good Life' it is the flock, the followers, that resuscitate the anthropomorphic socialism – socialism with a human faces – and guides and protects the socialist ideal. Put in Christian terms, socialism re-emerges, but not in the spirit of the father, or even the son. The figure of Christ the bedraggled shepherd, once maligned, persecuted and crucified, is resurrected and finds salvation among his disciples, his faithful flock. It is the disciples, the flock, that become the new leaders, socialism incarnate, discarding the idea that salvation is to be found in or through a single individual or group. It is not the vanguard that leads, nor the maximum leader. As the flock takes stock and gathers its forces, it resurrects the socialist ideal and carries forward the struggle for social change, but not with the shepherd as maximum leader or vanguard party at the helm. Like James's notion of the party (in fact the antithesis of a political party, with thousands and millions of people behind it) Johnson's flock is the new vanguard, an anti-vanguard mass party that is the opposite of a party.

As he writes in 'Tings an' Times', the new day, the new society, will require the participation of 'each an evrywan' as opposed to 'annahdah moses'[63] leading his flock of people to the promised land. Johnson returns to the notion of 'each an evrywan', a rendition of 'di people dem' of 'Reggae fi Radni'[64] that also appears in 'If I Waz a Tap-Natch Poet' in which the speaker refers to the subversive nature of 'candhumble/voodoo/kumina chant' and 'ole time calypso ar a slave song' which, despite being banned, could be recited by each and every slave, from grand-parent to grandchild.[65]

Unlike the Russian writer Vladimir Nabokov, who attempted to turn the 'we' of traditional Russian communalism into the Western 'I',[66] Johnson is concerned with the collective 'we', that is to say the flock or the 'masses'. In this sense, he is also at odds with Russia's Alexander Pushkin who argued that every individual is a Czar,[67] though clearly, if every individual is a Czar, then there are no Czars, in much the same way that if the flock are now leading their shepherds then they are all shepherds and, by extension, shepherds no longer exists. If Nabokov symbolizes the transition from the communal I – akin to the reflexive I-an-I of Rastafari – to the Western 'I' of individualism and compet-itiveness,[68] then Johnson embodies the opposite, a shift to the communal or socialistic 'we' that extends above and beyond the individual. This is not about making grand leaps into history through collectivism while ignoring the creative capacity of the individual. Nor is it what Marx described as 'completely crude and thoughtless communism'[69] that 'negates the *personality* of man in every sphere',[70] or a skewed socialist system that suppresses basic individual freedoms and presumes to level down each individual to a minimum equivalent without accounting for variation and the diverse needs and talents we may possess;[71] reducing human needs to basic provisions such as food, shelter, clothing or healthcare and education, while ignoring the reality that, as social beings, we have other mental, physical and metaphysical needs and aspirations. It is the collective 'we' that leads to the 'crucial scene' mentioned in 'Reggae fi Radni' where the people enter the stage, the site of the unfinished revolution, with the goal of building a new society. This is the idea, the aspiration, the exercise of a collective will towards a more egalitarian society in which we are all free to explore the world's possibilities and realize our potential as human beings.

Chapter 7

MORE TIME

The diminution of work life in the formal economy is going to mean decreased allegiance to the values, worldview, and vision that accompany the marketplace. If an alternative vision steeped in the ethos of personal transformation, community restoration, and environmental consciousness were to gain widespread currency, the intellectual foundation could be laid for the post-market era.

Jeremy Rifkin

And why rail I on this commodity,
But for because he hath not woo'd me yet.
Not that I have the power to clutch my hand
When his fair angels would salute my palm;
But for my hand, as unattempted yet,
Like a poor beggar, raileth on the rich.
Well, whiles I am a beggar, I will rail
And say there is no sin, but to be rich;
And being rich, my virtue then shall be
To say there is no vive but beggary.
Since kings break faith upon commodity,
Gain, be my lord, for I will worship thee.

William Shakespeare, *King John*

TIME IS a crucial element in Linton Kwesi Johnson's poetry. In his early 'blood poems' his phenomenal sense of time is framed in terms of rebels who linger in that liminal space between social life and death, before those moments when they channel their energies in the direction of their enemies. His cyclical sense of time is also evident in his imaginative mediation on the life, death and resurrection of socialism in which he informs us that 'evryting is jus fi a time' as 'soon'¹ the populace will assume its place as leaders. For Johnson, time engenders possibilities that are transformative and transcendental, and as he suggests in 'Di Anfinish Revalueshan', 'time cyaan steal but it can heal' and 'di time goin come agen' to march to preserve past gains or win unrealized freedoms.² It is through the protracted struggle for change that the Good Life is achieved. But what exactly is the Good Life? The images of a green pasture, a tropical balm and the quiet serenity of a cool running stream where life is pleasant and calm tempt the imagination, but what is it that gives meaning to life and makes life more meaningful? At a time when the human imprint on the natural environment imperils the very existence of what we consider to be natural, these questions assume an additional weight and sense of urgency, and it is this subject that Johnson addresses in the poem 'More Time'. In many respects the poem is an extension of themes articulated in 'Di Good Life', but whereas that poem uses biblical allegory to resuscitate socialism from the doldrums of despair, 'More Time' describes how the new society would be qualitatively different from the old. The poem was released on the album of the same name in 1998 and first published in the selection of poems, *Mi Revalueshanary Fren*, in 2002, that is to say after his socialist poems; and like the poem 'Story', several of the *More Time* poems are reflective and introspective, presenting a personal side of Johnson that we have scarcely seen in his poetry. In this sense, several *More Time* poems are less a dialectical reasoning on socialism and more of an inner reflection in which the poet probes the meaning of love, life and what lies in the inner sanctum of the soul.

More Time also includes poems on the familiar theme of violence in the form of police brutality and acts of genocide, but together they represent a 'more mature meditation' on life, in Johnson's words, that bears the signature of a middle-aged poet³ who is perhaps conscious that there is more life behind him than ahead. 'Liesense fi Kill' is the most biting of the *More Time* poems. Using the dialogical approach established in 'Reggae fi Radni' and 'Mi Revalueshanary Fren', the poem narrates a fictitious conversation between two colleagues about the number of blacks killed in police custody in Britain. The speaker suggests that his 'crazy' co-worker is a victim of conspiracy theories, that there is no proof that the police have a licence to kill blacks. But when Kristeen recalls the names of multiple black victims killed in police custody and indicts the police and the authorities for their actions, including former prime ministers Margaret Thatcher and Tony Blair, it is her male co-worker who appears to be irrational and unreasonable, turning the gender-biased rational-emotional binary on its head.[4]

In 'New Word Hawdah' the poet returns to the theme of violence and bloodshed in *Dread Beat an' Blood*. As the poet has remarked, he took umbrage with 'the fact that as we move in towards the twentieth century, rather than moving towards a greater humanitarianism or a greater humanization of society, we seem to be moving in the opposite direction'.[5] But while the earlier poems focused on police and internecine violence, 'New Word Hawdah', a linguistic play on the term New World Order made infamous by George H.W. Bush, represents a scathing attack on the sanitizing of the bloodletting in the former Yugoslavia and Rwanda – along with the massacre of Palestinians in Sabra and Shatila – characterized in the 'brand new langwidge a barbarity',[6] shielding our emotions and psyche from the gruesome horrors of mass carnage.

Both 'Hurricane Blues' and 'Seasons of the Heart' meditate on the meaning of life and love, themes that, though not entirely foreign in Johnson's earlier work, nonetheless betray a more introspective and spiritual tone than what we have come to expect from him. In 'Seasons of the Heart' time is entwined with memories that fade into the past 'like grey clouds I in the sombre winter sky' as 'all our yesterdays are now become I the springtime of our days'.[7] This deep sense of loss as we pass our prime and into our twilight years is also captured when the poet returns to the familiar elegy in 'Reggae fi May Ayim'. Here Johnson hints at an intimate relationship with Ayim, letting us in behind the mask that he referred to in the poem 'Story'. Context is important for the decoding of poetry, but this is perhaps especially true in the case of elegies, and in order to more fully appreciate the Ayim whom Johnson writes about in the poem we need to know something about May Ayim's life and the circumstances surrounding her death. Who was May Ayim? How did she die? And what does her life embody for her elegist, and his audience?

We know that May Ayim was born in Hamburg in 1960 to a German mother, Ursula Andler, and Ghanaian father, Emmanuel Ayim, that she was adopted as a child and that she inherited the family name Opitz from her foster parents. As a child, she struggled to forge an identity for herself as an Afro German woman, and as an adult she challenged racial exclusion in Germany through her work as a community organizer and in her essays and poetry, including her book *Showing Our Colours: Afro-German Women Speak Out*, translated from German and published in English in the UK and US in 1992.[8] Along with other Afro Germans, she drew inspiration from Audre Lorde who, during her sojourn in Germany, had encouraged members of the Afro German population to organize themselves.[9]

Afro German struggles became even more acute following the collapse of the Berlin Wall, as old prejudices surfaced with a heightened sense of German nationalism and the resurrection of the spirit of the *Volk* (the people) and *Vaterland* (fatherland), resulting in increased acts of xenophobia and physical, verbal and psychological abuse towards Afro Germans and people of colour in the united Germany.[10] This situation was compounded by the fact that, according to Ayim, the German left and Euro German feminists failed to recognize how deeply embedded racial exclusion was in Germany.[11] Ayim captured the sense of dread that Afro Germans experienced in the early 1990s in the poem 'Blues in Black-and-White':

> the re-united germany re-celebrates in 1990
> without immigrants refugees jewish and black people ...
> it celebrates among close friends it celebrates in white

Ayim's 'Borderless and Brazen: A Poem Against the German "u-not-y"' also confronts the invisibility of Afro German identity in Germany:

> i will be african
> even if you want me to be german
> and i will be german
> even if my blackness does not suit you

and

> i will go
> yet another step further and
> another step and will return
> and remain
> borderless and brazen[12]

The speaker is defiant and resolute in her refusal to be defined by the dominant Germanic culture, instead claiming both sides of her ancestry, and on terms of her choosing. In another English translation of the poem, the form is slightly altered:

> even if you
> would like me
> to be
> german
> even if
> my blackness
> annoys you[13]

In this version the word 'German' is enjambed, emphasizing the in-between-ness of the speaker's identity, but particularly the fact that, even as a person of African descent, the speaker is German and will remain German, and that there is no contradiction between these identities. This, combined with the poem's sparse lineation, highlight the duality and oppositional dynamic tied to the speaker's identity.

192 / Dread Poetry and Freedom

Ayim committed suicide in 1996, jumping from the thirteenth floor of an apartment building after being diagnosed with multiple sclerosis and following a series of what appear to have been psychotic episodes.[14] As a result, Germany lost a valiant voice that had reminded 'Germans and the North of the fact that the racial cleansing carried out in the Third Reich did not only concentrate on the Jews, Roma and Sinti, but also other minorities such as people of African descent', and that these histories should be publicly known.[15] Moreover, while there is always an element of *Geist* in the elegiac form, and notwithstanding the haunting sense of dread in many of Johnson's earlier poems, the tone of 'Reggae fi May Ayim' is more spiritual and emotive than what we have come to expect from him. Its inaugural refrain sets the tone when it describes the conspiracy between life and death to shatter hope and the heart's fragile desires, while history and biography collude and bring anguish and despair into our lives. In May Ayim's case, the conspiracy between life and death ends tragically when she jumps 'thirteen stanzas' to her death, her final poem 'in blood pan di groun'.[16] She eventually flies away 'pon a wan way tickit to ghana'[17] to her final resting place to reside among her West African ancestors. The poem's liturgical ending adds to the elegy's spiritual sensibility as the soul of the 'afro-german warrior woman' presumably finds the inner peace in Ghana that evaded her in life in Germany.

The relationship between the two poets was both political and personal and we are left with the distinct sense from the poem that they were paramours, making 'Reggae fi May Ayim' one of those rare occasions in which Johnson shares his intimate personal life with his audience. Not even in his elegy for his father, 'Reggae fi Dada', does he expose himself as he does in this poem. Despite the poem's mournful tone, politics takes precedence over the personal as Dada becomes the incarnation of Jamaica's social and political decay. But 'Reggae fi May Ayim' conveys a combination of vulnerability, doubt, love, regret and spirituality, and there is a solemn sense of loss devoid of solace to the poem that is punctuated by the fact that Ayim's death was unexpected and that Johnson was clearly oblivious to the fact 'dat di kaizah a darkness' had captured her heart.[18]

The poet clearly wishes that he could have had 'more time' with May Ayim, or that he could go back in time. Time is naturally a crucial part of the elegiac form because it involves remembering, a liminal process of dwelling between the past and present in order that the bereaved may come to terms with the deceased's absence. In Jamaican speak, 'more time' can mean, among other things, 'see you later' and perhaps there is a small part of poet that is hopeful that his spirit will meet hers in the afterlife. In addition to his personal ties with her, Ayim's death embodies eclipsed possibilities in terms of the desire to transform German society for Afro Germans, and particularly Afro German women, as part of the transformation of German society on the whole. But while the tragic circumstances of her death cast a shadow over her life, they do not overshadow it, and this accounts in part for the poem's liturgical ending in which the poet gives thanks for her love, life, light and memories. An elegy can be as much about the elegist as it is about the elegized, and when we consider the *More Time* poems together, we are left with the distinct impression that the then middle-aged Johnson was more conscious of the fragility of life, and no doubt his recent bout with prostate cancer has added to his cosmic sense of mortality.[19] As the poet himself admitted as he approached 50 years of age, 'When you're involved in revolutionary struggle, you're wondering if you're going to die in a police cell'. He never imagined a long life, and as time has passed he has become increasingly aware of his mortality, a reality that he acknowledges has impacted his ability to write poetry.[20] Put another way, 'As things have changed, the urgency' to write 'has diminished'

More Time

Mourning is about acknowledging loss, according to Sigmund Freud in his famous 1917 essay 'Mourning and Melancholia', and the absence of mourning reflects a refusal to detach the libido-desire from the deceased, resulting in melancholia or pathological mourning.[21] In a sense, the mourner attempts to buy more time with the deceased by holding on to the past. Freud's view that mourning is principally about the mourner's ego and not about the deceased's has come under criticism, and as critic Tammy Clewell has argued, Freud reassessed his ideas in later work such as *The Ego and the Id*, arguing that mourning is an ongoing process that involves accepting and welcoming the idea that mourning is never complete; that melancholia (though not as an internal conflict within the ego) is an integral part of this ongoing process as the deceased, or at least the memory of the deceased, remains attached to the ego as the mourner works through death.[22] This said, I am somewhat partial to the Freud of 'Mourning and Melancholia', taking my cue from Leslie Chamberlain's description of Freud as an artist whose creative mind and research led to discoveries that can serve as important points of departure for understanding the human condition.[23] This Freud also equated mourning and melancholia with poverty, or at least the fear of being poor.[24] If we add to this the anxiety associated with political instability and take the liberty of stretching Freud's analysis from the mourning that is characteristic of an elegy to the mourning and melancholia associated with economic and political instability (and it is worth noting that Freud wrote the essay in 1915 amid the crisis and instability of the First World War), the question then becomes what would a world beyond the contemporary experience of economic and political neurosis look like? And how do we get beyond the collective sense of economic and political melancholia that characterizes our time?

May Ayim died in the aftermath of official socialism that the collapse of the Berlin Wall and the reunification of Germany symbolized. While this heightened moment of German nationalism evoked a sense of dread for Ayim and other Afro Germans, as we know from Johnson's socialist poems, this moment also symbolized a break from totalitarianism that, Johnson argued, augured new possibilities for genuine freedom, and this is the theme that the poet tackles in the poem 'More Time'. Having spent the last 20 years chronicling black struggles and working-class movements, and advocating for a new social and political order, the poet now gives us a sense of what a more equitable society would be like.

'More Time' posits an image of humanity on the move, marching into the twentieth century armed with modern technology and the increased level of productivity that new technology affords, and the prosperity that the revolution in the means of production promised:

> Wi mawchin out di ole towards di new centri
> arm wid di new technalagy
> wi gettin more an more producktivity
> some seh tings lookin-up fi prasperity
> but if evrywan goin get a share dis time
> Ole mentality mus get lef behine[25]

The monorhythmic sequence of the first four lines – technology, productivity and prosperity – is hardly coincidental. The compelling rhyme scheme registers in our consciousness the idea that technological innovation and productivity are require-ments for the kind of progress to which Johnson alludes. The image of a collective march into the twentieth century alongside the repetitive drumbeat keeps time and even sustains our sense of time in the recorded version,[26] while capturing the monotony and drudgery characteristic of mundane labour. Meanwhile, an upbeat melody signals the sense of movement, possibility and hope embedded in the shift from the old century to the new, from one stage of society to another, and towards a society in which we have more time for leisure, pleasure, reflection and introspection. In this sense, the poem has the feel of a march into a modernity that harkens back to 'Reality Poem' in which reality and modernity are counterposed with mythology and antiquity. However, the march towards progress is not a given: 'but if evrywan goin get a share dis time | ole mentality mus get lef behine'.[27] Returning to the 'evrywan' of his earlier work, the poet argues that everyone should share in the presumed prosperity, but that this is only possible if society abandons the outmoded mentality that governs the capitalist work ethos. The poem also calls for the abolishment of unemployment, for labour deployment to be revolutionized, the banishment of overtime and what he calls, in Rasta speak, 'a highah quality a levity'.[28] But what is the 'share' and 'livity' that Johnson refers to? He calls for more time to experience those things in life in which we take pleasure – time to live, breathe and reflect – but where do we find this extra time, particularly when the application of new technology has led to displacement, deskilling, capital flight and the *enforced* leisure that increasingly leaves labour in the lurch without compensation?[29]

Perhaps part of the answer to this question is proffered by another figure who was closely associated with Johnson. While C.L.R. James, Frantz Fanon and Aimé Césaire were important political and aesthetic influences on the poet, no figure was of more importance to his overall development as an artist than his mentor and close personal friend John La Rose. In a 2007 obituary, Johnson described the late poet and publisher as Black Britain's 'elder statesman':

> Like Marcus Garvey, C.L.R. James, George Padmore, Fidel Castro and Frantz Fanon, John belongs to a Caribbean tradition of radical and revolutionary activism whose input has reverberated across continents. The depth and breadth of his contribution to the struggle for cultural and social change, for racial equality and social justice, for the humanization of society, is unparalleled in the history of the black experience in Britain. He was a man of great erudition whose generosity of spirit and clarity of vision and sincerity inspired people like me. John was not only my mentor, friend, comrade, he was like a father to me. He was the most remarkable human being I have ever known.[30]

Johnson's respect for La Rose is also captured in 'Beacon of Hope', a poem he dedicated to his 'nocturnal friend' who is embodied in the image of the *peeni waali* (the Jamaican word for a firefly):

tonight fear fades to oblivion
as you guide us beyond the stars
to a new horizon[31]

It is worth noting that before he released *More Time*, Johnson's most intimate poem, 'Story', was inspired by a La Rose poem, and that it was La Rose who, among other things, exposed Johnson to the world of Afro diasporic and African literature when he was a young aspiring poet.

La Rose was an autonomous socialist who had been actively involved in the Trinidadian labour movement and left politics before moving to London in the early 1960s. Unlike C.L.R. James, he was somewhat sympathetic to the Soviet Union and acknowledged the role that it played in anti-imperialist struggles.[32] In addition to founding the bookstore and publishing house New Beacon, he served as chairman of the Institute of Race Relations which published the journal *Race Today* before it was taken over, with La Rose's complicity, by Darcus Howe and transformed into the magazine of the Race Today Collective. As a political organizer in Britain he was at the forefront of a number of anti-racist campaigns, including against police brutality, and was actively involved in the British labour movement and the African solidarity movement.[33] He also co-founded the George Padmore Institute, a research and education centre in London, the Caribbean Artist Movement, the Black Education Movement, the Black Parents Movement and London's International Book Fair of Radical Black and Third World Books (1985–95). According to Johnson, 'More Time' was inspired by a discussion in the 1980s during the book fair about the potential benefits of the revolution in modern technology and increased productivity, and how this had the potential to produce full employment by reducing the workday and freeing up workers to realize their creative potential.[34]

La Rose was an astute political thinker who possessed an acute understanding of international political economy, and in his 1996 essay, 'Unemployment, Leisure, and the Birth of

Creativity', he made the following assessment of the contemporary political moment:

> As the 20th century ends, the world we inhabit is living through tempestuous times. Old specters of fascism and nazism, religious and ethnic conflict haunt us, even in Europe, once again. In other continents, the ravages of communalism and modern fundamentalisms, subsumed in the earlier visions of progressive national and social change, resurface in all their barbarism. The promise and struggles of the early post-war years, though producing major advances in most areas of the globe, now face new dilemmas.[35]

La Rose's essay reads like a manifesto, echoing the spirit of Marx and Engels' famous 1848 book. His chief argument is that, with the incessant reordering and reorganizing of the global economy and the phenomenal part played by technology in the increased productivity of labour, there exists the potential for 'a shorter working day, a shorter working life, and more time for rest, recreation and cultural activity'. La Rose then juxtaposes this possibility to the less palatable alternative: the continuous crisis of the 'international underclass', the drug economy and ongoing 'social exclusion'.[36] These are the choices, and La Rose's clever play of dialectic suggests that 'Out of the terror and dislocation of time without work, without visible income, out of the womb of originally unwelcome leisure also emerge prodigious marvels of creativity.'[37]

In other words, La Rose argues that the forced exclusion and normalized 'leisure' of the underclass fosters creativity, offering hope that the world's socially excluded possess the potential to invent new possibilities of freedom, or what he describes as 'marvels of reality' that can eventually lay the seeds for a creative alternative to the contemporary global political economy.[38] In his analysis, political economy and poetics converge in an imaginative attempt to think through the contemporary global moment. La Rose argues that it was leisure time that facilitated the development of drama, philosophy and democracy in ancient

Greece, although he acknowledges that slave labour made this leisure time possible.[39] For evidence of this phenomenon, we only have to observe poor artisans in Port-au-Prince who have built beautiful works of art out of scraps of metal, or, as La Rose suggests, the steel pan music in Port of Spain, the emergence of reggae music from Kingston's urban ghettos, the blues and jazz out of the experience of slavery and segregation in the US, and the creative expression of rap music and hip-hop culture, for evidence of this phenomenon. Social exclusion, or 'enforced leisure', can serve as a catalyst for creativity that, when channelled into politics, may lead to creative alternatives to the prevailing system as opposed to mere 'social death', and liberating labour from the eight-hour workday and five-day working week offers the possibility of freeing up our time to develop our mental and physical aptitudes and to reimagine the meaning of politics and economics.[40]

'More Time' might be described as a poetic equivalent of La Rose's prosaic manifesto. In an age when our concept of time is rapidly being reduced to milliseconds; in a society where the use of technology has the capacity to considerably lighten our workload by shortening the number of hours that we work in a lifetime; at a time when technology also has the capacity to dramatically increase the productivity of labour at the expense of our physical, mental and spiritual health, and deplete and destroy the world's natural resources while toying with the very essence of nature; in this time, Johnson and La Rose bring us back to a simple truism: life is for the living and, as human beings, we all need the time and the freedom to develop our abilities and explore our potential. We need more time, not to simply exist, but to genuinely live and create.

In this spirit, Jonathon Martineau's recent book, *Time, Capitalism, and Alienation: A Socio-Historical Inquiry into the Making of Modern Time*, is timely. Drawing on Marx's conception of alienated labour-time under capitalism, Martineau highlights the transition from 'concrete time' in the pre-capitalist era to 'abstract time' under capitalism in Europe. Concrete time, as the term suggests, is associated with the material processes necessary for reproduction and is linked to natural processes such as digestion, pregnancy, sleep, childbirth, seasons, death, sex and agrarian cycles, among others.[41] Abstract time is specific to capitalist production, a system in which human labour is fused with and regulated by the hegemony of clock time – seconds, minutes, hours, etc. – and the constant need to increase productivity in accordance with the demands of capitalist commodity production.[42] In this sense, as Marx reminded us, capital is congealed labour, or human labour that is invested in products that are sold on the market – commodified labour that is disciplined and punished in order to control labourers and the labour process.

The response to the imposition of abstract time – not only in Europe, but across the globe as a consequence of colonialism and imperialism – is the desire for more time. This is, in part, literally a call for more leisure and pleasure, but also for a return to, or least the desire to be more in tune with, life's natural cycles, both human and environmental, which diverge from conceptions of time tied to the market; a desire to recapture alienated labour-time and surplus labour, the source of surplus value, through the recapture of time and the range of social practices attached to it that have been alienated and colonized by capitalism.[43]

Recapturing alienated time is tied to the persistence of resistance, which has been complicated in more recent times by the reality that surplus labour is no longer as essential to capitalist reproduction, part of the 'moving contradiction' of capital, in David Harvey's words, as the centrality of technology in the workplace takes precedence, leaving labour with a surplus of time.[44] However, if the process of creating the new society involves resistance and creativity and an appreciation of labour's compromised context, it is precisely this point that seems to be lost in 'More Time'. This absence leaves Johnson vulnerable to the accusation that the poem's politics present a plea to the powers that be, and that he no longer believes in human self-activity. In this sense, as a kind of poetic-political manifesto for our time, 'More Time' lacks the dialectical sense of possibility and creativity that is characteristic of his earlier poetry. The poet's appeal fails to even hint at a viable means of realizing the society he desires and describes in these dread times. But again, as La Rose reminds us, society's surplus labour, as a restive and precarious population, is full of creative potential. Capital's capacity to produce a vast array of consumer items could auger the possibility of a society free from want, but the whole point of the capitalist arrangement is to create wants that translate into the demand for commodities, both based on necessities and desires, desires that are often translated, through clever marketing, as needs. However, for capital and capitalism to fulfil the promise of fostering the leisure time in which we are free to live, be creative and develop our aptitudes, capitalism would have to be non-capitalistic. This suggests that modern technology would no longer be in the hands of predatory capitalists who exercise tremendous influence on governments. In other words, capitalism would have to be other than itself if it were to grant more human time for leisure and pleasure.

As Wolfgang Streeck suggests in *Buying Time: The Delayed Crisis of Democratic Capitalism*, capitalism has been buying more time since the crisis of the 1970s, biding its time by reinventing itself in-between economic crises, through incremental changes that have had a profound impact on the welfare state. Capital borrows time and lives on borrowed time by way of inflationary measures and accumulating debt,[45] but if capitalism has proven itself to be more durable, flexible and insidious than the generic left has historically understood, how does the more time that Johnson alludes to come into being? Where is the sense of self-activity? In 'More Time' the 'each and everyone' of his earlier poems is conspicuously absent, replaced by the appeal, a plea even – 'gi wi more time'.

I certainly do not want to suggest that Johnson should harp on the same themes, and in the same way, that have preoccupied him over the past 25 years. On the contrary, his capacity to evolve and innovate, to adapt both the style and the content of his poems to the ever-shifting political moods of our time, while also remaining true to his convictions, is one of the admirable features of his work. In this spirit, the poems of *More Time* include a new departure for the poet within continuity of his earlier work, and the 'new' is particularly true, as I have suggested, in terms of how he touches on the themes of love, life and mortality – all of which are tied to the concept of time. However, these themes seem to have come at the expense of the more phenomenological conception of tension, contradiction and change, all of which is, perhaps, a product of the fact that the poet's creativity is no longer fuelled by the poetics and politics of the 1970s and 1980s – the impact of reggae, the exuberance tied to his discovery of various Afro diasporic and African writers, black radical politics and socialism, and his direct involvement in grassroots political movements.

In a 1999 interview I asked Johnson to compare the more guarded optimism of *More Time* with the revolutionary musings of *Tings an' Times*. His response: 'what is clear is that we are not living in a revolutionary period now. I think a decade has passed and people on the left really have no reason to be despondent ten years later. There's always hope and it depends on the kind of changes that you're looking for.' He then added, 'There can be change outside of revolutionary changes; there can be other changes and change is what we're after. Sometimes these changes might be piecemeal, but if we can consolidate ... them they will present a good foundation for another time in history when more transformations can take place on a more decisive scale.'[46] In other words, the changes that we desire may not come about in a sweeping, cataclysmic fashion, but small gains today can and do lay the groundwork for greater social triumphs and successes tomorrow. When asked specifically about what change means to him, Johnson responded that 'Change is about altering the way in which we live, our relations with each other, the relationships between workers and employers, between people themselves, between classes and it's about giving people power; it's about realizing the ideals of a greater humanity, of humanizing our social relations and empowering people and eradicating all forms of exploitation and oppression.'[47]

Johnson emphasizes the everydayness of the struggle for change and recognizes the significance of smaller gains as a prelude to the broader social opportunities that may present themselves down the road. For him, this broader change is the result of a process in which, along the way, smaller victories are won, leading to larger ones, paving the way for more far-reaching changes. The political context has changed, and so has the tenor and tone of the poet's poetry and politics, but this should not surprise us. In fact it is perfectly normal. However, as he recently remarked to a journalist, Britain is 'still very much a class-ridden society', but 'I can tell you that I'd rather live here than a lot of other places I've seen. As a place, it's home for me.'[48] It is not clear what other countries Johnson was referring to, but his comment prompts the question, can the better living conditions in England be divorced from the history of slavery, empire and the persistence of underdevelopment, social inequalities and instability across the globe? In other words, his remark seems to ignore the reality that the relative affluence in Europe and North America has come at a terrible price for the world's dispossessed through the hyper-exploitation of their labour, the extraction of their natural resources and the economic, civil, political and military instability that the extraction and exploitation of these human and natural resources have caused.

Johnson's politics clearly cannot be limited to a single interview or remark. In a 2004 interview, for example, he argued that revolutionary advances in technology 'could create the objective basis for guaranteeing full employment in modern societies. If only we could have a shorter working day, the shorter working week and so on.' He went on to discuss the situation in Germany where trade unions have won the right to a 35-hour week as an example of the direction that things could take 'if there was a political will to allow masses to reap the benefits from it'.[49] But how is this political will fostered? Here the poet added an important proviso: 'You have to organize, you have to fight to get the political will. You have to bring about those changes because the status quo are not going to just keel over and surrender. That's not how capitalism works. People have to agitate and fight in the way that the trade unions are fighting for the shorter working day and the shorter working week.'[50] Clearly, then, when the poet speaks of political will it is not in the naive belief that government and corporations will, through some form of spontaneous humane epiphany, make sweeping changes that are in the interest of society's dispossessed. As I have said, his sense of movement and possibility, the belief that people have the capacity to make change has been the most enduring characteristic of his poetry. He has consistently projected the idea that social change is possible: that when the prospects for radical social change appear to be hopeless, new forces can emerge to bring about a new day, to make history. This, more than any other element, has been the distinguishing mark of his poetry and politics. But while he has held on to this perspective politically, in this particular instance his poetry has lost some of its political allure.

I might justifiably be accused of demanding too much from a poet and from a single poem. Poetry does not proffer economic-political programmes, nor should we expect it to. Notwithstanding the depths to which he has carried us so far, is it possible that we have reached the limits of the poet's ability to inform our understanding of the dynamics of social change and the nature of the new society? Poetry can inspire us to imagine beyond the present and to dream of possibilities that appear to be impossible, and Johnson has carried us far in this sense. As La Rose has suggested, any process of social change will no doubt have to approximate the kind of creativity and imagination that is characteristic of poetry and art in general. But a poem is not a substitute for the practice of politics or what we might loosely, and with some reservation, describe as a political programme. The challenge, then, is to capture the creative spirit that poetry and the arts embody, and to translate this sensibility, this potential, into political practice, into human possibility, but without forgetting that art is a component part of this process.

As we have already discussed, the worst and most far-reaching consequence of the power and prominence of the capitalist juggernaut is its tendency to alienate people from their immediate surroundings and reduce them to mere fragments of themselves. The alienation we refer to here is not only economic, and we only have to observe the lives of the affluent to realize the extent to which financial prosperity is not a protective shield from modern social disorders. It is precisely this injurious living that Hannah Arendt was referring to when she spoke of a 'twofold loss of the world – loss of nature and the loss of human artifice in the widest sense', a world of alienation in which we 'either live in desperate lonely separation or are pressed together into a mass',[51] an amorphous heap that lacks an independent identity and creative spirit of its own.

The struggle for more time and against alienation and commodification, then, is at the core of the struggle for human freedom and our need to be more attuned to ourselves as individuals who exist within a collective cosmos. Johnson understands this, and this is also the point that Jonathon Martineau makes in *Time, Capitalism and Alienation*:

> Reclaiming human concrete times of emotions, work, social relationships, human bodies, friendships, love, parenting, childhood, laughter, sleep, childbirth, childrearing, food production, art, the concrete time of our ecosystems and so on, thus forms an integral part of the reclaiming of our lives and our world. The struggle for 'decommodification', to employ a somewhat rebarbative term, also entails a struggle for the decommodification of human and socio-natural concrete times, the end of temporal alienation and the subjection of human and social lives to the dictates of the capitalist market, capitalist abstract clock-time compulsions and capital accumulation. As such, temporal struggles figure prominently in 'value struggles' over the very forms in which social relations as well as social life are reproduced. From this perspective, humans appear not only as world-making beings, but also as time-making beings, and if we conceive of history as a concrete process of becoming, the reclaiming of the concrete times of human and socio-natural life might also lead to a reclaiming of history and historical time by those who make it.[52]

Adding to this conversation, and in an effort to point a way forward, David Harvey writes in *Seventeen Contradictions and the End of Capitalism*: 'Alienation from nature is alienation from our own species' potential. This releases a spirit of revolt in which words like dignity, respect, compassion, caring and loving become revolutionary slogans, while values of truth and beauty replace the cold calculus of social labour.' In other words, and as John La Rose's writing implies, the contradictions within capital – crisis, precarious labour and alienation – might also help to create the space for revolutionary possibilities that groups and movements can take advantage of, if they are sufficiently creative and organized.[53] This is the hope.

Chapter 8

SEARCHING FOR THE FANTASTIC

A calabash does not need magic to stay afloat.

African proverb

WHAT DOES the 'we' embodied in Linton Kwesi Johnson's 'each an evrywan a wi' represent? What does it mean to be part of a collective? What is solidarity? Does it exist? Can it exist? And how is it tied to identity and difference? These are some of the questions that were posed during a conversation between the Martiniquan poet, novelist and theorist Édouard Glissant and Johnson in the short 2007 film, *Making History*. In the slightly disjointed discussion Glissant suggests that in the search for 'roots without roots', our sense of identity is ultimately tied to our social function, or perhaps better put, it is tied to our search for a mission in life in terms of what do we live for, and what we, presumably collectively, are working towards? The dynamics of capitalist alienation, the permanent sense and incertitude as we nonetheless drift deeper into political and economic dislocation raises these central issues, and times like these demand creative responses.

As Robin D.G. Kelley has argued, 'now is the time to think like poets, to envision and make visible a new society, a peaceful, cooperative, loving world without poverty and oppression, limited only by our imaginations'.[1] Kelley also cautions that 'unless we have the space to imagine and a vision of what it means fully to realize our humanity, all the protests and demonstrations in the world won't bring about our liberation'.[2] In other words, if we are to move past the present, we will need to creatively create and imagine social alternatives that transcend our understanding of what is normal, to extend beyond the deep sense of despair and woe. To paraphrase Audre Lorde's statement that 'poetry is a necessity', the artist's sensibility is essential to our sense of being.

In his thought-provoking 1999 book *Transforming Ourselves/ Transforming the World: An Open Conspiracy for Social Change*, the Canadian internationalist Brian Murphy draws on decades of experience in international solidarity work to remind us that 'just as technology is the extension of the human soma and rationality, so art is the extension of the human psyche, and the combined power of intellect and emotion'.[3] Art 'is the expression of the emotional integration of perception, of aesthetic and moral values, of enduring beauty and knowledge. Art is the expression of human vision. Art', says Murphy, 'personalizes life and reality, infusing existence with passion and significance'. Finally, 'Art is the avant-garde of human psyche, continually breaking ground on the frontiers of the possible, creating new modes of perception and *recreating the future before its time*. The artistic character of humankind is the most mysterious of capacities; subjective, emotional, intuitive, unruly and brash, yet refined and penetrating; radically individual, yet profoundly universal. If our technology and our use of it tell us what we are, art tells us who we are, and could be.'[4] Art, then, is life and it embodies the essence of creativity, the very kind of creativity that is necessary for thinking about, through and beyond the present predicament. In practice, this process involves thinking and acting in creative ways and developing a critical analysis of the particular political juncture that we find ourselves in.

Perhaps it has not been obvious, but written through Johnson's poetry, this book, as a meditation on social transformation in response to callous capitalism is, in many ways, about socialism, but with an important proviso: by socialism, I do not mean it in the coarse ideological sense of the word with all of its attendant baggage; not as a pure noun, but in the active sense, a pseudo-verb that represents a process, the desire for social change and the struggle to bring into being a just and equitable society, an egalitarian society devoid of the crass accumulation of wealth that is rooted in the exploitation of human labour and various modes of discrimination, and the attendant social alienation. This is what the combination of Johnson's socialist poems and the poem 'More Time' represent. While I am not beholden to the word 'socialism' it is important to define what I mean by it: a social, political and economic way of living that provides, but is not limited to meeting, the basic material needs of the population; a set of ideas, beliefs and values tied to the collective will of a society in which the majority of the population plays the defining role in determining its fate while striking the delicate balance between collective rights and the freedom of individuals to develop and realize their creative potential as human beings. In the final analysis, in practice it involves creative creating in ways that nourish the human spirit while not being wholly subsumed to the collective will; to be able to live without fear of discrimination, recrimination or reprisal based on gender, sex, race, sexuality, class, abilities or any other form of exclusion that denies us our humanity. To the extent that this is socialism, in this sense we can speak of it as a universal ideal that cannot simply be reduced to a set of ideas, debates and practices that have evolved within the context of Europe or limited to a Western conception of the world tied to pseudo-social and pseudo-scientific notions of progress and development.

It is this vision that represents the unfinished revolution that is lurking behind the scenes, waiting to make its appearance, and *Dread Poetry and Freedom* was written with this revolution in mind, beginning with the premise that poets often possess that unique capacity to perceive the seemingly imperceptible; the ability to hone in on the spirits and vibrations that emerge from within society, translating them into artistic expressions, often long before members of the public, theorists and social scientists are able to articulate their significance. Linton Kwesi Johnson has been one such artist, combining his literary talents with his political ideals. In many ways, his life embodies what it means to (as described in another context) 'intuitively engage creative transformative forces'.⁵ It is as a result of working and writing through Johnson's poetry that we have arrived at this under-standing of the meaning of the unfinished revolution. However, while, as a poet-*engagé*, he has been at the forefront of the movement for a just society in the UK and internationally via his poetry, Jamaican poet Mutabaruka's 'Revolt Ain't a Revolution' cuts through the flawed notions of development and progress as measured and determined by technological development and economic indicators in ways that anticipate 'More Time'.⁶

Mutabaruka repudiates Western rationalism, cultural chau-vinism and ideas of progress while raising issues such as illiteracy and the need to build schools at the local community level. He also challenges the idea that foreign aid is the solution to economic problems in the Global South. His pointed criticism of the false panacea of foreign aid echoes Paget Henry, the Antiguan author of *Caliban's Reason: Introducing Afro-Caribbean Philosophy*. Speaking on the prospects for Caribbean devel-opment in the current stage of global capitalism, Henry has argued that, given the current global crisis and its impact on the Caribbean, 'we will have to fall back on what is incontesta-bly ours', which includes 'food, land, beaches, territorial space, capacities for learning and for creative self-transformation', and of course music.⁷

Mutabaruka's message was ultimately written for the people of Haiti in 1989, but his philosophy is rooted in the spirit of the reflexive dread dialectic of the I-and-I of Rastafarian cosmology. As Velma Pollard, the Jamaican novelist and author of *Dread Talk: The Language of Rastafari*, suggests, the I-and-I represents, among other things, the relationship between the individual and the collective in ways that downplay individuality and emphasize 'oneness' or the idea that the pronominal subject and object are one and the same.⁸ These are all basic tenets of Rastafari, a religious movement grounded in the practice of self-reliance and a disengagement from the West's modernist mission.

In turning to the poem 'Revolt Ain't a Revolution' I am suggesting that many of the elements necessary for creating a new society, socialistic society, are explicitly stated: a communal sense of community, economic self-sufficiency (to the extent that an economy can be completely self-sufficient) within an 'embedded' economy à la Karl Polanyi, the sustenance of a healthy ecology and a more holistic relationship between human beings and between human beings and the cosmos. While, aesthetically, Mutabaruka's poetry generally lacks that alluring dynamic tension and sense of movement that is characteristic of much of Johnson's work, what Mutabaruka consistently does well is cut through the political miasma by speaking pointedly to power and to the prevailing politics of our time.

The new society demands that we reconceptualize the world in which we live and explore new possibilities and new ways of being. It then also means that we must, in our own ways, become artists capable of dreaming of and imagining the seemingly impossible in ways that I have suggested poetry permits us to pursue. By this I do not mean that we all need to paint, write poetry or perform music or some other form of art, but that we need to tap into that creative and artistic energy, to creatively create new communities and new ways of being and thinking in the world in order to break with outmoded ideas, notions, visions and practices that have outlived their time and which, even in their prime, served to benefit a few to the detriment of the many. At the dawn of the 1990s, Ambalavaner Sivanandan raised these issues in his inimical, not to mention polemical, way in his now classic essay, 'All that Melts into Air is Solid: The Hokum of New Times'. The essay's tone is characteristic of the time in which it was written, but Sivanandan's basic argument is that there are still 'communities of resistance' that have retained some of the values of the working-class movement such as 'loyalty, comradeship, generosity, a sense of community and a feel for internationalism, an understanding that unity has to be forged and reforged again and again and, above all, a capacity for making other people's fights one's own – all the simple things that make us human'.[9] These communities come together 'over everyday cases of hardship to help out each other's families, setting up informal community centres to help them consolidate whatever gains they make. These are not great big things they do, but they are the sort of organic communities of resistance that, in a sense, were prefigured in the black struggles of the 1960s and 1970s and the insurrections of 1981 and 1985'.[10] An argument could perhaps be made that, in the twenty-first century, much of what Sivanandan describes is more of an aspiration than a reality, but if so, it is precisely the aspirational aspect of his argument that is important here. It is this aspiration that allows us to imagine how communities can be organized to resist the contemporary craze of capitalist fundamentalism that discards environmental and human needs. In England, this 'new class' is comprised of diverse groups: women, men, Asians, blacks, whites, the young, the old, shopkeepers and householders,[11] and these groups represent movements that 'throw up, by their very nature' what Sivanandan describes as 'a multi-faceted political culture which finds authority in practice, tests theory in outcome, and works towards a wider political movement commensurate with our times but', he adds, is 'unrelenting still of its struggle against Capital. The point is to overthrow capitalism, not to join it in order to lead it astray into socialism.'[12]

During a 1998 public speak-out against the establishment of gambling casinos in Detroit under the guise of job creation, the activist-theorist James Boggs emphasized the importance of creatively reimaging the meaning of community and working towards building a new sense of community that challenges the logic of the market and materialism:

> We, the People, have to see ourselves as responsible for our city and for each other, and especially for making sure that our children are raised to place more value on social ties than on material wealth. …
>
> We have to get rid of the myth that there is something sacred about large-scale production for the national and international market. … We have to begin thinking of creating small enterprises which produce food, goods and services for the local market, that is, for our communities and our city. Instead of destroying the skills of workers, which is what

large-scale industry does, these small enterprises will combine craftsmanship, or the preservation or enhancement of human skills, with the new technologies which make possible flexible production and constant readjustment to serve the needs of local customers ...

In order to create these new enterprises we need a view of our city which takes into consideration both the natural resources of our area and the existing and potential skills and talents of Detroiters.[13]

The philosopher-activist Grace Lee Boggs echoed James Boggs's sobering words, arguing that the alternative to prevailing social disorder is to 'build resistance to the global economy by producing for our own needs, growing our own food, and producing our own clothing and shelter in environmentally friendly worker-owned and cooperative enterprises, thus setting an example of productive work for our youth and at the same time creating community and empowering people'.[14] According to Lee Boggs, people in Detroit have long argued that 'we have to bring life back into our neighbourhoods by producing for ourselves and creating our own community markets. We can't keep going to the suburbs to purchase our basic needs. We have to restore reverence for life in our young people by involving them in nurturing living things.'[15] Once again we are brought back to the significance of local initiatives in response to the economic and social decay that plagues communities as a result of neoliberal capitalism. No sweeping movement or single cataclysmic event is going to bring about the social changes that we are so direly in need of. There is no great leap forward.

To create, creation and creativity are optimal words here, and genuine, deep-seated, far-reaching change stems from assiduous, consistent, incremental work that starts at the community level as we foster a spirit of cooperation and interdependence. 'We have to create schools which are an integral part of the community,' according to James Boggs, 'in which young people naturally and normally do socially necessary and meaningful work for the community, for example, keeping the school grounds and the neighborhood clean and attractive, taking care of younger children, growing gardens which provide food for the community, etc., etc.'[16] As a final note from Grace Lee Boggs, we learn that 'quietly but unmistakably out of the devastation created by de-industrialization and years of grasping at straws ... *a new concept of economics* as if people, communities, nature and spirit matter is emerging in the center of the First World as it is emerging at the grassroots level in Africa and Bangladesh'.[17]

This is what the Boggses proposed in response to the historic decline of Detroit, their antidote to the Motown to Ghost Town, plantation-to-plant-to-prison pipeline phenomenon and the persistence of a permanent underclass in what was once the industrial centre of the US. Their analysis encourages us to imagine, envision and create the kinds of communities we desire and to commit to the kinds of actions we need to take in order to bring them into being: people-oriented communities in which the very social and economic relations we have come to accept and take for granted as the normal practice are altered and ultimately abolished.

Some may argue that we are being asked to dream the impossible, but as Hannah Arendt once wrote, it is the seemingly improbable that has historically made the probability of our existence possible:

> It is in the very nature of every new beginning that it breaks into the world as an 'infinite improbability,' and yet it is precisely this infinitely improbable which actually constitutes the very texture of everything we call real. Our whole existence rest, after all, on a chain of miracles, as it were – the coming into being of the earth, the development of organic life on it, the evolution of mankind out of the animal species.[18]

Others may argue that the challenges before us are insurmountable, that these initiatives and the values they engender are only local in effect and fail to respond to the urgent need for substantive global change. After all, who could have imagined in the nineteenth century that humankind would soon develop the capacity to destroy the world virtually at the push of a button, that clean water, the most essential necessity of life, would become a commodity over which, as some project, major wars will ultimately be fought, or that genetically modified produce would redefine the meaning of 'natural' and in the process jeopardize the existence of actual natural vegetation while taking a yet unaccounted for toll on our health? If the scientific achievements of the past 400 years, and especially those of the last 100 years, have affirmed human creative potential, they have also demonstrated the human capacity for tremendous destruction. Developments in science have facilitated the ability to navigate the universe and cure age-old ailments, and yet countless people die each year of preventable diseases, malnutrition and a host of other disorders. At least since the detonation of the first atomic bomb and the subsequent decimation of Nagasaki and Hiroshima, it has been abundantly apparent that scientific advances in the wrong hands can lead to unparalleled devastation.

Creating change begins with individuals who are part of communities. This is where change matters most to people. The local struggle is the international struggle, or more accurately, is constitutive of the international struggle, and by consciously making this link we find the makings of a genuine global movement in which grassroots struggles in cities such as Dhaka, Kingston, Accra or Cape Town are linked to similar initiatives in Montreal, Saskatoon Detroit, or Auckland. In other words, local initiatives do not preclude global change or an international movement, but are in fact a precondition for it. As people across the globe begin to take hold of their communities – while linking their efforts with those of other communities in their city, region, country and internationally – local developments become component parts of a global movement for our moment.

There are no guarantees of success in this world of exorbitant living in which the servile worship of material things is the standard. But we are speaking of a more profound commitment to life that sustains us, that is intellectually, spiritually and physically enriching, and one that is more appreciative of the simple things that make life meaningful. As Frantz Fanon put it, humankind is a *Yes*, full of endless possibilities, but we live with the knowledge that there are no guarantees other than the fact that if we do not make the effort to radically change the terms under which we inhabit the earth, and the logic that governs it, the future of humankind is doubtful.

Searching for the Fantastic

The seeds of this book were planted 25 years ago when the late Richard Iton introduced me to Linton Kwesi Johnson's *Dread Beat an' Blood*. Johnson's poetry and music brought me back to my early childhood in the London districts of Peckham and later Walthamstow, listening and dancing to reggae and R&B, but also evoked memories of National Front terror – that, as a person of African or Asian descent, you could lose your life if you ventured into one of 'their' neighbourhoods. But the introduction to Johnson was also part of a larger set of discussions and debates with Richard about politics and music, some of which have found their way into this book in ways that are not always easy to discern, even for me as the author. In a way, we are still posthumously engaged in those conversations, and even disagreements, and it is then fitting that I end this book by drawing on his critical analysis of popular culture, art and aesthetics, and politics.

In his celebrated book, *In Search for the Fantastic: Politics and Popular Culture in the Post-Civil Rights Era*, Richard had this to say about the relationship between art, creativity and politics, and overcoming the limitations of stifled imaginations in the modern world:

At the beginning of the twenty-first century, we seem to have agreed that there is no escaping this modernity – so wide we can't get around it – and accordingly, its problematics and implicit margins. Even our references to alternative modernities suggest a primary template that might at best allow certain variations on a relatively fixed score. My goal here is to understand what role popular culture has played in getting us to this point, and perhaps pushing against the grain, the potentially transformative, thickly emancipatory and substantively post-colonial visions these black performances might offer in their lower registers; their capacity to displace modernity as a master signifier within black and global discourse, along with its norms and modal infrastructures.[19]

'By bringing into view and into the field of play practices and ritual spaces that are often cast as beyond the reasonable and relevant – to the point, indeed, of being unrecognizable as politics – these visions might help us gain normative traction in an era characterized by the dismissal of any possibilities beyond the already existing.'[20] Richard is referring to the 'fantastic', that is to say the role of popular culture and aesthetics in the lives of African Americans and Afro diasporic peoples in general, a role that has been overdetermined in black life as a result of exclusions in the realm of citizenship and from conventional political structures. However, whereas these exclusions have historically been lamented, Richard suggests that we think of popular culture and the role of art as a part of the creative political possibilities, outside of the conventional boundaries, that have so far been largely neglected. In other words, he suggests that what we often imagine as being outside of the realm of politics – in this particular case the sometimes subterranean black popular culture and arts – holds the key, or at least a key, to imagining possibilities within the realm of politics in ways that supersede our understanding of what is possible; that get us beyond the lived reality of what is, and into the realm of what can be.

In light of his untimely passing in 2013, Richard has bequeathed us a message that encourages us to think beyond the performance of politics and persistent pessimism – beyond what Cornel West referred to back in 1991 as the 'tidal wave of popular cynicisms' and the haunting spectre of 'nihilism about the capacities of people to imagine, create, and sustain alternatives to the world-encompassing capitalist order'.[21] In so doing, Richard brings us closer to a more fluid and emancipatory conception of freedom by encouraging us to look past – but not ignore – the present in which black life chances are proscribed; past the strictures of dogma that confine human potential and towards a place where the fantastic is not a phantasm but a source of creativity and imagination that is invoked for the fulfilment of a future beyond the fickle and feckless politics of the present.

However, as he cautions in his parting, meditative essay 'Still Life', 'black reflexive politics' is strategic, and avoiding the pitfalls of political conventions is neither a simple or obvious process. Drawing on examples of the use of space and silence in the work of musicians and artists such as Miles Davis, Erykah Badu in the music video for her song 'Window Seat' and Toni Morrison in her novel *Home*, he suggests the following: 'If the expectation is noise and the commitment to visual ubiquity, a deeply radical politics might be correlated with aesthetic humilities, ablative disjunctions, intentional silences, hesitations, and invisibilities, among other means of confusing politics', or what he calls 'deorchestration', that is to say 'a reflexive and deliberate strategy according to which various confounding options are alternately chosen and false happy endings rejected'.[22] In other words, politics, like art, is a creative and strategic art form that necessarily avoids the obvious, routine, predictable and banal while embracing the imaginative and irreverent, manipulating space and silence as the examples of Badu and Davis suggests.[23] Put another way, what he describes as reflexive politics requires nuance, subtlety, temper, tone and an abandonment of teleos and, sometimes, those things that we consider sacred, including speech and the choice to scream and shout (yes, subaltern silence can also speak).

Lastly, in the final words of *In Search of the Black Fantastic*, we are encouraged to think about, through and beyond the categories that separate human beings and to investigate 'the way certain things are kept apart, and the capacity of the substances and processes associated with the cultural realm to deepen our understanding of these operations'.[24] Richard was in part probing how we might get beyond or cut through the boundaries that hinder solidarities, including 'intra-racial' solidarities, across ethnic and class lines. Some have argued that achieving these lofty goals are impossible, and there is no doubt that solidarity, particularly across racial lines and in light of the depths and persistence of anti-black racism, has thus far mainly proven to be illusive, as Afro-pessimists have contemplated and as Richard himself demonstrated in his book *Solidarity Blues: Race, Culture, and the American Left*.[25] The apparent impossibility of solidarity, a failure of many on the left – and in this instance I mean the white left that continues to derisively use the term identity politics to frame the experience of its Other – has led to identity entrenchment out of fear of cultural erasure and misrecognition. The white left and liberals consistently fail to recognize this, and continue to perpetuate an adherence to what Aimé Césaire described as a 'pseudo-humanism'[26] and, we might add, a pseudo-universalism and a pseudo-socialism (I say this without ignoring the dynamics that differentiate 'people of colour' in general, or people of African descent in particular), all of which negate the particular experiences of the world's condemned and dispossessed, in this particular instance people of African descent who are by no means homogeneous. Put another way, the thickness of whiteness and anti-blackness is all-pervasive, and until the depths and gravity of this reality, among others, is grasped, universal solidarities and the mission to build a more egalitarian world will continue to elude us.

History suggests that life is predicated on invention, which implies the kind of creativity that eschews skewed conceptions of society that reduce life to a preconceived common minimum standard at the expense of a genuine egalitarian society; a society in which creativity is not stifled by or sacrificed for the ideal of sameness; a society that, in turn, would engender new possibilities that are beyond what we imagine possible. If, in our daily lives and struggles, we can generalize a capacity to creatively create then, perhaps, humanity stands a chance; perhaps there is a possibility of recreating a world in which to be human is open-ended and not reduced to the limits of our presumed limitations and ethno-cultural or other filiations. The challenge, then, is to allow ourselves to continuously imagine and to translate our imaginings into actions that stretch the limits of what we think to be intellectually and materially possible, but in the spirit of not only doing what is best for humankind, but doing so in tune with the global ecosystem of which we are an integral but disproportionately influential part. If we can imagine such a world, and work towards it with a sense of urgency that is commensurate to the current reality, then perhaps we stand a chance at arriving at a place and time in which future generations will look backwards at the current historical moment as both a major turning point and a minor historical blip, and not simply as a time of feigned happiness and genuine dread.

POST-APARTHEID POSTSCRIPT

N October 2017, while I was in the process of fine-tuning *Dread Poetry and Freedom* for publication, I was invited to give a series of talks in Cape Town on the work of C.L.R. James. Given that I had begun writing the book after my first visit to South Africa in 2001, the fortuitous timing of the trip could not have been a better, more convenient finale to a journey that had begun there 17 years before.

A great deal has unravelled in South Africa since 2001, and the Cape Town that I encountered in 2017 was radically different from and frighteningly similar to the city that I had visited 17 years before. South Africa is a heavily contested political terrain where discussions about the relevance of race and/versus class, feminism, Afro-pessimism, Marxism, communism and socialism, among other issues and ideas, are debated with a sense of urgency, perhaps especially among the younger, 'post-apartheid' generation as they attempt to make sense of their society and its place on the African continent and in the world.

Following one of the talks, a student from the University of Cape Town, whom I later found out had been involved in the #FeesMustFall student protest movement, approached me. He questioned the relevance of James's ideas and the need to discuss race, class and solidarity. Wasn't it now passé in light of the work of Sylvia Wynter and Afro-pessimism? The dialogue ended abruptly, perhaps because I questioned some of the underlying assumptions embedded in his questions, including the idea that the work of Sylvia Wynter was incompatible with James's ideas.

During a talk on James's *The Black Jacobins*, I described the aftermath of a revolt in the north of Haiti against the leadership of Toussaint L'Ouverture. The revolt was carried out in the name of his of his nephew, Moise, and in response Toussaint had Moise, perhaps the most popular figure in all of Haiti, executed. I then discussed how Toussaint increasingly became an autocratic ruler, concentrating absolute power in his hands. A palpable moment of silence ensued. The audience in the room had clearly interpreted Toussaint's actions in relation to their own experience in South Africa, a bitter Fanonian lesson about how revolutions often eat their own, and how liberation leaders often betray the aspirations of the population.

On my last day in Cape Town I met with some young women and men who had been actively involved in the student movement. I listened to their stories, as I had over the course of the week that I was there, impressed with the level of political acuity and commitment, and conscious that they – even as they attempted to break with South Africa's recent, and devastatingly disappointing past – were part of a long tradition of political engagement in South Africa that had roots in the struggles of their predecessors.

Towards the end of the discussion I mentioned that I was heading to Preston, UK where Linton Kwesi Johnson would be delivering a poetry reading. Roshila, a middle-aged South African educator-activist, could hardly contain her excitement as she mellifluously spoke about the importance of his poetry for her generation as it struggled against apartheid. In those challenging times, poetry, song and music were like a political lifeline – yet another reminder of the impact of art as it crosses borders, through time and space.

NOTES

Preface

1. See postscript.
2. Of course the so-called Cold War was actually a hot one in which Soviet and US geo-politics played themselves out with disastrous consequences throughout the southern hemisphere.
3. Andrew Salkey, Interview with Estaban Montego, in *Havana Journal* (London: Penguin Books, 1971), 172–3.
4. Salkey, Interview with Estaban Montego, 173.

Prologue

1. C.K. Williams, *Poetry and Consciousness* (Ann Arbor: University of Michigan Press, 1998), 15.
2. Johnson intended to record a reggae rendition of his favourite T.S. Eliot poetry but the project did not materialize due to copyright restrictions. See Steve Heilig, 'London Calling: Riots, Reactionaries, and Reggae', *Huffington Post*, 25 August 2011, www.huffingtonpost.com/steve-heilig/london-riots-reggae_b_925870.html, accessed 10 December 2017.
3. Gaston Bachelard, *The Poetics of Space* (New York: Penguin Books, 2014 [1958]), 7.
4. Ibid., 11.
5. T.S. Eliot, *On Poetry and Poets* (London: Faber and Faber, 1957), 30.
6. Eliot, *On Poetry and Poets*, 31, 114.
7. Bachelard, *The Poetics of Space*, 11.
8. Sylvia Wynter, 'We Must Learn to Sit Down Together and Discuss a Little Culture: Reflections on West Indian Writing and Criticism', in Allison Donnell and Sarah Lawson Welsh (eds), *The Routledge Reader in Caribbean Literature* (London and New York: Routledge, 1996), 308–9.

Chapter 1

1. Kamau Brathwaite, in Chris Searle, *Words Unchained: Language and Revolution in Grenada* (London: Zed Books, 1984), 236.

2. C.L.R. James, interviewed by Robert A. Hill, 'On Literature, Exile, an Nationhood', in David Austin (ed.), *You Don't Play with Revolution: The Montreal Lectures of C.L.R. James* (Oakland: A.K. Press, 2009), 225.

3. J. Edward Chamberlain, *Come Back to Me My Language: Poetry and the West Indies* (Urbana and Chicago: University of Illinois, 1993), 88.

4. David Austin, 'Interview with Kamau Brathwaite', 21 July 2005.

5. Michael Dash and Quincy Troupe, 'An Interview with Édouard Glissant, March 22, 2006', *Black Renaissance/Renaissance noire*, 6(7) 2006, 50 (emphasis in original).

6. Dash and Troupe, 'An Interview with Édouard Glissant', 50, 52.

7. Ibid., 55.

8. Adrienne Rich, quoted in Chamberlain, *Come Back to Me My Language*, 153.

9. Dash and Troupe, 'An Interview with Édouard Glissant', 54–5.

10. Jacques Derrida, 'Language is Never Owned', in Thomas Dutoit and Outi Pasanen (eds), *Sovereignties in Question: The Poetics of Paul Celan* (New York: Fordham University Press, 2005), 107 and T.S. Eliot, *On Poetry and Poets* (London: Faber and Faber, 1957), 31, 32.

11. C.K. Williams, *Poetry and Consciousness* (Ann Arbor: The University of Michigan Press, 1998), 9.

12. James Joyce, quoted in Chamberlain, *Come Back to Me My Language*, 153.

13. bell hooks, *Wounds of Passion: A Writing Life* (New York: Henry Holt & Company, 1997), 109.

14. Jean Binta Breeze in 'Riddym Ravings', *Marxism Today*, November 1988, 44.

15. Carolyn Cooper, *Noises in the Blood: Orality, Gender, and the 'Vulgar' Body of Jamaican Popular Culture* (Durham, NC: Duke University Press, 1995), 82.

16. Williams, *Poetry and Consciousness*, 15.

17. Gaston Bachelard, *The Poetics of Space* (New York: Penguin Books, 2014 [1958]), 7.

18. Ibid., 7–8.

19. Mahmoud Darwish, *La Palestine comme metaphor* (Paris: Actes Sud/ Babel, 1997), 53.

20. Fred Moten and Charles Henry Rowell, '"Words Don't Go There": An Interview with Fred Moten', in Fred Moten, *B. Jenkins* (Durham, NC: Duke University Press, 2010), 98–100.

21. For analysis of this process see Christopher Small, *Musicking: The Meanings of Performance and Listening* (Middletown: Wesleyan University Press, 1998) and *Music of the Common Tongue: Survival and Celebration in African American Music* (Hanover: Wesleyan University Press/University Press of New England, 1998), 13, 357.

See also Rob Rosenthal and Richard Flacks, *Playing for Change: Music and Musicians in the Service of Social Movements* (Boulder and London: Paradigm Publishers, 2011), 114.

22. Cooper, *Noises in the Blood*, 118.

23. Aimé Césaire, 'Poetry and Knowledge', in Michael Richardson and Krzysztof Fijalkowski (eds), *Refusal of the Shadow* (London and New York: Verso, 1996), 138, 139.

24. Césaire, 'Poetry and Knowledge', 139, 140, 142, 143.

25. I'm grateful to Yael Margalit for pointing out these particular parallels.

26. Césaire, 'Poetry and Knowledge', 146.

27. Eliot, *On Poetry and Poets*, 31, 32.

28. Martin Heidegger, 'The Origin of the Work of Art', in *Poetry, Language, Thought* (New York: Harper and Row, 1971), 72.

29. Aristotle, *The Politics of Aristotle* (New York: Mentor, 1963), 419.

30. Pablo Neruda, 'Poet's Obligation', in Mark Eisner (ed.), *The Essential Neruda: Selected Poems* (San Francisco: City Lights Books, 2004), 147.

31. Alain Badiou, *The Age of Poets* (London: Verso, 2014), 25, 55, 56, 58.

32. Audre Lorde, 'Poetry is Not a Luxury', in *Sister Outsider* (Freedom: The Crossing Press Feminist Series, 1984), 37.

33. David Austin, 'Interview with Amiri Baraka', 21 June 2004.

34. Jeff Dolven and Joshua Kotin, interview with J.H. Prynne, 'The Art of Poetry No. 101', *The Paris Review*, no. 218, 195.

35. Martin Heiddegger, 'What Are Poets For?' in *Poetry, Language, Thought* (New York: Harper Perennial Modern Thought, 2013), 89–92.

36. Martin Heidegger, 'The Origin of the Work of Art', in *Poetry, Language, Thought*, 70.

37. Césaire, 'Poetry and Knowledge', 143, 144.

38. Darwish, *La Palestine comme metaphor*, 78.

39. Octavio Paz, *Selected Poems* (New York: New Directions Books, 1984), 21.

40. Alain Badiou, 'Poetry and Communism', in *Lana Turner: A Journal of Poetry and Opinion*, www.lanaturnerjournal.com/blog/alain-badiou-poetry-and-communism, accessed 29 October 2017.

41. Alejo Carpentier quoted in Cobas Amate, 'Lam: A Visual Arts Manifesto for the Third World', in *Cuba: Art and History from 1868 to Today* (Montreal: Montreal Museum of Fine Arts, 2008), 199.

42. Suzanne Césaire, cited in Linsley, 'Wifredo Lam: Painter of Negritude', in Kimberly N. Pinder (ed.), *Race-ing Art History: Critical Readings in Race and Art History* (London: Routledge, 2002), 293.

43. Terry Eagleton, *Criticism and Ideology: A Study in Marxist Literary Theory* (London: Verso, 1978), 88, 89, 98, 101.

44. Jacques Derrida, 'Language is Never Owned', 104, 106–7.

45. Williams, *Poetry and Consciousness*, 15.

46. Ibid., 28.

47. Simon Zhu Mbako, 'Introduction', in *Tell Them of Namibia: Poems from the National Liberation Struggle* (London: Karia Press, 1989), 8.

48. Searle, *Words Unchained*.

49. See Andrew Salkey, in Salkey (ed.), *Writing in Cuba Since the Revolution: An Anthology of Poems, Short Stories and Essays* (London: Bogle-L'Ouverture Publications, 1977).

50. See Barry Feinberg, 'Introduction', in Feinberg (ed.), *Poets to the People: South African Freedom Poems* (London: George Allen & Unwin Ltd., 1974), 17–18.

51. Linton Kwesi Johnson quoted in Maya Jaggi, 'Poet on the Frontline', *The Guardian*, 4 May 2002, www.theguardian.com/books/2002/may/04/poetry.books, accessed 2 December 2017.

52. Joe Lowndes, 'Linton Kwesi Johnson and Black British Struggle', *Africa is a Country*, 26 May 2017, http://africasacountry.com/2017/05/linton-kwesi-johnson-and-black-british-struggle/, accessed 22 August 2017.

53. Fred D'Aguiar, 'Chanting Down Babylon', in Linton Kwesi Johnson, *Mi Revalueshanary Fren: Selected Poems* (London: Penguin Books, 2002), xiv.

54. Linton Kwesi Johnson, 'Writing Reggae: Poetry, Politics and Popular Culture', *Jamaica Journal* 33(1–2), 50–1.

55. See Amilcar Cabral, untitled poem and 'Island', 'Return' in *Unity and Struggle* (London: Heinemann, 1980), xxi, 3–4.

56. Lowndes, 'Linton Kwesi Johnson and Black British Struggle'.

57. Amilcar Cabral, 'National Liberation and Culture', in *Unity and Struggle*, 141.

58. D'Aguiar, 'Chanting Down Babylon', xiii.

59. Sarah Morrison, 'Linton Kwesi Johnson: "Class-Ridden? Yes, But This Is Still Home"', *The Independent*, 2 December 2012, www.independent.co.uk/news/people/profiles/linton-kwesi-johnson-class-ridden-yes-but-this-is-still-home-8373870.html, accessed 30 June 2017.

60. Dred Fred, 'Dread Fred Interviews Linton Kwesi Johnson', *Race Today*, 9(1), February 1977, 23 (my emphasis).

61. For poet Fred D'Aguiar, Johnson represents the ideals of social justice and transformation that 'were true during the French and American revolutions and in a radical lineage of poetry that runs from Swift to Shelley to Clare' and 'remain as true today though banished from the political arena and confined to the arts of the imagination'. D'Aguiar, 'Chanting Down Babylon', xiii–xiv.

62. The term refers to the use of language and rhythm designed to raise the political consciousness of its target audience. See Amor Kohli,

The Demands of a New Idiom: Music, Language, and Participation in the Work of Amiri Baraka, Kamau Brathwaite, and Linton Kwesi Johnson, in partial fulfilment of the requirements for the degree of Doctor of Philosophy in English, Tufts University, August 2005, 2.

63. June D. Dobbs, *Beating a Restless Drum* (Trenton: Africa World Press, Inc., 1998), 111.

64. In 'Colonization Reverse' Louise Bennett writes: What a devilment a Englan! | Dem face war an brave de worse; | But ah wonderin how dem gwine stan | Colonizin in reverse'. *Selected Poems* (Kingston: Sangster's Book Stores, 1996), 107.

65. See Lloyd Bradley, *Bass Culture: When Reggae was King* (London: Penguin Books, 2001), 151–3.

66. The existence of blacks in Britain appears to predate the advent of slavery. According to the nineteenth-century Scottish historian David MacRitchie, there has been a strong African presence in Britain dating back to antiquity. In *Ancient and Modern Britons*, a two-volume work published in 1884, MacRitchie suggests that the progenitors of a number of Scottish clans were African. As early as 1596, the British Privy Council expressed concern about the number of blacks residing in England, despite the fact that having black servants and courtiers (many of whom married their employers) was considered a status symbol by the wealthy and British nobility. By 1764 there were estimates of 20,000 'blackamoors' living in England, and by 1789 the number had allegedly doubled with an estimated quarter of the British Navy being staffed by Africans. In addition to the African navy officers, the rest of the black population was comprised primarily of mixed-race slaves who accompanied their masters to Britain from the West Indies, Africans brought to Britain by British slave ships and black American loyalists who had fought alongside the British during the American War of Independence. Unlike white loyalists from the United States, black loyalists were generally refused social assistance in England, a situation which in no small way contributed to the miserable living conditions in which they found themselves.

Black servants in Britain frequently escaped to the city streets of London, joining the existing population of black vagrants. As the number of these vagrants increased, their conditions became so deplorable that, in an effort to rid England of its 'black problem' altogether, in 1787 351 Blacks were sent to the settlement of Sierra Leone along with Jamaican Maroons who had been deported to Nova Scotia, Canada, and some 60 English sex workers. These blacks became the first Africans of the diaspora to resettle in Sierra Leone, and incredibly some of them were able to reconnect with their African families.

Other individuals of African descent who helped shaped the political culture in Britain include Robert Wedderburn, who has been described as an 'anarchist, Jacobin, ultra-radical, and Methodist heretic'. Wedderburn was the son of a slave dealer and a slave woman in Jamaica. He migrated to London in 1778 at the age of 17 and became a prominent, and to the state authorities frightening, spokesperson for slaves in the Caribbean. Wedderburn defended the inherent rights of Caribbean slaves to slay their owners and even promised to write home to encourage slaves to murder their masters at their convenience. For detailed accounts of the black presence in Britain see Peter Fryer, *Staying Power: The History of Back People in Britain* (London: Pluto Press, 2010) and Ron Ramdin, *The Making of the Black Working Class in Britain* (Aldershot: Gower Publishing Company Limited, 1987).

67. Caron Wheeler, 'UK Black', *UK Black*, EMI, 1990.
68. Andrea Levy, *Small Island* (London: Headline Book Publishing, 2004).
69. See Ashley Dawson, 'Linton Kwesi Johnson's Dub Poetry and the Politics and Aesthetics of Carnival in Britain', *Small Axe*, 10(3), October 2006, 60–1.
70. Brian Alleyne, *Radicals Against Race: Black Activism and Cultural Politics* (Oxford: Berg, 2002), 31.
71. Stuart Hall, Chas Critcher, Tony Jefferson, John Clarke and Brian Roberts, *Policing the Crisis: Mugging, the State, and Law and Order* (London: Macmillan Press, 1982), 12–13, 34–9. See also Paul Gilroy, *There Ain't No Black in the Union Jack: The Cultural Politics of Race and Nation* (Chicago: University of Chicago Press, 1991), 82–111.
72. See Giorgio Agamben, *Means Without Ends: Notes on Politics* (Minnesota: University of Minnesota Press, 2000), 4–6, *Homo Sacer: Sovereign Power and Bare Life* (Stanford: University of Stanford Press, 1998), 119 and David Austin, *Fear of a Black Nation: Race, Sex, and Security in Sixties Montreal* (Toronto: Between the Lines, 2013), 159–60.
73. Gilroy, *There Ain't No Black in the Union Jack*, 80.
74. Fryer, *Staying Power*, 391–4.
75. For an analysis of biosexuality in the afterlife of slavery see Austin, *Fear of a Black Nation*, 11, 167, 182, 187168–176.
76. Hall et al., *Policing the Crisis*, 38–47, 121–3.
77. Peter Hitchcock, '"It Dread Inn Inglan": Linton Kwesi Johnson, Dread, and Dub Identity', *Postmodern Culture*, 4(10), 1993, 19.
78. Linton Kwesi Johnson, 'Fite Dem Back', *Inglan is a Bitch* (London: Race Today Publications, 1980), 20.
79. Ashley Dawson, 'Linton Kwesi Johnson's Dub Poetry and the Politics of Carnival in Britain', *Small Axe*, 10(3), October 2006, 61.

80. Mervyn Morris, 'Linton Kwesi Johnson' *Jamaica Journal*, 20(1), February–April 1987, 17–18.
81. Alleyne, *Radicals Against Race*, 156, and Roxy Harris and Sarah White (eds), *Changing Britannia: Life Experience with Britain* (London: New Beacon Books, 1999), 57–8.
82. Linton Kwesi Johnson, 'Sonny's Lettah', *Mi Revalueshanary Fren: Selected Poems* (London: Penguin Books, 2002), 27. Unless otherwise indicated, all cited Johnson poems are from this Penguin edition.
83. Prince Buster, 'Madness/Ghost Dance', Prince Buster Music, 1972.
84. See George Jackson, *Soledad Brother* (Middlesex: Penguin Books, 1971).
85. Robin Bunce and Paul Field, 'Obi B. Egbuna, C.L.R. James and the Birth of Black Power in Britain', *Twentieth Century British History*, 22(3), 1 September 2011, 407.
86. The Clash, 'The Guns of Brixton', *London Calling*, CBS, 1979.
87. Gilroy, *There Ain't No Black in the Union Jack*, 125.
88. For more on this see Vivien Goldman, 'Culture Clash: Bob Marley, Joe Strummer and the Punky Reggae Party, *The Guardian*, 14 September 2014, www.theguardian.com/music/musicblog/2014/sep/19/clash-bob-marley-joe-strummer-punky-reggae-party, accessed 9 December 2017.
89. In Queen's rock-operatic song 'Bohemian Rhapsody' the speaker informs his mother that he has killed someone and resigns himself to his fate with a sense of fatalism that is embedded in the tissue of Mercury's extraordinary voice and the protagonist's nihilistic view that 'nothing really matters'. In Ella Fitzgerald's rendition of Cole Porter's 'Miss Otis Regrets' the singer's incredible sense of time both normalizes and dramatizes tragedy. Violence is expressed in the measured control of her voice. In the beginning, we think we are listening to a love song or an innocent ballad, but before we have time to reflect we are abruptly transitioned to the shooting of a would-be lover by a woman and her subsequent lynching by a mob.
90. For a brief analysis of the poem see John McLeod, *Postcolonial London: Rewriting the Metropolis* (London: Routledge, 2004), 134 and 135.
91. d'bi young, 'Dear Mama', in *Rivers ... and Other Blackness ... Between* (Toronto: Women's Press, 2007), 21–2.
92. young, 'Dear Mama', 22.
93. For a comprehensive analysis of black organizations and politics dating back to the inter-war period in Britain see A. Sivanandan, 'From Resistance to Rebellion: Asian and Afro-Caribbean Struggles in Britain', *Race & Class*, 23(2/3), Autumn/Winter 1981/2, 111–52.
94. Harris and White, *Changing Britannia*, 64.

95. Keanna Williams and Lydia Amoabeng, 'Interview with Linton Kwesi Johnson', in *The British Black Panthers and Black Power Movement: An Oral History and Photography Project* (London: Photofusion, 2013), 75; Morris, 'Linton Kwesi Johnson', 18, 54; Harris and White, *Changing Britannia*, 55.

96. Morris, 'Linton Kwesi Johnson', 19 and Harris and White, *Changing Britannia*, 55. For an analysis of how the state, including the police, responded to black political groups in this period see Gilroy, *There Ain't No Black in the Union Jack*, 90–3.

97. Morris, 'Linton Kwesi Johnson', 18.

98. Williams and Amoabeng, 'Interview with Linton Kwesi Johnson', 76.

99. Ibid., 75 and Morris, 'Linton Kwesi Johnson', 19.

100. Lowndes, 'Linton Kwesi Johnson and Black British Struggle'.

101. Anne-Marie Angelo, 'The Black Panthers in London, 1967–1972', *Radical History Review*, 103, Winter 2009, 19.

102. Michael Eldridge, 'The Rise and Fall of Black Britain', *Transition*, 74, 1997, 34, 37.

103. Stuart Hall, 'Conclusions: The Multicultural Question', in Barnor Hesse (ed.), *Un/settled Multiculturalisms: Diasporas, Entanglements, Disruptions* (London: Zed Books, 2000), 222–3 and also Stuart Hall, 'New Ethnicities', in David Morley and Kuan-Hsing Chen (eds), *Stuart Hall: Critical Dialogues in Cultural Studies* (London: Routledge, 2005), 442–51.

104. Eldridge, 'The Rise and Fall of Black Britain', 38.

105. Ibid., 41.

106. Ibid., 43.

107. Williams and Amoabeng, 'Interview with Linton Kwesi Johnson', 75.

108. Morris, 'Linton Kwesi Johnson', 19.

109. See Austin, *Fear of a Black Nation*, 118, 138–46.

110. Bunce and Field suggest that it was BBPM members who chose to dissolve the organization because it had become too rigid in terms of internal discipline and the 'right moral codes', and *Race Today* was established in the aftermath of its demise. Bunce and Field, 'Obi B. Egbuna, C.L.R. James and the Birth of Black Power in Britain', 412.

111. Harris and White, *Changing Britannia*, 55; Morris, 'Linton Kwesi Johnson', 18.

112. Burt Caesar, 'Interview: Linton Kwesi Johnson Talks to Burt Caesar at Sparkside Studios, Brixton, London, 11 June 1996', *Critical Quarterly*, 38(4), December 1996, 64.

113. Fryer, *Staying Power*, 258, 259.

114. 'C.L.R. James and Studs Terkel Discuss *The Black Jacobins* on WFMT Radio (Chicago), 1970', in Charles Forsdick and Christian

Høgsbjerg (eds), *The Black Jacobins Reader* (Durham, NC: Duke University Press, 2016), 350.

115. Alexander G. Weheliye, *Phonographies: Grooves in Sonic Afro-Modernity* (Durham, NC: Duke University Press, 2005), 100–2, 202.

116. See Anne E. Carroll, 'Du Bois and Art Theory: *The Souls of Black Folk* as a "Total Work of Art"', *Public Culture*, 17(2), 2005, 236, 244, 249.

117. W.E.B. Du Bois, *The Souls of Black Folk* (New York: Dover Publications, 1994 [1903]), 9.

118. Du Bois, *The Souls of Black Folks*, 2. In *The French Revolution in San Domingo*, published in 1914, eleven years subsequent to *The Souls of Black Folk*, T. Lothrop Stoddard suggests that 'The world-wide struggle between the primary races of mankind – the "conflict of color", as it has been happily termed – bids fair to be the fundamental problem of the twentieth century, and great communities like the United States of America, the South African Confederation, and Australia regard the "color question" as perhaps the gravest problem of the future', (Houghton Mifflin Company, 1914), vii. We know how the three colonies that Stoddard mentions chose to deal with their native and black 'problems'. Stoddard's introduction serves as the backdrop to his account of the 'French Revolution in San Domingo', in which the author appears to be chiefly concerned with the treatment of whites by the former slaves in the colony.

119. Sylvia Wynter and Katherine McKittrick, 'Unparalleled Catastrophe for Our Species? Or, To Give Humanness a Different Future: Conversations', in Katherine McKittrick (ed.), *Sylvia Wynter: On Being Human as Praxis* (Durham, NC: Duke University Press, 2015), 46–7.

120. Wynter and McKittrick, 'Unparalleled Catastrophe for Our Species?', 47, 50, 51, 59, 60.

121. Anthony Bogues, *Black Heretics, Black Prophets: Radical Political Intellectuals* (New York: Routledge, 2003), 89, 91.

122. Eliot, *On Poetry and Poets*, 18–19.

123. Morris, 'Linton Kwesi Johnson', 18.

124. Johnson, 'Writing Reggae', 57.

125. Caesar, 'Interview', 65, 72.

126. Linton Kwesi Johnson, 'Dread Beat an' Blood' and 'Time Come', *Savacou*, 9/10, 1974, 26–8.

127. Caesar, 'Interview', 65.

128. Harris and White, *Changing Britannia*, 74.

129. David Austin, 'Interview with Linton Kwesi Johnson', 26 October 2004.

130. Alex Wheatle, 'A Conversation with Linton Kwesi Johnson', *Wasafiri*, 24(3), September 2009, 38.

131. C.L.R. James is the author *Toussaint L'Ouverture* (1936) that starred Paul Robeson in London; the groundbreaking Caribbean novel, *Minty Alley* (1933), and several short stories; two important books on socialism (or three if we consider the overall arch of his magisterial *The Black Jacobins*, a remarkable synthesis of history, revolutionary politics, socialism, Caribbean nationalism and Pan-Africanism) – *World Revolution, 1917–1936: The Rise and Fall of the Communist International* (1937) and *Notes on Dialectics* (1948), a Hegelian meditation on the contemporary meaning of socialism; and *Beyond a Boundary*, a philosophical reflection on the convergence of art and politics in cricket, a classic study of sport and a forerunner to the discipline of cultural studies. James was theorist and political practitioner who was a central figure in both pan-African and socialist circles in Europe collaborating with leading pan-African figures such as George Padmore, Amy Ashwood Garvey, and Kwame Nkrumah in the 1930s and 1940s and with Leon Trotsky in the 1930s, and eventually met with Trotsky in Mexico in 1939. His interventions in Caribbean politics in the 1950s and 1960s have a left an enduring legacy on the Caribbean and on the Caribbean left, and he assumed almost iconic status among the members of the New Left in the US and Britain while profoundly influencing Black and Caribbean politics in Canada in the 1960s. In short, James was a maverick whose work blazed a trail for subsequent generations and he is increasingly recognized as one of the great minds of the twentieth century.

132. C.L.R. James, *Minty Alley* (London: New Beacon Books Ltd., 1971 [1936]), 54.

133. Linton Kwesi Johnson appears to be referring to Dudley Randall (ed.), *The Black Poets* (New York: Bantam Books, 1971) but there were others, including Ted Wilentz and Tom Weatherly (eds), *Natural Process: An Anthology of New Black Poetry* (New York: Hill and Wang Pub., 1971).

134. Bob Marley, quoted in Richard Iton, *In Search of the Black Fantastic: Politics and Popular Culture in the Post-Civil Rights Era* (Oxford: Oxford University Press, 2008), 250–1.

135. Johnson, 'Writing Reggae', 56; Caesar, 'Interview', 66; Harris and White, *Changing Britannia*, 59.

136. Chris Jackson interview with Ishmael Reed, 'The Art of Poetry No. 100', *The Paris Review*, 218, 2016, 47.

137. Amiri Baraka, 'When We'll Worship Jesus', in *SOS: Poems, 1961–2013* (New York: Grove Press, 2014), 168. I am grateful to David Grundy for sharing his paper '"Hard Facts": Amiri Baraka and Marxism-Leninism in the 1970s', presented at The Red and Black – The Russian Revolution and the Black Atlantic, Institute for

Black Atlantic Research (IBAR), University of Central Lancashire, Preston, 13–15 October 2017.

138. Amiri Baraka, cited in Grundy, '"Hard Facts"'.
139. Amiri Baraka, 'Introduction', *Hard Facts* (excerpts) (Newark: Revolutionary Communist League, 1973–5), n.p.
140. Iton, *In Search of the Black Fantastic*, 9–10, 89.
141. For analysis of Baraka's shift towards Marxism-Leninism see Robin D.G. Kelley, *Freedom Dreams: The Black Radical Imagination* (Boston: Beacon Press, 2002), 102–7.
142. Amiri Baraka, 'Das Kapital', in *SOS: Poems, 1961–2013*, 162.
143. David Austin, 'Interview with Amiri Baraka', 21 June 2004.
144. Ibid.
145. Ibid.
146. Amiri Baraka, *Eulogies* (New York: Marsilio Publishers, 1996 [1983]), 44.
147. For a Baraka performance of the poem 'Wailers' within the reggae aesthetic see www.youtube.com/watch?v=NoknZIf3HLs, accessed 9 October 1970.
148. Johnson, 'Writing Reggae', 57. See Bongo Jerry, 'Sooner or Later', *Savacou*, 3–4, December 1970–March 1971, 12 and 'Mabrak', *Savacou* 3–4, December 1970–March 1971, 15.
149. The opening page of *Dread Beat an' Blood* begins with the following lines from Bongo Jerry's 'Mabrak': 'Ever now communicate, for now I and I come to recreate | sight, sounds and meaning to measure feeling | of BLACK HEARTS, alone.'
150. See Caesar, 'Interview', 68.
151. See Michael A. Gonzales, 'Gangster Boogie', *Waxpoetics*, 38, 2009, 90 and Elizabeth DiNovella, 'Linton Kwesi Johnson', *The Progressive*, February 2007, 35.
152. Sound systems were a crucial factor in the development and spread of Jamaican popular music, but as Dennis Howards demonstrates, before the sound system, juke boxes played a central role in spreading Jamaican music in the absence of significant airplay. See Dennis Howard, 'Punching for Recognition: The Juke Box as a Key Instrument in the Development of Popular Jamaican Music', *Caribbean Quarterly*, 53(4), 2007, 32–46.
153. Clinton Hutton, 'Forging Identity and Community Through Aestheticism and Entertainment: The Sound System and the Rise of the DJ', *Caribbean Quarterly*, 53(4), 2007, 19.
154. Ibid., 23.
155. Caesar, 'Interview', 66; Morris, 'Linton Kwesi Johnson', 20, 22.
156. Wheatle, 'A Conversation with Linton Kwesi Johnson', 38. More recently, Johnson has acknowledged the importance of William Blake as a poet, and Gerald M. Hopkins, the English Jesuit poet-priest whose innovative use of language struck a cord with Johnson

whose poetry, like Hopkins', according to critic Emily Taylor Merriman, resists the linguistic and rhythmic dominance of the English language. See Emily Taylor Merriman, 'We Naw Tek Noh More a Dem Oppreshan: Linton Kwesi Johnson's Resistant Vision', in Adrian Grafe and Jessica Stephens (eds), *Lines of Resistance: Essays on British Poetry from Thomas Hardy to Linton Kwesi Johnson* (Jefferson: McFarland & Company, Inc., Publishers, 2012), 227.

157. Wheatle, 'A Conversation with Linton Kwesi Johnson', 40. For more on Bogle-L'Ouverture see Margaret Andrews, *Doing Nothing is Not an Option: The Radical Lives of Eric and Jessica Huntley* (Middlesex: Krik Krak, 2014).

158. Linton Kwesi Johnson, 'Man Free', *Dread Beat an' Blood*, Virgin, 1978. For a full biography of Darcus Howe see Robin Bunce and Paul Field, *Darcus Howe: A Political Biography* (London: Bloomsbury, 2014).

159. The original *Race Today* was a 'race relations rag of the Institute of Race Relations', established by business and academic interests to 'study the natives'. According to Johnson, Darcus Howe, one-time member of the Black Panther Movement, was offered the editorship of *Race Today* and, 'with the collusion of John La Rose, then the Institute's chairman, and several others "hijacked" the journal's typesetter' and established a magazine and an organization in 1973. Morris, 'Linton Kwesi Johnson', 19.

160. For an account of the importance of John La Rose's life and work see Alleyne, *Radicals Against Race*, 111–44.

161. Caesar, 'Interview', 70.

162. Linton Kwesi Johnson cited in Bunce and Field, *Darcus Howe*, 150.

163. Morris, 'Linton Kwesi Johnson', 20.

164. Johnson cited in Bunce and Field, *Darcus Howe*, 161.

Chapter 2

1. Édouard Glissant, *Caribbean Discourse: Selected Essays* (Charlottesville: University of Virginia, 1989), 120.

2. Linton Kwesi Johnson, 'Jamaica Rebel Music', in *Race & Class*, 17(4), 1976, 406.

3. Linton Kwesi Johnson, 'The Politics of the Lyrics of Reggae Music', *The Black Liberator*, 2(4), 1975, 363.

4. James Baldwin, 'Song', *Jimmy's Blues and Other Poems* (Boston: Beacon Press, 2014), 21.

5. Johnson, 'The Politics of the Lyrics of Reggae Music', 363–5.

6. Joseph Owens, *Dread: The Rastafarians of Jamaica* (Kingston: Sangster's Book Stores, 1976), 2.

7. Linton Kwesi Johnson, 'It Dread Inna Inglan', *Mi Revalueshanary Fren: Selected Poems* (London: Penguin Books, 2002), 25–6.

8. Mervyn Alleyne, *Roots of Jamaican Culture* (London: Pluto Press, 1989), 146–7. For an in-depth study of 'dread talk' and its contribution to the Jamaican lexicon see Velma Pollard, *Dread Talk: The Language of Rastafari* (Montreal and Kingston: McGill-Queen's University Press, 2000).

9. Johnson, 'Yout Scene', *Mi Revalueshanary Fren*, 3.

10. Johnson, 'Double Scank', *Mi Revalueshanary Fren*, 4.

11. Johnson, 'Dread Beat an Blood', *Mi Revalueshanary Fren*, 6.

12. Johnson, 'Five Nights of Bleeding', *Mi Revalueshanary Fren*, 7.

13. Johnson, 'Street 66', *Mi Revalueshanary Fren*, 9–10.

14. Louis Chude-Sokei, *The Sound of Culture: Diaspora and Black Technopoetics* (Middletown: Wesleyan College, 2016), 187–8.

15. Gordon Rohlehr, 'West Indian Poetry: Some Problems of Assessment I', Allison Donnell and Sarah Lawson Welsh (eds), *The Routledge Reader in Caribbean Literature* (London and New York: Routledge, 1996), 320.

16. Rohlehr, 'West Indian Poetry', 322.

17. Sylvia Wynter, 'The Counterdoctrine of Jamesian Poiesis', in Paget Henry and Paul Buhle (eds), *C.L.R. James Caribbean* (Durham, NC: Duke University Press, 1992), 72.

18. Owens, *Dread*, 3.

19. Paget Henry, 'Rastafarianism and the Reality of Dread', in Lewis R. Gordon (ed.), *Existence in Black: An Anthology of Black Existentialist Philosophy* (New York: Routledge, 1997), 157–8.

20. Henry, 'Rastafarianism and the Reality of Dread', 158.

21. Ibid., 159. According to Horace Campbell, in addition to Marcus Garvey's *The Blackman*, which operated out of London, another major influence on early Rastafarian beliefs was the Ethiopian World Federation (EWF) and its newspaper, *Voice of Ethiopia*. The EWF was founded by the cousin of Emperor Haile Selassie, Dr Malaku Bayen, in order to mobilize support against the Italian invasion and occupation of Ethiopia. Campbell suggests that 'adherents of black nationalism accepted literally the claim of the Ethiopian World Federation that Haile Selassie was the Elect of God and Light of the World. When the *Voice of Ethiopia* added that the true Israelites were black and that Africans formed the Twelve Tribes of Israel, giving an historical account of the Falashas who, it claimed, had carried the Ark of the Covenant back to Ethiopia, many Rastas believed that blacks were indeed children of Israel.' Horace Campbell, *Rasta and Resistance: From Marcus Garvey to Walter Rodney* (Trenton: Africa World Press, 1987), 77. In the 1950s, African liberation movements, notably the Land and Freedom Army, the Mau Mau of Kenya, also influenced and inspired Rastas.

236 / *Dread Poetry and Freedom*

In fact, the locks that have become the most identifiable physical
feature of Rastafari are said to have been inspired by Rastas who
saw pictures of members of the Mau Mau who wore their hair
in locks (Campbell, *Rasta and Resistance*, 95). They also found
justification in the Bible, Numbers 6:5, which reads 'All the days
of the nazirite vow no razor shall come upon the head; until the
time is completed for which they separate themselves to the Lord,
they shall be holy; they shall let the locks of the head grow long.'
In addition to Emperor Haile Selassie, other African leaders whose
work would later inspire Rastafari include Kwame Nkrumah of
Ghana, Patrice Lumumba of the Congo, and Jomo Kenyatta of
Kenya. Campbell also claims that King Ja Ja of Opobo, an Ibo ruler
in part of what is present-day Nigeria, also had an influence on
Rastafari. King Ja Ja fought valiantly against the European traders
and the British government and in 1887 he was finally exiled to
the Caribbean (Barbados and St Vincent) where his memory is
preserved in folk songs. Even in exile, King Ja Ja challenged British
colonial authority. Campbell suggests that Rastas linked the biblical
meaning of Jah with that of King Ja Ja, hence the common Rasta
chant, Jah Rastafari! (Campbell, *Rasta and Resistance*, 102, 103).

22. Nathaniel Samuel Murrell and Lewin Williams, 'The Black
Biblical Hermeneutics of Rastafari', in Nathaniel Samuel Murrell,
William David Spencer and Adrian Anthony McFarlane (eds),
Chanting Down Babylon: The Rastafari Reader (Philadelphia: Temple
University Press, 1998), 329–30.

23. Burning Spear, 'Marcus Garvey Dread', *Marcus Garvey*, Island
Records, 1976.

24. Big Youth, 'Marcus Garvey Dread', *Dreadlocks Dread*, Front Line,
1978.

25. Murrell and Williams, 'The Black Biblical Hermeneutics of
Rastafari', 324–5, 335–6, 337, 340.

26. Maya Jaggi, 'Poet on the Frontline', *The Guardian*, 4 May 2002,
www.theguardian.com/books/2002/may/04/poetry.books, accessed
2 December 2017.

27. Linton Kwesi Johnson, 'Writing Reggae: Poetry, Politics and
Popular Culture', *Jamaica Journal*, 33(1–2), December 2010, 56.

28. Dred Fred, 'Dread Fred Interviews Linton Kwesi Johnson', *Race
Today*, 9(1), February 1977, 23; Alex Wheatle, 'A Conversation
with Linton Kwesi Johnson', *Wasafiri*, 24(3), September 2009, 41.
This autonomous creative spirit guided his work and his attitude
towards publishing and he refused to seek literary recognition from
mainstream publishers. Instead he sought acknowledgement from
the culture and community that inspired his work, and to this end
his early work was published by Bogle-L'Ouverture and other small
independent presses. See Wheatle, 'A Conversation with Linton

Kwesi Johnson', 40. For more on Bogle-L'Ouverture see Margaret Andrews, *Doing Nothing is Not an Option: The Radical Lives of Eric and Jessica Huntley* (Middlesex: Krik Krak, 2014).

29. Mervyn Morris, 'Linton Kwesi Johnson' *Jamaica Journal*, 20(1), February–April 1987, 22.

30. Tony Whyton, *Beyond a Love Supreme: John Coltrane and the Legacy of an Album* (Oxford: Oxford University Press, 2013), 25.

31. Chude-Sokei, *The Sound of Culture*, 196; Michael Eldridge, 'The Rise and Fall of Black Britain', *Transition*, 74, 1997, 43.

32. Peter Hitchcock, '"It Dread Inn Inglan": Linton Kwesi Johnson, Dread, and Dub Identity', *Postmodern Culture*, 4(10), 1993, 22.

33. Phanuel Antwi, 'Dub Poetry as Black Atlantic Body-Arcive', *Small Axe*, 48, November 2015, 68–9.

34. Chude-Sokei, *The Sound of Culture*, 162–3.

35. The poet was nonetheless surprised to discover some years later that Onuora was using the term dub poetry to describe what was, in essence, what he had initially labelled reggae poetry. The term was later generically applied, incorporating the work of a number of poets, including Johnson, Mutabaruka, Michael Smith, Jean Binta Breeze and Canadian-based poets Lillian Allen and Clifton Joseph, among others. The last two adopted the term dub poetry when Allen met Oku in Cuba at the International Festival of Youth and Students in 1978. Christian Habekost, *Verbal Riddim: The Politics and Aesthetics of Afro-Caribbean Dub Poetry* (Amsterdam: Editions Radophi, 1993), 33.

36. Morris, 'Linton Kwesi Johnson', 25.

37. Shalini Puri, 'Beyond Resistance: Notes Toward a New Caribbean Cultural Studies', *Small Axe*, 7(2), September 2003, 33.

38. Kwame Dawes, *Natural Mysticism: Towards a Reggae Aesthetic* (Leeds: Peepal Tree, 1999), 83.

39. Ibid., 18, 69–70, 82.

40. Ibid., 81.

41. Robert J. Stewart, 'Linton Kwesi Johnson: Poetry Down a Reggae Wire', *New West Indian Guide*, 67(1/2), 1993, 71.

42. J. Edward Chamberlain, *Come Back to Me My Language: Poetry and the West Indies* (Urbana and Chicago: University of Illinois, 1993), 143.

43. Burt Caesar, 'Interview: Linton Kwesi Johnson Talks to Burt Caesar at Sparkside Studios, Brixton, London, 11 June 1996', *Critical Quarterly*, 38(4), December 1996, 64.

44. Caesar, 'Interview', 65.

45. Morris, 'Linton Kwesi Johnson', 20; Caesar, 'Interview', 64–5.

46. Keanna Williams and Lydia Amoabeng, 'Interview with Linton Kwesi Johnson', in *The British Black Panthers and Black Power Movement: An Oral History and Photography Project*, 26 July 2013, 73.

47. Morris, 'Linton Kwesi Johnson', 17; Johnson, 'Writing Reggae', 51–2; Brian Alleyne, *Radicals Against Race: Black Activism and Cultural Politics* (Oxford: Berg, 2002), 153; and Roxy Harris and Sarah White (eds), *Changing Britannia: Life Experience with Britain* (London: New Beacon Books, 1999), 55 and Morris, 'Linton Kwesi Johnson', 52.

48. See Barry Chevannes' summary of research carried out for the Sistren Theatre Collective in Barry Chevannes, *Rastafari: Roots and Ideology* (Syracuse: Syracuse University Press, 1994), 258–9.

49. Imani M. Tàfari-Ama, 'Rastawoman as Rebel: Case Studies in Jamaica', in Murrell, Spencer and McFarlane, *Chanting Down Babylon*, 91, 96, 98, 99, 104, 92, 100–1.

50. Ibid., 91, 96, 98, 99, 104.

51. Robin D.G. Kelley, *Freedom Dreams, The Black Radical Imagination* (Boston: New Beacon Press, 2002), 151–2.

52. Johnson, 'Jamaican Rebel Music', 407.

53. David Scott, 'The Archaeology of Black Memory: An Interview with Robert A. Hill', *Small Axe*, 3(1), 1999, 132–45. For a detailed history of the origins of Rastafari see Robert Hill's *Dread History: Leonard P. Howell and Millenarian Visions in the Early Rastafarian Religion* (Chicago and Kingston: Research Associates School Time Publications/Frontline Distribution Int'l Inc. and Miguel Lorne Publishers, 2001).

54. I am simplifying a rather complex discussion of Badiou's conception of democracy, but Wright argues that Badiou's stateless notion of democracy and liberation – centred on the idea that the state (socialist, communist, and capitalist states) co-opts and corrupts aspirations for liberation and obstructs the development of axiomatic truths such as human equality and that cultural identity politics, including gender, race and even class politics are incompatible with democracy because they are particularistic and depend on the state for recognition and inclusion. In fairness to Badiou, Wright does suggest that the French philosopher makes a distinction between his more anthropological conception of culture from art, including music, poetry and drama. Colin Wright, 'Badiou's Axiomatic Democracy Against Cultural Politics: A Jamaican Counter-Example', *Culture, Theory, & Critique*, 50(1), 2009, 79, 80–1.

55. Ibid., 87.

56. Stewart, 'Linton Kwesi Johnson', 78.

57. Johnson, 'Come Wi Goh Dung Deh', *Mi Revalueshanary Fren*, 18–19.

58. Johnson recited some of his early poems to the drumming of Rasta Love, including a bass drum, a funde which the poet would sometimes play, a repeater drum, and at times a bass guitar or a

soprano saxophone in schools, libraries and youth clubs. Morris, 'Linton Kwesi Johnson', 19.

59. Morris, 'Linton Kwesi Johnson', 19; Caesar, 'Interview', 67; Johnson, 'Writing Reggae', 58.

60. Edward Said, *Culture and Imperialism* (New York: Vintage Books, 1994), 228. For a critique of Said's perspective on Rastafari and the Caribbean in general see David Austin, 'Inside-Outside: Edward Said's Caribbean and Dilemma's in Contrapuntalism', in May Telmissany and Tara Schwartz (eds), *Counterpoints: Edward Said's Legacy* (Cambridge: Cambridge Scholars Publishing, 2010), 123–48.

61. Hill, *Dread History*, 46 (emphasis in the original).

62. Sylvia Wynter uses the term epistemological imperialism in David Scott, 'The Re-enchantment of Humanism: An Interview with Sylvia Wynter', *Small Axe*, 4(2), 2000, 159.

63. See Aaron Kamugisha, 'Reading Said and Wynter on Liberation', in Anthony Bogues (ed.), *After Man, Towards Human: Critical Essays on Sylvia Wynter* (Kingston and Miami: Ian Randle Publishers, 2006), 145.

64. See 'Text of Speech by Walter Rodney delivered at Sir George Williams University', Montreal, 18 October 1968. A text of this speech was also included in Rodney's, *The Groundings With My Brothers* (London: Bogle-L'Ouverture Publications, 1990), 67.

65. Wright, 'Badiou's Axiomatic Democracy Against Cultural Politics', 86. Walter Rodney, the Guyanese historian and pan-African Marxist, expressed his profound respect for the wisdom of Jamaica's Rastas when he recounted his 'groundings' with them in 1968. Rodney, *The Groundings With My Brothers*, 67.

66. Maya Jaggi suggests that these poems represent an ironic spin on the collapse of the former Soviet Union in in her article, 'Poet on the Frontline', *The Guardian*, 4 May 2002, www.theguardian.com/books/2002/may/04/poetry.books, accessed 2 December 2017.

67. Johnson has resigned himself to the idea that 'God is the answer to all the questions that science can't answer, so God, like science, is here to stay', Linton Kwesi Johnson, quoted in 'What God Means to Me', *New Statesman*, 2 April 2009, www.newstatesman.com/religion/2009/04/believe-god-human-peter-faith, accessed 2 December 2017.

68. Jerome C. Branche, 'Speaking Truth, Speaking Power: "Of Immigrants," Immanence, and Linton Kwesi Johnson's "Street 66"', *The Poetics and Politics of Diaspora: Transatlantic Musings* (New York: Routledge, 2015), 87–92.

69. Linton Kwesi Johnson, 'Reggae Sounds', *Mi Revalueshanary Fren*, 17.

70. Emily Taylor Merriman, 'We Naw Tek Noh More a Dem Oppreshan: Linton Kwesi Johnson's Resistant Vision', in Adrian Grafe and Jessica Stephens (eds), *Lines of Resistance: Essays on British Poetry from Thomas Hardy to Linton Kwesi Johnson* (Jefferson: McFarland & Company, Inc., Publishers, 2012), 220–1. Here Merriman speaks of the music as both a source of joy and a political force that complements the voice; and Hitchcock, '"It Dread Inn Inglan"', 12.

71. Johnson, 'Bass Culture', *Mi Revalueshanary Fren*, 14–16.

72. Johnson, 'Street 66', *Mi Revalueshanary Fren*, 9–10.

73. John McLeod, *Postcolonial London: Rewriting the Metropolis* (London: Routledge, 2004), 134 and 135.

74. Stuart Hall, Chas Critcher, Tony Jefferson, John Clarke and Brian Roberts, *Policing the Crisis: Mugging, the State, and Law and Order* (London: Macmillan, 1982), 357.

75. Johnson, 'Street 66', *Mi Revalueshanary Fren*, 10.

76. Kwame Dawes, 'New Sounds', in *Shook Foil: A Collection of Reggae Poems* (Leeds: Peepal Tree Press, 1997), 64–5.

77. According to Marley biographer Stephen Davis: 'As winter descended on North America in October 1979 the Wailers began a tour in support of *Survival* at the Apollo Theater in Harlem, an appropriate address since in Bob's mind the purpose of the tour was to cultivate his most elusive audience, black America. He had seen a quote from the writings of W.E.B. DuBois ... that stirred him: "if the young black American is going to survive and live a life, he must face the fact that however much he is an American, there are interests which draw him nearer to the dark people outside America than to his fellow white citizens". To this end, Bob was touring to establish a Rasta presence in black America that would evolve into his ideal alternative to the rigors of socialism and capitalism.' Stephen Davis, *Bob Marley: Conquering Lion of Reggae* (London: Plexus, 2006), 218.

78. Caesar, 'Interview', 68.

79. Bob Marley, 'Bob Marley', in Gordon C., *The Reggae Files: A Book of Interviews* (London: Hansib Publications Ltd., 1988), 39–41.

80. Bob Marley, quoted in Richard Iton, *In Search of the Black Fantastic: Politics and Popular Culture in the Post-Civil Rights Era* (Oxford: Oxford University Press, 2008), 247–8.

81. Iton, *In Search of the Black Fantastic*, 247–8; Davis, *Bob Marley*, 217.

82. Linton Kwesi Johnson, 'Reality Poem', Linton Kwesi Johnson, 'It Dread Inna Inglan', *Mi Revalueshanary Fren: Selected Poems* (London: Penguin Books, 2002), 36.

83. Paul Gilroy, 'Could You Be Loved? Bob Marley, Anti-politics and Universal Sufferation', *Critical Quarterly*, 47(1–2), July 2005, 229.

84. Gerhard Dilger, 'Interview with Mutabaruka: "The Link of Spirit with Man is Necessary"', *Ruptures*, 10, October–December 1995, 180.

85. See 'Great Queens of Afrika', *Blakk Wi Blak ... K ... K ...*, Shanachie, 1991. Mutabaruka's Rastafarian anthem 'Dispel the Lie', for example, might be read in the same spirit as Marley's religiosity and dedication to Emperor Haile Selassie ('Dispel the Lie', *Blakk Wi Blak ... K ... K ...*, Shanachie, 1991).

86. Billy Bob Hargus, 'Linton Kwesi Johnson: Interview January 1997', www.furious.com/perfect/lkj.html, accessed 15 August 2017. For some unknown reason, the name associated with the interview on this site is Jason Gross.

87. Hargus, 'Linton Kwesi Johnson', January 1997.

88. Linton Kwesi Johnson, quoted in Maya Jaggi, 'Poet on the Frontline'.

89. Albert Murray, 'Art and Propaganda', *Paris Review*, 219, 2016, 188 and 191.

90. Paul Gilroy, *Black Atlantic: Modernity and Double Consciousness* (Cambridge: Harvard University Press, 1993), 188. Wilson Jeremiah Moses poses the same questions in *Afrotopia: The Roots of African American Popular History*, indicting Afrocentrists for their 'oversimplifications' of black contributions to the Bible or ancient cultures and empires and 'the romanticization of pharaohs' while ignoring what he refers to as the 'real' Africa of war, famine and 'cruel illiterate thugs who terrorize the populations of cities lacking plumbing, electricity, or hospitals'. Wilson Jeremiah Moses, *Afrotopia: The Roots of African American Popular History* (Cambridge: Cambridge University Press, 1998), 227–8, 229, 230. However, Moses too is guilty of oversimplification as he reduces an entire continent to strife and illiteracy, reproducing dominant tropes that ignore external forces that have helped to undermine African governments, as well as genuine efforts to confront the challenges of post-colonial discord on the continent from within. He also ignores the fact that most histories are romantic and contrived, highlighting the virtues of the victors and the ruling elite. Rarely are histories written from below. For a concise analysis and overview of debates centred on the ethno-racial make-up of ancient Egypt see Aaron Kamugisha, 'Finally in Africa: Egypt from Diop to Celenko', *Race & Class*, 45(1), 2003, 31–60.

91. According to Diop the rebellion lacked the level of coordination and direction and the degree of popular education that is characteristic of more modern movements and, coupled with the size of the territory which permitted the monarchy to take refuge in neighbouring provinces, the rebellion failed. The next few passages are important because, perhaps more than any

other individual, Diop's work has profoundly contributed to our appreciation of ancient African history, and yet clearly, his interest here is in the value of that history for understanding revolutionary possibilities in the present: considering 'the failure of a revolution during Antiquity, it is evident that the non-revolutionary character of the social structure is less important than the size factor. In reality, whatever may have been the "virtues" of Egypt's social organization, it finally created, like Greece, intolerable abuses and uprisings as virulent as the Greco-Latin revolts. These revolts in Egypt would surely have triumphed if the territorial dimensions had been the same. Only the size of the kingdom condemned the insurrections in advance.' Cheikh Anta Diop, *The African Origins of Civilization: Myth or Reality* (Chicago: Lawrence Hill Books, 1974 [1955]), 207. Diop, *The African Origins of Civilization*, 207–8.

92. Linton Kwesi Johnson, 'Roots and Rock: The Marley Enigma', *Race Today*, 7(10) October 1975, 237–8.

93. Michael Denning, *Noise Uprising: The Audiopolitics of a World Musical Revolution* (London: Verso, 2015), 228–9.

94. Johnson, 'Roots and Rock', 238.

95. Ibid.

96. Johnson, 'The Marley Debate', 20–1.

97. Dred Fred, 'Dread Fred Interviews Linton Kwesi Johnson', *Race Today*, 9(1), February 1977, 22.

98. Denning, *Noise Uprising*, 142, 144, 148.

99. For an intriguing discussion on the evolution of 'Redemption Song' see Robert A. Hill, 'Redemption Works: From "African Redemption" to "Redemption Song"', *Review: Literature and Arts of the Americas*, 43(2), 2010, 200–7.

100. David Scott suggests that the term 'black' is not a fixed entity but is open to interpretation over time, as are the terms 'radical' and 'tradition', and that the joining of the terms 'radical' and 'tradition' are counterintuitive, as radical suggests a break or a breach whereas tradition suggests sameness and continuity shaped by the desire to be framed by a particular set of experiences. See David Scott, 'On the Very Idea of a Black Radical Tradition', *Small Axe*, 17(1), March 2013, 1–3. See also Nijah Cunningham, 'A Queer Pier: Roundtable on the Black Radical Tradition', *Small Axe*, 17(1), March 2013, 84–95.

101. Anthony Bogues, *Black Heretics, Black Prophets: Radical Political Intellectuals* (New York and London: Routledge, 2003), 188 (emphasis in the original).

102. Carolyn Cooper, *Noises in the Blood: Orality, Gender, and the 'Vulgar' Body of Jamaican Popular Culture* (Durham, NC: Duke University Press, 1995), 134.

103. According to Johnson, the sole contact that Simon Draper, the label's founder, had with black people was with the black servants who cooked for his family in South Africa and, consequently, he had difficulty relating to blacks who were free and independent. Miguel Cid, 'Linton Kwesi Johnson: 20 ans de lutte poétique', in *Vibrations*, 9, November 1998.

104. Linton Kwesi Johnson, 'Bob Marley and the Reggae International', *Race Today*, 9(4), June/July 1977, 92.

105. Darren Jenkins, 'Linton Kwesi Johnson', *WUSB 90.1 Program Guide*, 3(2), Spring 1987, n.p.

106. Linton Kwesi Johnson, 'Introduction: The People Speak', in Roger Steffens, *So Much Things to Say: The Oral History of Bob Marley* (New York: W.W. Norton & Company, 2017), xiii–xv.

107. As an example, the Normans were originally Scandinavian Norsemen who occupied what is now the region of Normandy, giving up their language for a rural dialect of French which became the language of ruling aristocracy during the Norman conquest of England. This French dialect contributed some 10,000 words to what we now know as English between 1066 and 1399. In other words, even *if* we were to concede that Jamaica's national language is a dialect of English, English and French have had their dialects too, and have their roots in dialects. Bill Bryson, *The Mother Tongue: English and How it Got That Way* (London: Penguin, 2009), 45–6.

108. Edward Kamau Brathwaite, *History of the Voice: The Development of Nation Language in Anglophone Caribbean Poetry* (London: New Beacon Books, 1984), 13.

109. Mervyn Morris, 'Nation Language', *Race Today*, 16(3), January 1985, 45. See also Matthew Hart's *Nations of Nothing But Poetry: Modernism, Transnationalism, and Synthetic Vernacular Writing* (Oxford: Oxford University Press, 2010), 133, 135.

110. Winston James, *A Fierce Hatred of Injustice: Claude McKay's Jamaica and His Poetry of Rebellion* (London and New York: Verso, 2000), 140.

111. Brathwaite, *A History of the Voice*, 16–18. For Brathwaite, the term represents 'the *submerged* area of that dialect' which, for him, is 'much more closely allied to the African aspect of experience in the Caribbean', resembling 'an English which is like a howl, or a shout, or machine-gun fire or the wind or a wave ... like the blues'. Brathwaite, *A History of the Voice*, 13 (emphasis in the original). Note that Brathwaite uses the word dialect in his description, perhaps reflecting his reluctance to refer to Creoles as languages. Nation-language suggests an underlying unity between the various Creoles spoken across the Anglo Caribbean, languages that are the product of the 'tidalectic' (Brathwaite's term) cultural to and fro between the African continent in the Caribbean because, as he has

famously proclaimed, 'the hurricane does not roar in pentameters' (*A History of the Voice*, 13). Brathwaite's pan-Caribbean linguistic nationalism has also been criticized for Afrocentric essentialism and even ethnocentrism, but in his defence, critic Matthew Hart points out that despite the pitfalls associated with homogenizing identity, revolutionary figures like Frantz Fanon and Amilcar Cabral acknowledged the importance of nationalism and the nation state in liberation struggles. Hart, *Nations of Nothing but Poetry*, 123, 134–6.

112. Alleyne, *Roots of Jamaican Culture*, 130, 134.
113. Ibid., 120, 132.
114. Ibid., 132, 145.
115. Hart, *Nations of Nothing but Poetry*, 57, 59, 65.
116. See Manuela Coppola, 'Spelling Out Resistance: Dub Poetry and Typographic Creativity', *Anglistica AION*, 17(2), 2013, 7–18; Mervyn Morris, 'Printing the Performance', *Jamaica Journal*, 23(1), February–April, 1990, 22; Mark Sebba, 'How Do You Spell Patwa', *Critical Quarterly*, 38(4), 50–63.
117. Glissant, *Caribbean Discourse*, 121.
118. Antonin Artaud, *The Theater and It's Double* (New York: Grove Press, 1958), 78. Artaud wrote: 'We must get rid of our superstitious valuation of texts and *written* poetry. Written poetry is worth reading once, and then should be destroyed. Let the dead poets make way for others' (78).
119. Some poets have elected to write in vernacular in ways that are legible to English readers, and given the false divides that has separated so-called print poetry from performance poetry – print poetry presumably represents the true poetry and performance poetry the pretender – Morris has encouraged poets who write in Jamaican to take the literary side of their poetry as seriously as the performance and not to succumb to idea that only so-called print poetry deserves serious attention to the written craft. See Kwame Dawes, 'The Dichotomies of Reading "Street Poetry" and "Book Poetry"', *Critical Quarterly*, 38(4), 3–19, and Morris, 'Printing the Performance', 25. Morris is perhaps not only concerned with literary merits, but also the literary audience and the reception of Caribbean poetry by the English literary establishment, and perhaps underestimates that, in terms of resistance, the use of language is as important as the message, resistance is embedded in the language and unconventional spelling of English-sounding words forces the reader to confront the presumed aesthetic and literary superiority of the English language, and to creatively engage the meaning embedded in both the *orthography* and *phonology* of Jamaican, meaning that it cannot simply be translated into English without sacrificing, to use a tautology, meaning. This is perhaps

true of any language, but given the close proximity of Jamaican to English, with some effort, to an extent, translation is not necessarily any more challenging than translating Shakespearean English into the modern language would be. Resisting standardization of the language means dwelling in the creative spaces of the language and remaining open to the creation of new words and meanings (here it is worth noting that Shakespeare not only significantly contributed to the creative use of the English language, but also made an important contribution to the English lexicon, coining some 2,000 words and countless phrases). Bryson, *Mother Tongue*, 57, 69.

120. Fred Moten, 'The Phonographic *mise-en-scène*', *Cambridge Opera Journal*, 16(3), 2004, 270.

121. Johnson, 'Writing Reggae', 51. See also Maya Jaggi's article, 'Poet on the Frontline'.

122. Unlike Johnson, McKay was born into an affluent family as his parents combined thrift and a keen business sense in order to acquire large tracts of land, elevating themselves into the planter class. James, *A Fierce Hatred of Injustice*, 18.

123. Johnson, 'Writing Reggae', 51.

124. Winston James, 'A Race Outcast from Class: Claude McKay's Experience and Analysis of Britain', in Bill Schwarz (ed.), *West Indian Intellectuals in Britain* (Manchester: Manchester University Press, 2003), 88–9.

125. Ibid., 74.

126. Ibid., 80.

127. Ibid., 82–3.

128. James, *A Fierce Hatred of Injustice*, 130.

129. Ibid., 28, 46, 60–4, 72, 100–13, 124–7, 150.

130. Mervyn Morris, 'Introduction', in Mervyn Morris (ed.), *Louise Bennett: Selected Poems* (Kingston: Sangster's Book Store, 1996), xiv.

131. Lillian Allen, 'Language', in *Selected Poems of Lillian Allen* (Toronto: Women's Press, 1993), 44.

132. Lillian Allen, 'Wings', in *Selected Poems of Lillian Allen*, 45.

133. Susan Gingell, 'Coming Home Through Sound: See-Hear Aesthetics in the Poetry of Louise Bennett and Canadian Dub Poets', *Journal of West Indian Literature*, 17(2), 2009, 34, 36. Louise Bennett first saw her language printed in English when she was about seven years of age when a teacher at a Calabar School in Kingston presented her with a copy of Claude McKay's *Constab Ballads*. Moved by the sight of the poems in her native tongue, she memorized some of them and began to recite them in front of friends and relatives, and she soon began writing her own poetry in Jamaican. Her poems were met with a combination of ridicule and praise. For some, particularly among the literary establishment and the ruling elite, she was seen as an embarrassment and was

ridiculed for degrading English literary standards. But she also received popular support from the poor and working class whose language was now being represented on the page and the stage, not in mock appreciation, but in abiding appreciation of the language's intelligence and lyricism. For an introduction to Bennett's life and work see Mervyn Morris, *Miss Lou: Louise Bennett and the Jamaican Culture* (Kingston and Miami: Ian Randle Publishers, 2014).

134. Bennett, 'Bans a Killin', 5.

135. Cooper, *Noises in the Blood*, 139–40.

136. Louise Bennett, 'Jamaica Language', cited in Mervyn Morris, *Miss Lou: Louise Bennett and Jamaican Culture* (Kingston: Ian Randle Publishers, 2014), 5.

137. Brathwaite, *A History of the Voice*, 20, 30.

138. For the video clip from *Upon Westminster Bridge* see www.youtube.com/watch?v=NE3kVwyY2WU, accessed 2 February 2017.

139. Mervyn Morris, 'Introduction', in Mervyn Morris (ed.), *Louise Bennett: Selected Poems* (Kingston: Sangster's Book Stores, 1996), xiv–xv.

140. Louise Bennett, 'Dutty Tough', *Selected Poems* (Kingston: Sangster's Book Stores, 1996), 25.

141. Klive Walker, *Dubwise: Reasoning from the Reggae Underground* (Toronto: Insomniac Press, 2005), 13, 74.

142. Belinda Edmondson, *Caribbean Middlebrow: Leisure Culture and the Middle Class* (Ithaca: Cornell University Press, 2009), 96.

143. In his many interviews over the years, Johnson has rarely mentioned Bennett as an important influence on him. This is perhaps understandable given his early departure from Jamaica and his poetic-political formation in England. Yet, given her stature on the one hand, and his obvious appreciation for Jamaican culture on the other, her absence is surprising. In a 2007 interview he acknowledges Bennett for giving 'aesthetic weight' to Jamaica's language. See Elizabeth DiNovella, 'Linton Kwesi Johnson', *The Progressive*, February 2007, 35. This said, in a 2010 article published in *Jamaica Journal*, the poet recalls reading Bennett's 'Colonisation in Reverse' in *Breaklight*, an anthology edited by Andrew Salkey although, based on his comments, it is impossible to discern the extent to which her work touched his. In the same article, he also recalls joining Louise Bennett in a 1983 performance at the Lyric Theatre in London. On stage, their rapid Jamaican call and response dialogue sounds natural and almost spontaneous as they recite the children's song 'Mawning Buddy'. But in their playful exchange during the song 'Coconut Tree', Johnson sounds somewhat stiff, which perhaps has something to do with the fact that 'Coconut Tree' is a folk love song involving flirtatious sexual innuendo. Johnson, 'Writing Reggae', 53. See Miss Lou, *Yes M'Dear*, Island Records, 1983.

144. Louise Bennett, 'Bans o' Ooman', *Jamaican Labarish* (Kingston: Sangster's Book Stores, 1975), 41.

145. Ibid., 41.

146. See Carolyn Cooper, '"That Cunny Jamma Oman": The Female Sensibility in the Poetry of Louise Bennett', *Jamaica Journal* 18(4), November 1985–January 1986, also published in *Noises in the Blood*, 47–67.

147. See Phanuel Antwi, 'Dub Poetry as Black Atlantic Body-Archive', *Small Axe*, 48, November 2015, 74–6.

148. Ibid., 75–6.

149. Afua Cooper, *Utterances and Incantations: Women, Poetry, and Dub* (Toronto: Sister Vision Black Women and Woman of Colour Press, 1999), 7.

150. Puri, 'Beyond Resistance', 33 (emphasis in the original).

151. Jean Binta Breeze, 'Can a Dub Poet Be a Woman?', in Alison Donnell and Sarah Lawson Welsh (eds), *The Routledge Reader in Caribbean Literature* (London: Routledge, 1996), 499.

152. See Cooper, *Noises in the Blood*, 136–73.

153. Cooper, '"That Cunny Jamma Oman"', 47–67.

154. Puri, 'Beyond Resistance', 35.

155. Ibid., 35.

156. Ibid., 38.

157. Jean Binta Breeze, 'Ordinary Mawning', *Tracks*, LKJ Records, 2000.

158. d'bi young, 'Notes on the Cyclical Nature of Cycles', in *blood.claat* (Toronto: Playwrights Canada Press, 2005), 3.

159. d'bi young, 'Artist's Statement' and 'Di Dub', in *Art on Black* (Toronto: Women's Press, 2006), 1, 5, and Ric Knowles, 'To Be Dub, Female and Black: Towards a Woman-Centered Afro-Caribbean Diasporic Performance Aesthetic in Toronto', *Theatre Research in Canada*, 33(1), 2012.

160. Knowles, 'To Be Dub, Female and Black', 91. d'bi work includes: seven plays, including the sankofa trilogy: *blood.claat*, *benu*, & *word! sound! powah!* and The Orisha Trilogy: *Esu Crossing The Middle Passage*, *She Mami Wata & The Pussy WitchHunt*, and *Bleeders*; three collections of poetry including *Art on Black*, *Rivers and Other Blackness Between*, and six dub poetry albums (including wombanifesto, 333, and #CivilRightsMixtape), and a comic book set in Jamaica called *Shemurenga: Back Supah Shero*.

Chapter 3

1. Linton Kwesi Johnson, 'Yout Rebels', in *Mi Revalueshanary Fren: Selected Poems* (London: Penguin Books, 2006), 22.

2. Burt Caesar, 'Interview: Linton Kwesi Johnson talks with Burt Caesar at Sparkside Studios, Brixton, London', in *Critical Quarterly*, 38(1), 11 June, 1991, 66.

3. David Austin, 'Interview with Linton Kwesi Johnson', 26 October 2004.

4. Rebecca Dyer, 'Immigration, Postwar London and the Politics of Everyday Life in Samuel Selvon's Fiction', *Cultural Critique*, 52, Fall 2002, 139–40.

5. *From Mento to Lovers' Rock*, BBC Radio Six Music, episodes 1–10, www.bbc.co.uk/programmes/b00sf8sb, accessed 5–7 July 2017 (originally broadcast in 1983).

6. Linton Kwesi Johnson, 'Jamaican Rebel Music', *Race & Class*, 17(4), 1976, 398–9.

7. Johnson, 'Jamaican Rebel Music', 400. See also David Austin, 'Tings An' Times: Fanon and the Poetry of LKJ', *Serai*, 9(5), Spring 1996, 12–14.

8. Johnson, 'Jamaican Rebel Music', 400.

9. Frantz Fanon, *The Wretched of the Earth* (Harmondsworth: Penguin Books, Grove Press, 1967), 42.

10. Ibid., 42.

11. Given Fanon's description, the great wonder is why – considering the poor socio-economic conditions and the degree of social alienation that exists in our societies – we don't have a greater amount of and more severe violent outbreaks. The causes of much of the social madness that plagues us are often neglected while emphasis is instead placed on symptoms. Meanwhile poverty, oppression, social alienation and general inequality, the root causes – 'the subsoil' – of violent phenomena and auto-destructive behaviour, are not addressed.

12. Caesar, 'Interview', 65.

13. Johnson, 'Dread Beat an Blood', *Mi Revalueshanary Fren*, 5.

14. Fanon, *The Wretched of the Earth*, 44.

15. Ibid., 44.

16. Ibid., 44.

17. Ibid., 44.

18. Ibid., 45.

19. Ibid., 45.

20. Johnson, 'Jamaican Rebel Music', 400.

21. Ibid., 400.

22. Darren Jenkins, 'Linton Kwesi Johnson', *WUSB 90.1 Program Guide*, 3(2), Spring 1987, n.p.

23. Fanon, *The Wretched of the Earth*, 42.

24. Ibid., 42.

25. Christian Lapoussinière, 'Equisse d'une etude comparée de l'œuvre d'Aimé Césaire et de Frantz Fanon: Le mâitre et l' élève', *Le Rebelle*, 5, 2004, 9–33.

26. Césaire taught Fanon at the Lycée Schoelcher where, among other things, he declared the virtues of Negritude, a celebration of the ancestry, culture and the humanity of people of African descent, and Fanon also participated in Césaire's political campaign that catapulted to the French National Assembly in 1946 as a representative of the Communist Party. For a detailed analysis of Fanon's debt to Césaire see Reiland Rabaka, *The Negritude Movement: W.E.B. Du Bois, Aimé Césaire, Leon Damas, Leopold Senghor, Frantz Fanon, and the Evolution of an Insurgent Idea* (Lanham: Lexington Books, 2015), 173–5, 177.

27. Frantz Fanon, 'West Indians and Africans', *Towards the African Revolution* (New York: Grove Press, 1967), 21, 26, and Frantz Fanon, *Black Skin, White Masks* (New York: Grove Press, 1967), 153.

28. Aimé Césaire, 'Flint Warrior Through All Words', in *Aimé Césaire: Lyrical and Dramtic Poetry (1942–1982)*, trans. Clayton Eshleman and Annette Smith (Charlottesville: The University of Virginia Press), 99.

29. Aimé Césaire, 'Homage to Frantz Fanon', in *Caribbean Symposium: West Indian Nation in Exile*, 6–8 October 1967, n.p.

30. Césaire, 'Homage to Frantz Fanon', n.p. Fanon makes several important allusions to his former teacher in *Black Skin, White Masks*, including a passage from Césaire's *Discourse on Colonialism* that indicts America for acts of barbarism practiced against blacks, and Europe for its savage crimes in its colonies – crimes that were eventually reproduced in Europe against Europeans in the form of Hitler and Nazism. Fanon, *Black Skin, White Masks*, 90–1.

31. Patrick Chamoiseau, 'Fanon, Côté Cœur, côté sève', in *Sur Fanon*, Bernard Magnier (ed.) (Montréal: mémoire d'encrier, 2016), 50–1.

32. Ibid., 48.

33. Alfred Alexandre, 'Fanon ou le lyricisme de la révolte?' in *Sur Fanon*, Bernard Magnier (ed.) (Montreal: mémoire d'encrier, 2016), 17.

34. Fanon, *The Wretched of the Earth*, 68.

35. Césaire, *Et les chiens se taisaient*, 68–9.

36. Linton Kwesi Johnson, 'Five Nights of Bleeding', in *Mi Revalueshanary Fren*, 6.

37. Césaire, quoted in Fanon, *The Wretched of the Earth*, 68.

38. Fanon, *The Wretched of the Earth*, 69.

39. Aimé Césaire *Discourse on Colonialism* (New York: Monthly Review Press, 2000), 83–4.

40. Rabaka, *The Negritude Movement*, 185.

41. Suzanne Césaire, '1943: Surrealism and Us', in Michael Richardson (ed.), *Refusal of the Shadow: Surrealism and the Caribbean* (London: Verso, 1996), 124.

42. Sylvia Wynter, 'Beyond the Word of Man: Glissant and the New Discourse of the Antilles', *World Literature Today*, 63(4), 1989, 639.

43. Richard Iton, *In Search of the Black Fantastic: Politics and Popular Culture in the Post-Civil War Era* (Oxford and New York: Oxford University Press, 2008), 16.

44. Robin D.G. Kelley, *Freedom Dreams, The Black Radical Imagination* (Boston: New Beacon Press, 2002), 158.

45. Ibid., 171.

46. Aimé Césaire, 'Wifredo Lam', in *Aimé Césaire: The Collected Poetry* (Berkeley and Los Angeles: University of California Press, 1983), 373.

47. Roberto Cobas Amate, 'Lam, A Visual Arts Manifesto for the Third World', in Nathalie Bondil (ed.), *Cuba: Art and History, from 1868 to Today* (Montreal: Montreal Museum of Fine Arts, 2008), 203.

48. René Depestre, 'An Interview with Aimé Césaire', in Aimé Césaire, *Discourse on Colonialism* (New York: Monthly Review Press, 2000 [1955]), 86.

49. Kelley, *Freedom Dreams*, 161. According to Kelley, poet Ted Joans referred to the music of Charlie Parker and Cecil Taylor as 'surrealizing' music; and in sharp contrast to the poetry of Ezra Pound and T.S. Eliot, Paul Garon's 1975 book *Blues and the Poetic Spirit* acknowledged that the erotic and transcendental framing of love, humour, the desire to be free from toil that is captured in the poetry of the blues is an expression of spirit of revolt that surrealism projected (Kelley, *Freedom Dreams*, 163–4).

50. Emily Taylor Merriman makes the same observation in her essay, 'Wi Naw Tek Noh More a Dem Oppreshan: Linton Kwesi Johnson's Resistant Vision', in Adrian Grafe and Jessica Stephens (eds), *Lines of Resistance: Essays on British Poetry from Thomas Hardy to Linton Kwesi Johnson* (Jefferson, NC: McFarland & Company, Inc. Publishers, 2012), 219.

51. Kelley, *Freedom Dreams*, 162.

52. Clifton Joseph with the Livestock Band, 'Night in Tunisia', *Oral/Trans/Missions*, LP, Verse to Vinyl, 1989.

53. Unfortunately, with the exception of *Oral/Trans/Missions*, Clifton Joseph's poetry is not widely available, although a number of his performances are posted on YouTube. I am grateful to him for sharing his work with me.

54. Linton Kwesi Johnson, 'Two Sides of Silence', *Bass Culture*, Island Records, 1980.

55. Roxy Harris and Sarah White (eds), *Changing Britannia: Life Experience with Britain* (London: New Beacon Books, 1999), 71.

56. For an in-depth study of Joe Harriott and his fellow musicians see Alan Robertson, *Joe Harriott: Fire in His Soul* (London: Northway Publications, 2011). See also Coleridge Goode and Roger Cotterrell, *Bass Lines: A Life in Jazz* (London: Northway Publications, 2002). Coleridge Goode was the bassist in Harriott's quintet.

57. Linton Kwesi Johnson, 'Two Sides of Silence', *Dread Beat an' Blood* (London: Bogle-L'Ouverture Publications, 1975), 36.

58. Johnson, 'Two Sides of Silence', 37.

59. Kelley, *Freedom Dreams*, 160.

60. Robert J. Stewart suggests that Johnson was inspired by the surrealism of the Ibo-Nigerian poet Christopher Okigbo and the Congo's Tchicaya U Tam'si, but surprisingly does not mention Césaire. Robert J. Stewart, 'Linton Kwesi Johnson: Poetry Down a Reggae Wire', *New West Indian Guide*, 67(1/2), 1993, 71.

61. Mireille Rosello, 'Introduction', in Aimé Césaire, *Notebook of a Return to My Native Land* (Highgreen: Bloodaxe Books, 1995), 13.

62. Malik Noël-Ferdinand, 'Les Corps perdu du créole chez Aimé Césaire et Derek Walcott', *Editions Présence Africaine*, 189, 2014, 113–28.

63. Derek Walcott, cited in Noël-Ferdinand, 'Les Corps perdu du créole chez Aimé Césaire et Derek Walcott', 113–14. I am grateful to Malik Noël-Ferdinand for pointing out the Walcott reference, for sharing his essay with me and for his feedback on this chapter.

64. André Breton, 'A Great Black Poet: Aimé Césaire', in Michael Richardson (ed.), *Refusal of the Shadow: Surrealism and the Caribbean* (London: Verso, 1996), 194.

65. Ibid., 196.

66. Fanon, *Black Skin, White Masks*, 39–40.

67. John Berger, *The Success and Failure of Picasso* (New York: Pantheon Books, 1989), 138–40.

68. Wynter, 'Beyond the Word of Man', 639.

69. Homi K. Bhabha, 'Foreword: Framing Fanon', in Fanon, *The Wretched of the Earth* (New York: Grove Press, 2004), xxxix.

70. Ibid., xl.

71. David Macey poses this question in David Austin, 'The Wretched of the Earth', *Ideas*, Canadian Broadcasting Corporation, 2006.

72. Tsenay Serequeberhan, *The Hermeneutics of African Philosophy: Horizon and Discourse* (New York: Routledge, 1994), 73, 82.

73. Ibid., 75–6.

74. Ibid., 76–7.

75. Ibid., 79.

76. Ato Sekyi-Otu, *Fanon's Dialectic of Experience* (Cambridge, MA: Harvard University Press, 1996), 11–12; Said, *Culture and Imperialism*, 269–70.

77. Frantz Fanon, *L'Œil se noie* and *Les Mains parallèles*, in Jean Khalfa and Robert Young (eds), *Frantz Fanon: Écrits sur l'aliénation et la liberté, Œuvres II* (Paris: Éditions La Découverte, 2015), 65–133.

78. Sekyi-Otu, *Fanon's Dialectic of Experience*, 4–5.

79. Ibid., 5, 53.

80. d'bi young, 'Blood', *Art on Black* (Toronto: Women's Press, 2006), 103.

81. young, 'Blood', 103.

82. young, 'Blood', 104.

83. d'bi young anitafrika, 'Notes on the Cyclical Nature of Cycles', in *Blood.Claat* (Toronto: Playwrights Canada Press, 2005), 7.

84. young, 'Blood', 104.

85. Ibid., 103.

86. For a classic study of Jamaican maroons see Orlando Patterson, *The Sociology of Slavery: An Analysis of the Origins, Development and Structure of Negro Slave Society in Jamaica* (Rutherford: Farleigh Dickinson University Press, 1969). See also Kenneth M. Bilby, *True-Born Maroons* (Kingston: Ian Randle Publisher).

87. See young anitafrika, *blood.claat* (Toronto: Playwrights Canada Press, 2005), 47–50.

88. young, 'Blood', 106, 'The Orisha Letters', 50–7, and 'Yemojah Moon Pheonix', 33, *Art on Black*.

89. Amor Kohli, *The Demands of a New Idiom: Music, Language, and Participation in the Work of Amiri Baraka, Kamau Brathwaite, and Linton Kwesi Johnson*, in partial fulfilment of the requirements for the degree of Doctor of Philosophy in English, Tufts University, August 2005, 18.

90. Linton Kwesi Johnson, *Voices of the Living and the Dead* (London: Race Today, 1988), 11.

91. Ibid., 19.

92. Ibid., 21.

93. Ibid., 27.

94. Fanon, *The Wretched of the Earth*, 42.

95. Tina Pippin, '"Behold, I stand at the Door and Knock": The Living Dead and Apocalyptic Dystopia', *The Bible and Critical Theory*, 6(2), 2010, 40.3.

96. Jacqueline Foertsch, 'Last Man Standing: Interracial Sex and Survival in Post-Nuclear Films, 1951–2007', *Modern Language Studies*, 42(1), 39.

97. Pippin, '"Behold, I stand at the Door and Knock": The Living Dead and Apoocalyptic Dystopia', 40.6.

98. Ibid., 40.5.

99. Ibid., 40.8.

100. Johnson, *Voices of the Living and the Dead*, 31.

101. Ron Ramdin, *The Making of the Black Working Class in Britain* (Aldershot: Gower Publishing Company Ltd., 1987), 476.

102. According to Horace Campbell in his popular *Rasta and Resistance*, by 1980 black Britons, only 3 per cent of the total population, comprised 17 per cent of the prison population, a proportionately higher black incarceration rate than for blacks in the United States. Horace Campbell, *Rasta and Resistance: From Marcus Garvey to Walter Rodney* (Trenton: Africa World Press, Inc., 1987), 195. By 1981 blacks were five times more likely to find themselves imprisoned than whites. This is based on a report by *Abolitionist*, and is quoted in Campbell, *Rasta and Resistance*, 195.

103. Caesar, 'Interview', 69.

104. David Harvey, *Seventeen Contradictions and the End of Capitalism* (Oxford: Oxford University Press, 2014), 263.

105. Hannah Arendt, *On Violence* (New York: Harcourt Brace Jovanovich, 1969), 65. After exhausting all official and legal methods of redress under apartheid, the South African struggle against white domination was characterized by both violent and non-violent methods, culminating in the official end of apartheid. That South Africa today has one of the highest homicide rates in the world attests to the depth of social alienation and destitution that plagued the country under apartheid, the extent to which these conditions are yet to be alleviated, the difficulty in doing so and the absence of the will to do so among the ruling elite. Far too often, mention is made of violence in South Africa without referring to its historic and social roots. The system of apartheid was one of the most pathologically oppressive systems of colonial dispossession the world has seen, and in its afterlife no one has walked away unscathed. Post-apartheid South Africa ails from the effects of the old regime while struggling to face the challenges represented by the new. Fanon implores us to go beyond the mere appearance of violence, such as in the case of South Africa, or Jamaica for that matter, in order to fully appreciate the subsoil of violence in order to envision how a society might move beyond devastation and decay and towards a vision of genuine freedom.

106. William Blake, 'London', *William Blake: Selected Poetry* (London: Penguin Books, 1988), 48.

107. W.H. Stevenson, 'Introduction', in William Blake, *William Blake: Selected Poetry*, 17.

108. Johnson, 'Five Nights of Bleeding', *Mi Revalueshanary Fren*, 7.

109. Linton Kwesi Johnson, *Dread Beat an' Blood* (London: Bogle-L'Ouverture Publications, 1975), 22.

110. Ibid., 22.

111. Ibid., 23.

112. Johnson, 'All Wi Doin is Defendin', *Mi Revalueshanary Fren*, 12.

113. Ibid., 12.
114. Johnson, 'Time Come', *Mi Revalueshanary Fren*, 23.
115. Michael Smith, 'It a Come', in *It a Come* (San Francisco: City Lights Books, 1989), 20.

Chapter 4

1. Linton Kwesi Johnson, 'Independant Intavenshan', *Forces of Victory*, Island Records, 1979.
2. Alissa Trotz, 'Walter Rodney's Example: Lessons for Our Times', *Symposium to Commemorate the 30th Anniversary of the Assassination of Walter Rodney*, Queen's College Alumni Association, New York and WBAI-Pacifica Radio, York College, Brooklyn, New York, 12 June 2010, 14 (unpublished paper).
3. James Baldwin, 'Staggerlee Wanders', *Jimmy's Blues and Other Poems* (Boston: Beacon Press, 2014), 15.
4. Trotz, 'Walter Rodney's Example', 9, 13.
5. Peter Hitchcock, '"It Dread Inn Inglan": Linton Kwesi Johnson, Dread, and Dub Identity', *Postmodern Culture*, 4(10), 1993, 24.
6. The conversation unfolds in *Making History*, a short film directed by Karen McKinnon and Caecilia Tripp: www.youtube.com/watch?v=jql4ctFACwY, accessed 9 December 2017.
7. John McLeod, *Postcolonial London: Rewriting the Metropolis* (London: Routledge, 2004), 134.
8. Paul Gilroy, *There Ain't No Black in the Union Jack: The Cultural Politics of Race and Nation* (Chicago: University of Chicago Press, 1991), 39.
9. David Austin, 'Interview with Linton Kwesi Johnson', 26 October 2004.
10. Ibid.
11. David Austin, *Fear of a Black Nation: Race, Sex, and Security in Sixties Montreal* (Toronto: Between the Lines, 2013), 23; David Austin, 'Introduction to Walter Rodney', *Small Axe*, 5(2), 2001, 64; Linton Kwesi Johnson, 'Reality Poem', *Mi Revalueshanary Fren: Selected Poems* (London: Penguin Books), 35–6.
12. David Austin, 'Interview with Linton Kwesi Johnson', 26 October 2004; Linton Kwesi Johnson, 'Review Notes', *Race Today*, 9(7), November/December, 1977, 167.
13. Johnson, 'Review Notes', 167.
14. Martin Carter, 'Shape and Motion One', *Poems of Succession* (London: New Beacon Books, 1977), 55.
15. Walter Rodney, *Walter Rodney Speaks: The Making of an African Intellectual* (Trenton: Africa World Press, 1990), 8.

16. Martin Carter, 'I Come from the Nigger Yard', *Poems of Succession* (London: New Beacon Books, 1977), 38.

17. Ibid., 40.

18. Walter Rodney, 'Lecture 8a: [Pre-Revolutionary Russian Thinkers]', in *The Two World Views on the Russian Revolution: Reflections from Russia*, 16–17 (unpublished). These lectures will be published in the forthcoming Walter Rodney, *The Russian Revolution: A View from the Third World*, edited by Jesse Benjamin and Robin D.G. Kelley (London: Verso, 2018).

19. The study group with C.L.R. and Selma James involved regular meetings with a number of young Caribbean women and men, some of whom would go on to play significant political roles in the Caribbean or would emerge as prominent writers or intellectuals. Among those involved were Richard Small, Norman Girvan, Orlando Patterson, Robert Hill, Joan French, Adolph Edwards and John Maxell, all of Jamaica; Adolph Edwards, Margaret Carter Hope and occasionally Anne Cools from Barbados; Stanley French, St Lucia; and Walton Look Lai, Trinidad. The study group had a tremendous impact on Rodney who was then grappling with his own ideas and attempting to forge his own approach to historical and political work at the time. Finding nothing among the British left that was helpful, the study group was indispensable to his political development, affording him 'the opportunity … to acquire a knowledge of Marxism, a more precise understanding of the Russian Revolution, and of historical formulation'. James's keen ability to get to the heart of an issue appealed to Rodney, and both C.L.R. and Selma James came to 'exemplify the power of Marxist thought. That's what one got – a sense that a bourgeois argument could never really stand a chance against a Marxist argument, provided one was clear about it'. Rodney, *Walter Rodney Speaks*, 28–9.

20. Ibid., 15.

21. Ibid., 15.

22. Ibid., 15.

23. Ibid., 15–16.

24. *Race Today*, 15(1), 1983, 3.

25. Anon., *Race Today*, 8(1), January 1976, 7. We know from Andrew Salkey's *Guyana Journal* that Rodney closely followed Guyanese politics before he returned to Guyana in 1974. Andrew Salkey interviewed Rodney in London shortly after the historian had returned from a brief visit to Guyana. See Salkey, 'Appendix B: Interview with Walter Rodney', *Georgetown Journal: A Caribbean Writer's Journey from London via Port of Spain to Georgetown, Guyana, 1970* (London: New Beacon Books, 1973), 383–8. The interview was conducted on 4 June 1970.

26. Linton Kwesi Johnson, *Race Today*, February 1975, 46.

27. Andrew Salkey, 'Introduction', in David Dabydeen (ed.), *Walter Rodney: Poetic Tributes* (London: Bogle-L'Ouverture Publications, 1985).

28. See Austin, *Fear of a Black Nation*, 23–5.

29. George Lamming, 'Foreword', in *A History of the Guyanese Working People, 1881–1905* (Baltimore: Johns Hopkins University Press, 1981), xvii.

30. Georg Wilhelm Friedrich Hegel, *The Philosophy of History* (New York: Dover Publications, Inc., 1956), 91.

31. Robert Hill in Clairmont Chung (ed.), *Walter A. Rodney: A Promise of Revolution* (New York: Monthly Review Press, 2012), 65–6.

32. Paulo Freire, *Pedagogy of the Oppressed* (New York: Continuum, 2005).

33. Hill in Chung, *Walter A. Rodney*, 66.

34. Walter Rodney, *How Europe Underdeveloped Africa* (London: Bogle-L'Ouverture Publications, 1988 [1972]), 280.

35. Rodney, *How Europe Underdeveloped Africa*, 280.

36. See Walter Rodney, 'African Slavery and Other Forms of Social Oppression on the Upper Guinea Coast in the Context of the Atlantic Slave-Trade', *The Journal of African History*, 1(3), 1966, 431–43, 'Portuguese Attempts at Monopoly on the Upper Guinea Coast, 1580–1650', *The Journal of African History*, 6(3), 1965, 307–22, in which Rodney cites Karl Polanyi's article, 'Sortings and "Ounce Trade" in the West African Slave Trade', *Journal of African History*, 5(3), 1964, 381–93. See also *A History of Upper the Guinea Coast: 1545 to 1800* (New York: Monthly Review Press, 1980 [1970]), a book that is a product of his PhD thesis. A critical study of this book would perhaps include an analysis of Karl Polanyi's (in collaboration with Abraham Rothstein), *Dahomey and the Slave Trade: An Analysis of an Archaic Economy* (Seattle: University of Washington Press, 1966). See also David Austin, notes on 'Karl Polanyi and Africa', unpublished paper presented at The Relevance of Karl Polanyi for the 21st Century, 9–11 December 2008, Concordia University.

37. David Austin, 'Cabral, Rodney, and the Complexities of Culture in Africa', in Firoze Manji and Bill Fletcher Jr., *Claim No Easy Victories: The Legacy of Amilcar Cabral* (Montreal: Daraja Press, 2013).

38. See Walter Rodney, *The Groundings With My Brothers* (London: Bogle-L'Ouverture Publications, 1990), 60–68.

39. Rupert Lewis, *Walter Rodney's Intellectual and Political Thought* (Detroit: Wayne State University Press), 105.

40. Prince Buster and All Stars, 'Dr. Walter Rodney (Black Power)', FAB Records, 1968.

41. Lewis, *Walter Rodney's Intellectual and Political Thought*, 101.

42. This story is chronicled in John Masouri, *Stepping Razor: The Life of Peter Tosh* (London: Omnibus Press, 2013), 65 and Chris Salewicz, *Bob Marley: The Untold Story* (New York: Faber and Faber, 2009), 180.

43. Lloyd Bradley, *Bass Culture: When Reggae was King* (London: Penguin Books, 2001), 195, 231.

44. Rodney, *Walter Rodney Speaks*, 42–3.

45. See C.L.R. James, 'The Eighteenth Brumaire of Louis Bonaparte and the Caribbean', in David Austin (ed.), *You Don't Play with Revolution: The Montreal Lectures of C.L.R. James* (Oakland: AK Press, 2089), 128–31.

46. Martin Carter, 'There is No Riot', *Poems of Succession* (London: New Beacon Books, 1977), 116.

47. Walter Rodney, 'Race and Class in Guyanese Politics', www.youtube.com/watch?v=9szjOu-yIPs, accessed 17 October 2016.

48. Walter Rodney, *A History of the Guyanese Working People, 1881–1905* (Baltimore: Johns Hopkins University Press, 1981), 180.

49. Rodney, *A History of the Guyanese Working People*, 180, 181.

50. Rodney, 'Race and Class in Guyanese Politics'.

51. Carole Boyce Davies, *Left of Karl Marx: The Political Life of Black Communist Claudia Jones* (Durham, NC: Duke University Press, 2008).

52. Walter Rodney, *People's Power, No Dictator* (Georgetown, Guyana: Working People's Alliance, 1979), 7.

53. Lewis, *Walter Rodney's Intellectual and Political Thought*, 236.

54. Thirty-five thousand people turned out to join his funeral procession, which is partly captured in the Victor Jara Collective film that is named after a line from a Martin Carter poem, *In the Sky's Wild Noise*. The film eerily captures Rodney's thoughts in stark black and white images as he describes Guyana's volatile political context. Caribbean governments issued official statements on his death, memorial services were held in parts of Africa, England, Germany and the United States, and recriminations were heaped on Forbes Burnham and his government (Lewis, *Walter Rodney's Intellectual and Political Thought*, 246).

55. J. Edward Chamberlain, *Come Back to Me My Language: Poetry and the West Indies* (Urbana and Chicago: University of Illinois, 1993), 264.

56. J. Edward Chamberlain, *If This Is Your Land, Where Are Your Stories? Finding Common Ground* (Toronto: Alfred A. Knopf Canada, 2003), 183.

57. Fred Moten, *In the Break: The Aesthetics of the Black Radical Tradition* (Minneapolis: University of Minnesota Press), 68.

58. Peter M. Sacks, *The English Elegy: Studies in the Genre from Spencer to Yeats* (Baltimore: Johns Hopkins University Press, 1985), 20–1.

59. Sacks, *The English Elegy*, 22.
60. For more on elegies as criticism see Tammy Clewell's reading of J. Ramazani in 'Mourning and Beyond Melancholia: Freud's Psychoanalysis of Loss', *Journal of the American Psychological Association*, 52(1), 2004, 53–6.
61. Jacques Derrida, Thomas Dutoit and Outi Pasanen (eds), *Sovereignties in Question: The Poetics of Paul Celan* (New York: Fordham University Press, 2005), 139–40.
62. See, for example, Aimé Césaire's elegy for Frantz Fanon and his tribute to Wifredo Lam; various elegies for Bob Marley, including Rachel Manley's 'Bob Marley's Dead', James Berry's 'Sound of a Dreamer (*Remembering Bob Marley*)', John Agard's 'For Bob Marley' and Afua Cooper's 'Stepping to Da Muse/Sic (for Bob Marley)'; Mervyn Morris' 'Valley Prince', Lorna Goodison's 'For Don Drummond' and Norman Weinstein's 'Drummond's Lover Sings the Blues', 'The Ethiopian Apocalypse of Don' and 'The Migration of Drummond's Organs (*After Death*)' – all for the legendary Jamaican trombonist Don Drummond; Bob Stewart's 'Words is Not enough', ahdri zhina mandiela's 'Mih Feel It (*Wailin fih Mikey*)', Malik's 'Instant Ting', Norval Edwards' 'Poem for Michael' and Kamau Brathwaite's 'Stone (*For Mikey Smith stoned to death on Stony Hill, 1954–1983*)', which are dedicated to the memory of the Jamaican poet Michael Smith; and, among others, Andrew Salkey's homage to Grenada's Maurice Bishop (he also wrote elegy for Guineas-Bissau's Amilcar Cabral).
63. Shaka Rodney, 'Mother', in Dabydeen, *Walter Rodney*, 1.
64. Marina Omowale Maxwell, 'Pat, Mother, Be Strong', in Dabydeen, *Walter Rodney*, 8.
65. John Agard, 'Come from that Window Child', in Dabydeen, *Walter Rodney*, 9–10.
66. Grace Nichols, 'For Walter Rodney', in Dabydeen, *Walter Rodney*, 13.
67. Jan Carew, 'The History Maker', in Dabydeen, *Walter Rodney*, 44.
68. Ibid., 48.
69. Ibid., 45. It is not obvious to me why Carew exempts the meek from redemption, unless it is to suggest that redemption implies culpability and that it is perpetrators of crimes against humanity who must redeem themselves, not their victims. Nor is it obvious what the 'lumpen elite' implies.
70. Ibid., 50.
71. Martin Carter, 'For Walter Rodney', in Dabydeen, *Walter Rodney*, 51.
72. Andrew Salkey, 'Lime and Salt', in Dabydeen, *Walter Rodney*, 26.
73. Clifton Joseph, 'Rites/for Walter Rodney', in Dabydeen, *Walter Rodney*, 23, 24.

74. Edward Kamau Brathwaite, 'For Walter', in Dabydeen, *Walter Rodney*, 58.

75. Kamau Brathwaite, 'How Europe Underdeveloped Africa', in *Middle Passages* (Newcastle upon Tyne: Blood Axe Books, 1992), 43.

76. Ibid., 48.

77. For an account of the historical Jesus of Nazareth who became the theological Christ, see Reza Aslan, *Zealot: The Life and Times of Jesus of Nazareth* (New York: Random House, 2013).

78. Rebecca Dyer, 'Poetry of Politics and Mourning: Mahmoud Darwish's Genre-Transforming Tribute to Edward W. Said', *PMLA*, 112(5), 2007, 1450.

79. Sacks, *The English Elegy*, 23.

80. W.E.B. Du Bois, *The Souls of Black Folk* (New York: Dover Publications, 1994 [1903]), 156.

81. Alexadner G. Weheliye, *Phonographies: Grooves in Sonic Afro-Modernity* (Durham, NC: Duke University Press, 2005), 100–2, 202.

82. Moten, *In the Break*, 180.

83. Ibid., 98–9.

84. The 18 October 1968 speech is published as 'On the Banning of Walter Rodney from Jamaica', in David Austin (ed.), *You Don't Play with Revolution*, 299.

85. Walter Rodney, 'Towards the Sixth Pan-African Congress: Aspects of the International Class Struggle in Africa, the Caribbean and America', in Horace Campbell (ed.), *Pan-Africanism: Struggle against Neo-Colonialism and Imperialism* (Toronto: Union Labour/ Better Read Graphics, 1975), 19. Rodney's remarks are part of what remained a defining feature of his character throughout his short life. His uncompromising and no-nonsense political stance and his ability to pointedly articulate his political ideas, irrespective of whose feathers his convictions might ruffle, is one the traits that separated him from many of his contemporaries.

86. C.L.R. James quoted in Lewis, *Walter Rodney's Intellectual and Political Thought*, 171.

87. C.L.R. James, *Nkrumah and the Ghana Revolution* (Westport: Lawrence Hill & Co., 1977).

88. Tim Hector, 'Walter Rodney, the Dread Scene, There and Here', *The C.L.R. James Journal*, 8(1), 2000/1, 79.

89. Cited by C.L.R. James, *Walter Rodney and the Question of Power* (London: Race Today Publications, 1983), 5.

90. Ibid., 8.

91. James is certain that Rodney was aware that Burnham was prepared to use the army and the state apparatus in general against him ('prepare your wills') and 'became too anxious about it'. According to James, Rodney 'did not wait for the revolutionary people and the

revolutionary class to be in conflict with the government before he could start the question of the insurrection', adding that 'The working class by and large was with Walter, the leader, but they were not in any mortal conflict with the government' and were unprepared to push the struggle to its limits. They were not ready to directly contest Burnham's power. James, *Walter Rodney and the Question of Power*, 8.

92. Ibid., 9.

93. For an analysis of tragedy in relation to revolutionary politics see David Scott's *Omens of Adversity: Tragedy, Time, Memory, Justice* (Durham, NC: Duke University Press, 2014).

94. Johnson, 'Reggae fi Radni', *Mi Revalueshanary Fren*, 48.

95. James, *Walter Rodney and the Question of Power*, 9 (emphasis in original).

96. Ibid., 9.

97. Austin, *Fear of a Black Nation*, 119.

98. Rodney, *The Groundings With My Brothers*, 22.

99. Rodney, *Walter Rodney Speaks*, 45.

100. Colin Prescod, 'Guyana's Socialism', *Race & Class* 18(2), 1976, 125.

101. Ibid., 125–6 (emphasis added).

102. Johnson, *Voices of the Living and the Dead*, 31.

103. Prescod, 'Guyana's Socialism', 126.

104. Lewis, *Walter Rodney's Intellectual and Political Thought*, 168.

105. Rodney, 'Introduction' and 'Lecture 8b: [Trotsky as Historian of the Russian Revolution]', *The Two World Views of the Russian Revolution*, 1–8 (unpublished).

106. Horace Campbell, 'C.L.R. James, Walter Rodney and the Caribbean Intellectual', in Selwyn R. Cudjoe and William E. Cain (eds), *C.L.R. James: His Intellectual Legacies* (Amherst: University of Massachusetts Press, 1995), 407–8.

107. Prescod, 'Guyana's Socialism', 126.

108. Ibid., 126–7. In a recently declassified CIA memo documenting a late 1979 conversation between Rodney and a representative of the US embassy in Guyana, Rodney not only shares his view on Maurice Bishop and the revolutionary government of Grenada (he describes the government as a 'political embarrassment') but also appears to have, quite remarkably, shared his views on armed struggle. According to the memo, he told the representative that he was not sure whether or not the WPA would engage in acts of terrorism, which he abhorred, but that some kind of retaliation against the government would occur within the next year as all legitimate and legal channels of political opposition had been exhausted. The memo, dated 13 December 1979, is based on a conversation that appears to have taken place that month, six months before Rodney was killed, during which, in the classic Marxist conception of the

highly industrialized state and socialism, he reiterated the view that the US would one day become the most successful socialist state and expressed his appreciation for the country's democratic spirit and that a WPA-led government would seek to have friendly relations with the US. However, he also expressed his admiration for Cuba, discussed the ideological inflexibility of the PPP on economic matters and gave the impression that his death was imminent and that he was resigned to that fate. If the memo is authentic – and here I do not simply mean in terms of an accurate recording of the conversation, but more an accurate record of the spirit and tone of the conversation – it portrays an image of a somewhat vulnerable and even forlorn Rodney who is fully aware that his death is inevitable. He is concerned about what will happen to his family if he is eliminated and, as part of the transition of WPA to a political party, is attempting to clarify its position on a number of issues in order to avert misunderstanding with the US, allaying fears and attempting to minimize the political and personal fallout that would ensue in the event of his elimination. This said, it is hard to imagine that Rodney did not at least anticipate that his conversation would likely be shared with the Burnham government and that, given his acknowledgement that the WPA was preparing for armed struggle of some kind – if this is in fact the case – that the Burnham government would take steps to prevent this, including physically eliminating Rodney and other members of the WPA.

109. Anthony Bogues, *Black Heretics, Black Prophet: Radical Political Intellectuals* (New York: Routledge, 2003), 144 (emphasis in the original).

110. Tim Hector, 'Walter Rodney, Friend, Scholar and Caribbean Figure Extraordinary', *The C.L.R. James Journal*, 8(1), 2000/1, 67.

111. Bogues, *Black Heretics, Black Prophet*, 5.

112. Rodney, *Walter Rodney Speaks*, 10–11, 18–19.

113. Rupert Roopnarine, *Walter Rodney*, 111.

114. Ibid., 112–13.

115. Andaiye, quoted in Lewis, *Walter Rodney's Intellectual and Political Thought*, 243.

116. Johnson, 'Reggae fi Dada', 48, 49.

117. During a 1979 conversation in the US Robert Hill proposed plans for a speaking tour in 1980. Rodney ominously told Hill that he would not be around the following year, clearing suggesting that he would not be alive by that time. Hill in *Walter A. Rodney*, 68.

118. Ngũgĩ wa Thiongo, *The First Walter Rodney Memorial Lecture* (London: Friends of Bogle, 1987), 9.

119. Patricia Rodney, 'Walter Rodney and Black Liberation', Montreal, 25 May 1995 (unpublished).

Chapter 5

1. Michael Horovitz, 'Wi Noh Reach Mount Zion Yet', *New Statesman and Society*, 17 May 1991, 34.

2. Perhaps the combination of biblical lore as a metaphor for the vicissitudes of socialism is difficult for critics to disentangle or digest. Or, perhaps it is difficult for critics to reconcile Johnson, a British poet originally from Jamaica, with poems that are explicitly about socialism. Perhaps, for some, the poet appears to be out of place, as most black artists are defined by their ethno-racial makeup in ways that disavow their art on its own terms, situating it outside the social and cultural contexts that have produced it, or reducing it to the contexts in ways that reduce 'blackness' to an absolute existence. Of course, the validity of each of the propositions rests on ignoring the socialist politics of Johnson's earlier poetry.

3. Roberto Masone, *Marlene NourbeSe Phillip, Linton Kwesi Johnson and the Dismantling of the English Norm* (Cambridge: Cambridge Scholars Publishing, 2017), 103, 105.

4. Henghameh Saroukhani, 'Penguinizing Dub: Paratextual frames for transnational protest in Linton Kwesi Johnson's *Mi Revalueshanary Fren*', *Journal of Postcolonial Writing*, 51(3), 2015, 265.

5. Ibid., 266 (emphasis in original).

6. Ibid., 256.

7. Johnson's broad appeal is largely because his recorded poetry is accompanied by music, and that he was once recorded on Island Records at a time when reggae ruled 'world music'.

8. Richard Iton, *In Search of the Black Fantastic: Politics and Popular Culture in the Post-Civil War Era* (Oxford and New York: Oxford University Press, 2008), 202.

9. Walter Benjamin, 'The Task to the Translator', in *Illuminations* (New York: Schocken Books, 1977), 69, 70.

10. Jacques Derrida in Thomas Dutoit and Outi Pasanen (eds), *Sovereignties in Question: The Poetics of Paul Celan* (New York: Fordham University Press, 2005), 106–7.

11. Ibid., 67, 96–7, 165; Charles Henry Rowell, '"Words Don't Go There": An Interview with Fred Moten', in Fred Moten, *B. Jenkins* (Durham, NC: Duke University Press, 2010), 104.

12. Emily Taylor Merriman, 'We Naw Tek Noh More a Dem Oppreshan: Linton Kwesi Johnson's Resistant Vision', in Adrian Grafe and Jessica Stephens (eds), *Lines of Resistance: Essays on British Poetry from Thomas Hardy to Linton Kwesi Johnson* (Jefferson: McFarland & Company, Inc., Publishers, 2012), 228.

13. Amiri Baraka, 'The "Blues Aesthetic" and the "Black Aesthetic": Aesthetics as the Continuing Political History of a Culture',

in *Digging: The Afro-American Soul of American Classical Music* (Berkeley: University of California Press, 2009), 22.

14. Benjamin, 'The Task to the Translator', 71.
15. 'The spatial metaphor is apt, as efforts to contextualize or situate Johnson are, in effect, efforts to find a place for his work. Also, reading poetry spatially is a common technique for understanding form and its constraints. The word "stanza", for example, means room in Italian. Many Early Modern poets (e.g. Donne, Mary Wroth, Spenser) use self-reflexive spatial metaphors in which the text of the poem becomes a space to be navigated from left to right across the line, from top to bottom over the course of a stanza.' Yael Margalit in correspondence with the author.
16. Christian Habekost, *Verbal Riddim: The Politics and Aesthetics of African-Caribbean Dub Poetry* (Amsterdam: Editions Radophi, 1993). As a survey, the book is very useful and thanks to Habekost 'dub poetry' has at least one scholarly introduction. Habekost, who was once known as the poet-performer 'Ranting Chako', has been featured on the LP *Dread Poets Society: The Anthology of Contemporary Dub Poetry*, has promoted dub poets in his native Germany and has translated into German and edited the poetry of a number of dub poets for publication, including *Mutabaruka: The First Poems*, *Gedichte aus Jamaica*, and *Dub Poetry: 19 Poets from England and Jamaica*. As one reviewer of the *Verbal Riddim* argued, 'Indeed, in his awareness of the cultural, gender, and power relations of performance, it is difficult to see how this first study of dub poetry could be bettered as an introduction to the field'. Gerald Porter, 'Review', *The Journal of American Folklore*, 107(425), 1994, 459. But Bruce King's review is far less generous, and perhaps more accurate: 'This is a terrible book. It repeats a few obvious ideas over and over, is often unintelligible unless you already know what is being discussed, is advocacy scholarship at its most simple-minded, has the critical insight and selectivity of a fanzine, and, unbelievably, is dull reading.' However, in an effort to salvage something in his otherwise scathing review King writes: 'I nonetheless recommend that you order the book for your library or even for yourself; there are bound to be times when you will want to look up some of the biographical facts, the quotations from interviews, the discography, or perhaps show a student the Table of Contents as a possible model.' Bruce King, 'Review', *Research in African Literatures*, 26(2), 1995, 222.
17. Habekost, *Verbal Riddim*, 11.
18. June D. Dobbs, *Beating a Restless Drum: The Poetics of Kamau Brathwaite and Derek Walcott* (Trenton: Africa World Press, 1998), 28.
19. Ibid., 28.

20. Habekost, *Verbal Riddim*, 17.
21. Ibid., 212, 217.
22. Ibid., 212.
23. Ibid., 212.
24. Ibid., 216–17.
25. Ibid., 212.
26. Ibid., 29. The poet, critic, and musician Kwame Dawes would no doubt take issue with Habekost's comparison of Zephanaiah and Johnson. As Dawes argued in a review of Zephaniah's 2001 collection of poems *Too Black, Too Strong*: 'Where Linton Kwesi Johnson is sometimes vilified and feared for his hard-hitting reggae verse, Zephaniah is loved. Perhaps this may merely be a product of personality, but I suspect there is a great deal more going on there. One sometimes has the impression that Zephaniah is seen as harmless. Who knows if this is true? But what I miss in him is the irony to recognize that he may have actually been co-opted by the very system he denounces.' See Kwame Dawes, 'Review', *World Literature Today*, 76(2), 2002, 159–60. But for Habekost, *US and Dem* 'is marked by the dynamic expression of Zephaniah's militant political stance', a stance that 'has nothing in common with Linton Kwesi Johnson's nostalgic socialist attitude'. 'For Zephaniah', he goes on, 'it seems to be easier to stick to his revolutionary fervour since he has never linked his radical position with any particular ideology. Nor has his poetry been dominated by the grim seriousness of his dub poetry colleague.' Habekost, *Verbal Riddim*, 220.
27. Ibid., 218.
28. Ibid., 218.
29. For more on the use of Jamaican, including spelling, as a language of resistance see Manuela Coppola, 'Spelling Out Resistance: Dub Poetry and Typographic Creativity', *Anglistica AION*, 17(2), 2013, 9–10, 15–8, Mervyn Morris, 'Printing the Performance', *Jamaica Journal*, 23(1), February–April 1990, 22, and Mark Sebba, 'How Do You Spell Patwa', *Critical Quarterly*, 38(4), 54–6.
30. Horovitz, 'Wi Noh Reach Mount Zion Yet', 34, (my emphasis).
31. Habekost, *Verbal Riddim*, 217.
32. Ibid., 18.
33. Horovitz, 'Wi Noh Reach Mount Zion Yet', 34.
34. Robert J. Stewart, 'Linton Kwesi Johnson: Poetry Down a Reggae Wire', *New West Indian Guide*, 67(1/2), 1993, 86.
35. *Shake, Beat, and Dub*, BBC Two, 1992, www.youtube.com/watch?v=45XCNUGFsTA, accessed 11 July 2017.
36. Linton Kwesi Johnson in Maya Jaggi, 'Poet on the Frontline', *The Guardian*, 4 May 2002, www.theguardian.com/books/2002/may/04/poetry.books, accessed 2 December 2017.

37. Johnson, 'Story', *Mi Revalueshanary Fren*, 46.
38. *Shake, Beat, and Dub*, BBC Two, 1992, www.youtube.com/watch?v=45XCNUGFsTA, accessed 11 July 2017.
39. A Jamaican word for thin, or very thin.
40. David Austin, 'Interview with Linton Kwesi Johnson', 23 May 1999.
41. David Austin, 'Interview with Linton Kwesi Johnson', 26 October 2004.
42. C.L.R. James, *Beyond a Boundary* (Durham, NC: Duke University Press, 1993 [1963]), 19.
43. Writing in *State Capitalism and World Revolution* the trio argued: 'Theirs is a last desperate attempt under the guise of "socialism" and "planned economy" to reorganize the means of production without releasing the proletariat from wage-slavery. Historical viability they have none; for state-ownership multiplies every contradiction of capitalism.' C.L.R. James (in collaboration with Raya Dunayevskaya and Grace Lee), *State Capitalism and World Revolution* (Chicago: Charles H. Kerr Publishing Company, 1986 [1950]), 7.
44. As the highest form of cognition, Dialectic, or Reason is both negative and positive because it both destroys outmoded categories of thinking while creating new categories (new universals) out of the discarded ones. Whereas Reason is always in motion, negating old classifications while sublating (carrying over) the old categories to a higher ground, Understanding 'creates a Universal and sticks to it' as if holding on to the past for dear life. The category 'becomes abstract' and fossilized, unable to move with the flow of history. Objects, in our case the socialist movement, present 'knots' or 'crystalizations' that point the way forward from old categories of thought to new ones. Put another way, changes in the nature of political movements result in changes in consciousness as Reason assesses the 'signposts' that emerge from concrete actuality, and these 'coagulations' point the way forward towards understanding how and in what form a new society might emerge. C.L.R. James, *Notes on Dialectics: Hegel, Marx, Lenin* (London: Allison and Busby, 1980), 23, 30-32.
45. Ibid., 140.
46. For Hegel, 'Africa proper, as far as History goes back, has remained – for all purposes of connection with the rest of the World – shut up … the land of childhood, which lying beyond the day of self-conscious history, is enveloped in the dark mantle of Night', and 'The Negro … exhibits the natural man in his completely wild and untamed state' and 'all thought of reverence and morality – all that we call feeling' must be cast aside if Africans are to be understood.

Georg Wilhelm Friedrich Hegel, *The Philosophy of History* (New York: Dover Publications, 1956), 91, 93.

47. In this philosophic system there are three basic parts of the human persona: the *Okra* (soul), *sunsum* (ego), and *honan* (body). The '*Okra* is the divine spark of Onayame, the creator God, that exists in all human beings', and Hegel's *Supreme Being* or Absolute bears an uncanny resemblance to Onayame, as does his Dialectic to the *Okra*. The *Okra* often escapes the awareness of the ordinary individual whose consciousness is usually at the level *sunsum* or even *honan*, which loosely correspond to the Hegelian categories of Understanding, along with Simple, everyday, common sense, vulgar empiricism, and ordinary perception, respectively. Paget Henry, *Caliban's Reason: Introducing Afro-Caribbean Philosophy* (New York: Routledge, 2000), 28.

48. Kwame Gyekye, *An Essay on African Philosophical Thought: The Akan Conceptual Scheme* (Philadelphia: Temple University Press, 1995).

49. Edward Brathwaite, 'Masks', in *The Arrivants: A New World Trilogy* (Oxford: Oxford University Press, 1973), 89–157.

50. In his eightieth birthday lectures, published by *Race Today*, he highlighted the emergence of the women's movement and ethnically based organizations, adding them to his list of significant developments of the last part of the twentieth century. He recalled the importance of the work-to-rule movements in Hungary and Czechoslovakia in 1956 and 1968 respectively – both of which were crushed by Russian tanks – the Solidarity movement in Poland in the 1980s and the development of workers' and peasants' councils in Iran as important indicators of the new society emerging from the old. C.L.R. James, *C.L.R. James's 80th Birthday Lectures* (London: Race Today Publications, 1984), 67.

51. David Austin, 'Interview with Linton Kwesi Johnson', 26 October 2004.

52. Paul Gilroy, 'You Can't Blame the Youth', *Race & Class*, 23(2/3), Autumn/Winter 1981/2, 208–10.

53. Allison Blakely, *Russia and the Negro: Blacks in Russian History and Thought* (Washington: Howard University, 1986), 41–2.

54. See Joy Gleason Carew, *Blacks, Reds, and Russian: Sojourners in the Search of the Soviet Promise* (New Brunswick: Rutgers University Press, 2008), 15–26, and Eva Ulrike, 'The Unfinished Revolution: Black Perceptions of Eastern Europe', in Barbara Korte, Eva Ulrike and Sissy Helfe (eds), *Facing the East in the West: Images of Eastern Europe in British Literature, Film and Culture* (Amsterdam and New York: Rodopi, 2010), 125.

55. Claude McKay, *Selected Poems* (Mineola: Dover Publications, 1999), 27, and Claude McKay, *Selected Poems* (New York: A Harvest Book, 1953), 83.

56. René Depestre, 'An Interview with Aimé Césaire', in Aimé Césaire, *Discourse on Colonialism* (New York: Monthly Review Press, 2000 [1955]), 85–6.

57. Eva Ulrike, 'The Unfinished Revolution', 126; Carew, *Blacks, Reds, and Russian*, 115–39.

58. Ulrike, 'The Unfinished Revolution', 127–9.

59. The title for the US edition of the novel is *Green Winter*.

60. Ulrike, 'The Unfinished Revolution, 125, 130–3.

61. Malcolm X, *Malcolm X Talks to Young People* (Atlanta: Pathfinder Press, 2001) 91.

62. Karl Marx, *Capital: A Critique of Political Economy*, vol. 1 (New York: International Publishers, 1967), 233.

63. Malcolm X, *Malcolm X Speaks* (New York: Grove Press, 1966), 69. Also cited in Keeanga-Yamahtta Taylor, *From #BlackLivesMatter to Black Liberation* (Chicago: Haymarket Books, 2016), 197.

64. Other black or Caribbean figures and groups that engaged with the Soviet Union, socialism or Marxism in one form or another include: Elma Francois, Angela Davis, George Jackson, the Black Panther Party, the League of Revolutionary Black Workers and Walter Rodney. In fact, if we choose to include Forbes Burnham's People's National Congress to the list then Guyana is perhaps the only country in the world to boast three socialist parties at the forefront of the country's politics, the other two being the Working People's Alliance and Cheddi Jagan's People's Progressive Party. To this list of Caribbean communist/socialist parties and governments we can add the Worker's Party of Jamaica and the People's Revolutionary Government of Grenada.

65. Linton Kwesi Johnson cited in Habekost, *Verbal Riddim*, 216.

66. Linton Kwesi Johnson, *LKJ A Capella Live*, LKJ Records, 1996.

67. Burt Caesar, 'Interview: Linton Kwesi Johnson talks to Burt Caesar at Sparkside Studios, Brixton, London, 11 June 1996', *Critical Quarterly*, 38(4), December 1996, 76.

68. Linton Kwesi Johnson, 'Di Eagle an' Di Bear', *Making History*, Island Records, 1984.

69. Caesar, 'Interview', 76.

70. The early blood poems and the socialist poems of the 1990s represent arguably Johnson's best poetry, and given the not so obvious parallels between them – their dialectical form and evocative imagery – it is not coincidental that representatives of these poems, 'Five Nights of Bleeding' and 'Tings an Times', were

selected in the December 1996 issue of *Critical Quarterly* which also includes an extensive interview with the poet.

71. C.L.R. James, 'Letters to Literary Critics', in Anna Grimshaw (ed.), *The C.L.R. James Reader* (Oxford: Blackwell, 1992), 236.

72. Gordon Rohlehr, 'Afterthoughts', in Allison Donnell and Sarah Lawson Welsh (eds), *The Routledge Reader in Caribbean Literature* (London and New York: Routledge, 1996), 328.

73. Nothrop Frye, *Anatomy of Criticism* (Princeton: Princeton University Press, 1990), 143.

74. Ibid., 143.

75. For an analysis of the impact of the Bible on Bob Dylan see Seth Rogovoy, *Bob Dylan: Prophet, Mystic, Poet* (New York: Scribner, 2009).

76. Mahmoud Darwish, *La Palestine comme metaphor* (Paris: Actes Sud/ Babel, 1997), 23, 142.

77. Martin Heidegger, 'What Are Poets For?' *Poetry, Language, Thought* (New York: Harper Perennial Modern, Thought, 2013), 92.

78. Lloyd Bradley, *Bass Culture: When Reggae was King* (London: Penguin Books, 2001), 68.

79. Carolyn Cooper, *Noises in the Blood: Orality, Gender, and the 'Vulgar' Body of Jamaican Popular Culture* (Durham, NC: Duke University Press, 1995), 121–2.

80. Derrida in Dutoit and Pasanen, *Sovereignties in Question*, 105–7.

81. Austin, 'Interview with Linton Kwesi Johnson', 26 October 2004.

82. Amor Kohli, *The Demands of a New Idiom: Music, Language, and Participation in the Work of Amiri Baraka, Kamau Brathwaite, and Linton Kwesi Johnson*, in partial fulfilment of the requirements for the degree of doctor of philosophy in English, Tufts University, August 2005, 187–9.

83. Christopher Rowland, 'Face to Faith', *The Guardian*, 24 November 2007, www.theguardian.com/commentisfree/2007/nov/24/ comment.religion, accessed 22 January 2017.

84. David Austin, 'Interview with Linton Kwesi Johnson', 26 October 2004.

85. Fred Moten, *In the Break: The Aesthetics of the Black Radical Tradition* (Minnesota: University of Minnesota Press, 2003), 9–18.

86. For analyses of the black radical tradition which has historically combined black radical protest and socialism, see Cedric J. Robinson, *Black Marxism: The Making of the Black Radical Tradition* (Chapel Hill: University of North Carolina Press, 2000); Robin D.G. Kelley, *Freedom Dreams, The Black Radical Imagination* (Boston: New Beacon Press, 2002); Carole Boyce Davies, *Left of Karl Marx: The Political Life of Black Communist Claudia Jones* (Durham, NC: Duke University Press, 2008).

87. Darren Jenkins, 'Linton Kwesi Johnson', *WUSB 90.1 Program Guide*, 3(2), Spring 1987.

Chapter 6

1. Cornel West, *The Ethical Dimensions of Marxist Thought* (New York: Monthly Review, 1991), xii.
2. Ibid., xii–xiii.
3. Linton Kwesi Johnson, 'Tings an Times', *Mi Revalueshanary Fren: Selected Poems* (London: Penguin Books, 2006), 75.
4. Ibid., 76.
5. C.L.R. James, *Mariners, Renegades and Castaways: Herman Melville and the World We Live In* (Hanover: Dartmouth College, published by the University Press of New England, 2001).
6. Johnson, 'Tings an Times', *Mi Revalueshanary Fren*, 76.
7. Ibid., 77.
8. Ibid., 78.
9. Ibid., 79.
10. Ibid., 79.
11. Ibid., 79.
12. Ibid., 79.
13. Rob Nixon, '"An Everybody Claim Dem Democratic": Notes on the "New" South Africa', *Transition*, 54, 23–8.
14. Ibid., 34–5.
15. Johnson, 'Mi Revalueshanary Fren', *Mi Revalueshanary Fren*, 67–70. 'Mi Revalueshanary Fren' is certainly one of those poems for which the performance is more effective than reading it in silence. I have heard Johnson perform the poem twice, once in Toronto in October 2002 and again in October 2017. Each time I was struck by how with slight variation in intonation he was able to convey wit and a subtle sense of irony in the revolutionary's repetitive response to his friend.
16. Christian Habekost, *Verbal Riddim: The Politics and Aesthetics of African-Caribbean Dub Poetry* (Amsterdam: Rodopi, 1993), 212.
17. Johnson, 'Mi Revalueshanary Fren', *Mi Revalueshanary Fren*, 67.
18. Habekost, *Verbal Riddim*, 212.
19. Based on remarks by Linton Kwesi Johnson during a 14 October 2017 reading at 'The Red and Black: The Russian Revolution and the Black Atlantic' at the Institute for Black Atlantic Research (IBAR), University of Central Lancashire, Preston, 13–15 October 2017.
20. Burt Caesar, 'Interview: Linton Kwesi Johnson Talks to Burt Caesar at Sparkside Studios, Brixton, London, 11 June 1996', *Critical Quarterly*, 38(4), December 1996, 76.

21. Ibid., 76.

22. Richard Iton, *Solidarity Blues: Race, Culture, and the American Left* (Durham, NC: Duke University Press, 2000.

23. Johnson, 'Mi Revalueshanary Fren', *Mi Revalueshanary Fren*, 68.

24. This is a point that warrants more careful consideration as the allusion to glasnost and perestroika are a measure of a moment when it appeared as though the fate of the world lay in the balance, a time when, for many, the Soviet Union still represented a ray of hope, an alternative to capitalism. Great expectations accompanied Gorbachev's reform efforts when they were first introduced in the 1980s, and years after the USSR's demise he is equally heralded and castigated for his efforts. For champions of the unbridled free market system he, prompted by Ronald Reagan, initiated the process that opened the door to capitalism. For some supporters of the former Soviet Union, he betrayed the ideals of communism and paved the way for the crass consumer capitalism, stark inequality and robber baronism that is characteristic of Russia today. But Gorbachev envisioned an entirely different scenario. *Creative Effort of the People* was written for the All-Union Scientific and Practical Conference in Moscow in December 1984, just three months before he became the leader of USSR. For Gorbachev, the 'creative effort of the people is the essence of socialism and a fundamental factor in its emergence and consolidation', and that the 'perfection of developed socialism is, in the final analysis, a question of extending the opportunities for developing the personality, for developing the initiative of Soviet people as masters of their country, as working people and as citizens'. Any decision or steps 'in practical matters should be appraised above all from the point of view of what they would bring to the people, what their social and ideological consequences would be', and 'Disregard for the people's needs cannot be justified by any reference to objective circumstances'. Mikhail Gorbachev, *Creative Effort of the People* (Moscow: Novosti Press Agency Publishing House, 1985), 6–7. Ultimately, Gorbachev believed that: 'The increasing effective drawing of working people into the management of production and socio-political processes, and the extension of socialist democracy are a time-tested method for instilling in Soviet people a feeling of being complete and frugal masters of their country and a feeling of personal commitment to their affairs and concerns of the Party and the state.' Gorbachev, *Creative Effort of the People*, 7.

25. Johnson, 'Mi Revalueshanary Fren', *Mi Revalueshanary Fren*, 68–9.

26. Ibid., 69.

27. Johnson, 'Di Anfinish Revalueshan', *Mi Revalueshanary Fren*, 107.

28. Ibid., 108.

29. Ibid., 108.

30. Ibid., 108.

31. Mervyn Morris, 'Linton Kwesi Johnson', in *Jamaica Journal* 20(1), 20 February–April 1987 (the interview was conducted in 1982).

32. In her 1974 essay *Sex, Race, and Class*, Selma James, one of the leading spokespersons for wages for housework campaign for a fair wage for domestic duties, states: 'We demand wages for the work we do in the home. And that demand for a wage from the State is first a demand to be autonomous of men on whom we are now dependent. Secondly, we demand money without working out of the home, and open for the first time the possibility of refusing forced labor in the factories and in the home itself.' For James, wages for housework is also a 'basis for Black and white women to act together, "supported" or "unsupported", not because the antagonism of race is overcome, but because we both need the autonomy that the *wage and the struggle for the wage* can bring. Black women will know in what organizations (with Black men, with white women, *with neither*) to make that struggle. *No one else can know.*' Selma James, *Sex, Race, and Class* (Oakland: PM Press), 99.

33. Caesar, 'Interview', 73–4.

34. Ibid., 74.

35. Richard Iton, *In Search of the Black Fantastic: Politics and Popular Culture in the Post-Civil War Era* (Oxford and New York: Oxford University Press, 2008), 277. Iton also includes reggae and drum and bass artists within this tradition. See also Ric Knowles, 'To Be Dub, Female and Black: Towards a Woman-Centered Afro-Caribbean Diasporic Performance Aesthetic in Toronto', *Theatre Research in Canada*, 33(1), 2012, 84–5.

36. d'bi young, 'Revolushun I', in *Art on Black* (Toronto: Women's Press, 2006), 20. Hear also d'bi, *333*.

37. young, 'Revolushun I', 20–1.

38. Alain Badiou, *The Age of Poets* (London: Verso, 2014), 87.

39. Ibid., 87.

40. Maurizio Viano, 'The Left According to the Ashes of Gramsci', *Social Text*, 18, 1987–8, 54–5.

41. Badiou, *The Age of Poets*, 87.

42. Viano, 'The Left According to the Ashes of Gramsci', 59.

43. Badiou, *The Age of Poets*, 91.

44. Jerome C. Branche's insightful study of *Masks* and several Johnson poems does not make any direct link between Brathwaite and Johnson. See Jerome C. Branche, *The Poetics and Politics of Diaspora: Transatlantic Musings* (New York: Routledge, 2015), chapters 2 and 3. The same is true in of Amor Kohli's study of Amiri Baraka, Kamau Brathwaite and Johnson, 'The Demands of a New Idiom'.

45. As early as 1977 he suggested that while the poetry of Derek Walcott and Mervyn Morris did very little for him poetically (he has since

mentioned his admiration for Walcott), he felt close to Brathwaite's work because it 'combines both the classical with nuances of rhythm and speech which are particular to the Caribbean'. Dred Fred, 'Dread Fred Interviews Linton Kwesi Johnson', *Race Today*, 9(1), February 1977, 23.

46. Maureen Warner-Lewis, *E. Kamau Brathwaite's Masks: Essays and Annotations* (Kingston: Institute of Caribbean Studies, 1992), 10. For another critical reading of 'Mask' see Gordon Rohlehr, *Pathfinder: Black Awakening in the Arrivants of Edward Kamau Brathwaite* (Tunapuna, Trinidad: self-published, 1981), 109–63.

47. Warner-Lewis, *E. Kamau Brathwaite's Masks*, 11.

48. Ibid., 12.

49. Ibid., 12.

50. Ibid., 12. This cyclical view of life is also characteristic of d'bi young's work, and particularly the play *blood.claat* (see Chapter 3).

51. Warner-Lewis, *E. Kamau Brathwaite's Masks*, 15.

52. In the video, the poet donning his trademark trilby and wide-framed glasses engages in what might be described as a mild, mid-level skank to the jarring baseline of the Dennis Bovell band while slowly rotating away from and towards the camera as the backdrop transitions from scenes of warfare, vigorous dancing and a green pasture and a bright lavender cloudless sky that connotes the image of utopia/heaven that symbolizes the socialist land of milk and honey. See www.youtube.com/watch?v=UrKoyxdhjfs, accessed 23 November 2017.

53. Johnson, 'Di Good Life', *Mi Revalueshanary Fren*, 73.

54. Johnson, 'Reggae fi Radni', *Mi Revalueshanary Fren*, 47, 48.

55. Johnson, 'Di Good Life', *Mi Revalueshanary Fren*, 73.

56. Derrida in Dutoit and Pasanen, *Sovereignties in Question*, 18.

57. Ibid., 33.

58. Johnson, 'Di Good Life', *Mi Revalueshanary Fren*, 73.

59. Ibid., 74.

60. David J.A. Clines, *On the Way to the Postmodern: Old Testament Essay, 1967–1998*, vol. 2 (Sheffield: Sheffield Academic Press, 1998), 823–8.

61. Johnson, 'Di Good Life', *Mi Revalueshanary Fren*, 74.

62. Johnson, 'Tings An' Times', *Mi Revalueshanary Fren*, 79.

63. Ibid., 79.

64. Johnson, 'Reggae fi Radni', *Mi Revalueshanary Fren*, 49.

65. Johnson, 'If I Waz a Tap-Natch Poet', *Mi Revalueshanary Fren*, 95.

66. Nina L. Khrushcheva, *Imagining Nabokov: Russia Between Art and Politics* (New Haven: Yale University Press, 2007), 14.

67. Ibid., 17.

68. Ibid., 20.

69. Karl Marx, *Economic and Philosophic Manuscripts of 1844* (Moscow: Progress Publishers, 1974), 88.

70. Ibid., 88 (emphasis in original).

71. Ibid., 88.

Chapter 7

1. Linton Kwesi Johnson, 'Di Good Life', *Mi Revalueshanary Fren: Selected Poems* (London: Penguin Books, 2006), 74.

2. Johnson, 'Di Anfinish Revalueshan', *Mi Revalueshanary Fren*, 108.

3. David Austin, 'Interview with Linton Kwesi Johnson', 23 May 1999.

4. For an analysis of this poem alongside other Johnson poems see Jerome C. Branche, 'Speaking Truth, Speaking Power: "Of Immigrants," Immanence, and Linton Kwesi Johnson's "Street 66"', *The Poetics and Politics of Diaspora: Transatlantic Musings* (New York: Routledge, 2015), 87–92.

5. Linton Kwesi Johnson, 'Interview with Linton Kwesi Johnson', by David Austin, 23 May 1999.

6. Johnson, 'New Word Hawdah', *Mi Revalueshanary Fren*, 103.

7. Johnson, 'Seasons of the Heart', *Mi Revalueshanary Fren*, 83.

8. Tomi Adeaga, 'May Ayim Opitz and the Afro-Deutsche Body in Germany', in Joan Anim-Addo and Suzanne Scafe (eds), *I am Black/White/Yellow: An Introduction to the Black Body in Europe* (London: Mango Publishing, 2007), 199.

9. Karein K. Goertz, 'Showing Her Colors: An Afro-German Writes the Blues in Black and White', *Callaloo*, 26(2), 2003, 309; Adeaga, 'May Ayim Opitz and the Afro-deutsche Body in Germany', 197–8.

10. May Ayim, 'The Year 1990: Homeland and Unity from an Afro-German Perspective', in Antje Harnisch, Anne Marie Stokes and Friedmann Weidauer (eds), *Fringe Voices: An Anthology of Minority Writing in the Federal Republic of Germany* (Oxford: Berg, 1998), 107–8; Karein K. Goertz, 'Showing Her Colors', 306; Adeaga, 'May Ayim Opitz and the Afro-Deutsche Body in Germany', 202.

11. Ayim, 'The Year 1990', 109–10, 114.

12. May Ayim, 'Borderless and Brazen: A Poem Against the German "u-not-y"', *Affilia: Journal of Women and Social Work*, 23(1), February 2008, 92.

13. May Ayim, 'Unlimited and Outright – A Poem Against the (Hypocrisy) of German Unity', *Journal of Gender Studies*, 6(1), 1997, 71.

14. Goertz, 'Showing Her Colors', 202; Adeaga, 'May Ayim Opitz and the Afro-Deutsche Body in Germany', 203.

15. Adeaga, 'May Ayim Opitz and the Afro-Deutsche Body in Germany', 203.

16. Johnson, 'Reggae fi May Ayim', *Mi Revalueshanary Fren*, 92.

17. Ibid., 92.

18. Ibid., 92.

19. As the poet said in 2012, 'Once you have a disease like cancer, you look at life a bit differently. Some things that were important no longer seem as important as they were.' Sarah Morrison, Linton Kwesi Johnson: 'Class-ridden? Yes, But This is Still Home', *The Independent*, 2 December 2012, www.independent.co.uk/news/people/profiles/linton-kwesi-johnson-class-ridden-yes-but-this-is-still-home-8373870.html, accessed 29 June 2017.

20. Linton Kwesi quoted in Maya Jaggi, 'Poet on the Frontline', *The Guardian*, 4 May 2002, www.theguardian.com/books/2002/may/04/poetry.books, accessed 2 December 2017.

21. Sigmund Freud, 'Mourning and Melancholia', in James Strachey (ed.), *The Standard Edition of the Complete Psychological Works of Sigmund Freud, vol. 4 (1914–1916): On the History of the Psycho-analytic Movement Papers Metapsychology and Other Works* (London: The Hogarth Press and the Institute of Psycho-Analysis), 244–5, 250.

22. Tammy Clewell, 'Mourning and Beyond Melancholia: Freud's Psychoanalysis of Loss', *Journal of the American Psychological Association*, 52(1), 2004, 56, 60–1, 64–5.

23. Leslie Chamberlain, *The Secret Artist: A Close Reading of Sigmund Freud* (New York: Seven Stories Press, 2000).

24. Freud, 'Mourning and Melancholia', 252, 254.

25. Johnson, 'More Time', *Mi Revalueshanary Fren*, 86.

26. Emily Taylor Merriman, 'We Naw Tek Noh More a Dem Oppreshan: Linton Kwesi Johnson's Resistant Vision', in Adrian Grafe and Jessica Stephens (eds), *Lines of Resistance: Essays on British Poetry from Thomas Hardy to Linton Kwesi Johnson* (Jefferson: McFarland & Company, Inc., Publishers, 2012), 226.

27. Johnson, 'More Time', *Mi Revalueshanary Fren*, 86.

28. Ibid., 87.

29. David Harvey, *Seventeen Contradictions and the End of Capitalism* (Oxford: Oxford University Press, 2014), 111.

30. Linton Kwesi Johnson, 'John La Rose', *The Guardian*, 4 March 2006. www.theguardian.com/news/2006/mar/04/guardianobituaries.socialexclusion, accessed 21 September 2017. The obituary was also published in *The Black Scholar* as 'In Memoriam: John La Rose (1927–2006)', 37(2), 2007, 61.

31. Johnson, 'Beacon of Hope', *Mi Revalueshanary Fren*, 63.

32. Brian W. Alleyne, *Radicals Against Race: Black Activism and Cultural Politics* (Oxford: Berg, 2002), 127–8.

33. Johnson, 'In Memoriam: John La Rose (1927–2006)', 61–2.

34. Based on remarks by Linton Kwesi Johnson during a 14 October 2017 reading at The Red and Black: The Russian Revolution and the Black Atlantic, at the Institute for Black Atlantic Research (IBAR), University of Central Lancashire, Preston, 13–15 October 2017.

35. John La Rose, 'Unemployment, Leisure, and the Birth of Creativity', *The Black Scholar* 26(2), 1996, 29.

36. Ibid., 29.

37. Ibid., 29.

38. Ibid., 30.

39. Ibid., 30.

40. Ibid., 30–1.

41. Jonathon Martineau, *Time, Capitalism and Alienation: A Socio-Historical Inquiry into the Making of Modern Time* (Leidon and Boston: Brill, 2015), 114, 115.

42. Ibid., 120, 126, 127.

43. Ibid., 122, 132, 149.

44. David Harvey, *Marx, Capital, and the Madness of Economic Reason* (Oxford: Oxford University Press, 2018), 123, 200.

45. Wofgang Streeck, *Buying Time: The Delayed Crisis of Democratic Capitalism* (London: Verso, 2014), xii–xiv.

46. David Austin, 'Interview with Linton Kwesi Johnson', 23 May 1999.

47. Ibid.

48. See Sarah Morrison, 'Linton Kwesi Johnson: "Class-Ridden? Yes, But This Is Still Home"', *The Independent*, 2 December 2012, www.independent.co.uk/news/people/profiles/linton-kwesi-johnson-class-ridden-yes-but-this-is-still-home-8373870.html, accessed 30 June 2017.

49. David Austin, 'Interview with Linton Kwesi Johnson', 26 October 2004.

50. Ibid.

51. Hannah Arendt, *Between Past and Future* (Cleveland: Meridian Books, 1963), 89–90.

52. Martineau, *Time, Capitalism and Alienation*, 168.

53. Harvey, *Seventeen Contradictions and the End of Capitalism*, 69, 263.

Chapter 8

1. Robin D.G. Kelley, *Freedom Dreams: The Black Radical Imagination* (Boston: Beacon Press, 2002), 196.

2. Brian K. Murphy, *Transforming Ourselves/Transforming the World: An Open Conspiracy for Social Change* (London: Zed Books Ltd., 1999), 198.

3. Ibid., 48.
4. Ibid., 48 (my emphasis).
5. See Paget Henry, *Caliban's Reason: Introducing Afro-Caribbean Philosophy* (New York: Routledge, 2000), 259.
6. Mutabaruka, 'Revolt Ain't a Revolution (For the People of Haiti)'.
7. Henry, *Caliban's Reason*, 270. The veteran South African writer Peter Abrahams has written that the meaning of life that eludes us is to 'be found in the growing awareness that we ourselves can give meaning to life by the choice we make as individuals, communities, societies', and in so doing, 'acculturate ourselves out of the impulse to greed, destructiveness, disharmony into caring for each other. This is humanity's choice.' Peter Abrahams, *The Black Experience in the 20th Century: A Biography and Meditation* (Bloomington: Indiana University Press, 2001), 402. But while we can wholeheartedly share Abrahams optimism, it is hard to imagine that those who have a vested interest in holding on to power at all costs will relinquish their power through some form of self-imposed acculturation, and even harder to reconcile the spirit of Johnson's 'each an' evrywan' with Abrahams' rejection of homosexuality as an aberration of nature. However, these contradictions exemplify the challenges involved in the fight for social justice while appreciating humanity in all of its complexity.
8. Velma Pollard, *Dread Talk: The Language of Rastafari* (Montreal-Kingston: McGill-Queen's Press, 2000), 106–7.
9. Ambalavaner Sivanandan, 'All that Melts into Air is Solid', in *Communities of Resistance: Writings on Black Struggles for Socialism* (London: Verso, 1990), 50–1.
10. Ibid., 52.
11. Ibid., 52.
12. Ibid., 57.
13. James Boggs cited in Grace Lee Boggs, *Living for Change: An Autobiography* (Minneapolis: University of Minnesota Press, 1998), 220–221.
14. Ibid., 267–8.
15. Ibid., 251.
16. Ibid., 221.
17. Ibid., 272 (my emphasis).
18. Hannah Arendt, *Between Past and Future* (Cleveland: Meridian Books, 1963), 169.
19. Richard Iton, *In Search of the Black Fantastic: Politics and Popular Culture in the Post-Civil War Era* (Oxford and New York: Oxford University Press, 2008), 28.
20. Ibid., 16–17.
21. Cornel West, *The Ethical Dimensions of Marxist Thought* (New York: Monthly Review, 1991), xiii.

22. Richard Iton, 'Still Life', *Small Axe*, 17(1), March 2013, 39.
23. Ibid., 39.
24. Iton, *In Search of the Black Fantastic*, 290.
25. Richard Iton, *Solidarity Blues: Race, Culture, and the American Left* (Chapel Hill: University of North Carolina Press, 2000).
26. Aimé Césaire, *Discourse on Colonialism* (New York: Monthly Review Press, 2000), 36.

INDEX